Corruption in India
Agenda for Action

Michael Schulte
'Dee

(Given to me in Delhi following the course on Christian Political Involvement organised by Rajiv Abraham).

Corruption in India
Agenda For Action

Editors
S. Guhan
Samuel Paul

Vision Books
(Incorporating Orient Paperbacks)
New Delhi • Bombay • Hyderabad

ISBN 81-7094-277-2

© Public Affairs Centre, 1997

First Published in 1997 by
Vision Books Pvt. Ltd.
(Incorporating Orient Paperbacks)
24, Feroze Gandhi Road, Lajpat Nagar III
New Delhi - 110024, India.

Printed at
Rashtra Rachna Printers
C-88, Ganesh Nagar, Pandav Nagar Complex
Delhi-110092, India.

Contents

Preface	7
1. Introduction *S. Guhan*	9
2. Corruption in the Political Process: A Case for Electoral Reform *K. Ganesan*	29
3. Corruption, Political Interference and the Civil Service *Madhav Godbole*	60
4. The Role of Audit in Tackling Corruption *Ramaswamy R . Iyer*	88
5. The Right to Information *A. G. Noorani*	114
6. Corruption in Public Service Delivery *Samuel Paul and Manubhai Shah*	144
7. Corruption and Administrative Discretion *S.P. Sathe*	164
8. Lok Pal and Lok Ayukt *A. G. Noorani*	189
9. Commissions of Inquiry *A. G. Noorani*	218
10. Prevention of Corruption : Towards Effective Enforcement *C.V. Narasimhan*	251

11. Corruption in India : A Strategic Agenda for Action 286
    Samuel Paul

    Bibliography 305

    About the Contributors 309

    Index 311

Preface

The cancerous spread of corruption in India's public life has been a matter of great concern to its citizens in all walks of life. There is a growing literature in the country on the diagnosis of this phenomenon, and the print media, in particular, has provided extensive coverage to corruption scandals in high places. While the public awareness of this problem has increased over the years, significant progress has not yet been made in terms of developing and designing remedies that can adequately deal with its magnitude and severity. Government's initiatives in this regard have also been piecemeal and, more often than not, in response to the public criticisms that have erupted in the wake of periodic scandals. From time to time prominent public leaders and other concerned citizens have called for concerted efforts to fight corruption and, in some cases, have launched people's movements for this purpose. These laudable efforts have certainly kept the issue of corruption in the limelight. They have not, however, succeeded so far in generating a specific and feasible agenda for action to tackle corruption.

It was against this background that an effort was initiated under the auspices of the Public Affairs Centre, Bangalore, to examine the pervasive problem of corruption from multiple perspectives as a basis for evolving a strategic agenda for action. The project began with several rounds of informal discussions in Madras and Bangalore among civil servants, both retired and serving, scholars, lawyers and industrialists. These deliberations provided valuable guidance on the key issues to be probed and the specific steps to be taken towards the preparation of this volume. The topics identified for study as a result of these discussions were integrally related to good governance and had a strong focus on generating actionable ideas to tackle corruption. The project was fortunate in securing the ready and enthusiastic co-operation of an impressive array of experts who agreed to prepare papers for this volume.

In April 1996, a workshop was organised by the Public Affairs Centre to discuss and revise the papers commissioned under the project. The authors and a select group of participants spent a day-and-a-half on this exercise. The national elections held in April-May 1996 in which issues of corruption surfaced prominently lent a sense of urgency and timeliness to this endeavour. There was a consensus that the papers and the agenda for action emerging therefrom should be disseminated widely at an early date. We are fortunate that Vision Books, New Delhi, readily undertook to publish this volume in record time.

This project and the publication of this book reflects the interests of the Public Affairs Centre (PAC) in improving the quality of governance in our society. We are most grateful to the Board and Staff of the Centre for their support, both intellectual and financial. The assistance provided by Mr. K. Gopakumar of PAC who ably liaised with the editors, authors and publisher is gratefully acknowledged.

Many other friends have also contributed directly and indirectly to the timely completion of this effort. Mr. P. Sabhanayagam, former Chief Secretary of Tamil Nadu, played a lead role in the early discussions in Madras on tackling corruption. Mr. N. Ram, Editor, *Frontline* supported and facilitated this venture in its early stages. Mr. K.P. Geethakrishnan, former Executive Director for India at the IMF, and Professor A. Vaidyanathan of Madras Institute for Development Studies helped us in procuring the needed books and reports for which we are grateful. The discussants who spared their valuable time to participate in the April Workshop and several other friends who commented on this volume and offered useful suggestions also deserve our special thanks.

Finally, we would like to acknowledge the support provided by the National Foundation for India and its Executive Director, Mr. Shankar Ghose, in this endeavour.

Bangalore
January 26, 1997

S. GUHAN
SAMUEL PAUL

1
Introduction

S. Guhan

What is Corruption?

All those who are likely to read this volume can be assumed to be familiar with the phenomenon of corruption in India from their own personal experience or based on what they have heard and read. However, it is not easy to propose a compact and comprehensive formal definition of corruption. *The Oxford English Dictionary* offers as many as nine meanings of corruption which can be grouped into four main categories. Corruption may apply to an object (physical decomposition, putrefaction, spoiling of quality, adulteration); to the perversion of language or taste, to morals (to destroy moral purity, to debase, to defile); or to public office (to destroy or prevent the integrity or fidelity of a person in his discharge of duty, to induce to act dishonestly or unfaithfully, to make venal; to bribe). The last two aspects are captured in the etymology of the word, based on the Latin verb to break, *rumpere*, which implies that something is broken, such as a moral or social code of conduct or, more narrowly, a law or an administrative rule[1].

Corruption can straddle both the public and private sectors. However, given our focus on corruption in the public services, it might be useful to start with the narrow definition that corruption is the 'misuse of public power for private gain'[2]. Other definitions have been offered citing the misuse of public office, violation of public interest, disapproval of public opinion and the illegal use of public office for private gain. These and similar definitions have been critiqued on the ground that they tend to be too broad and indeterminate since there could be much debate on what constitutes "misuse" or "public power" or "public interest". On the other hand, definitions which link corruption narrowly to bribery have been faulted on the ground that they leave out forms of misconduct which can lead to or result from corruption, such as nepotism, patronage, and a variety of white collar offences which may or may not involve direct or immediate financial considerations[3].

Faced with this dilemma, it might be useful to look for an operational, rather than an abstract, definition. In India, the Prevention of Corruption Act, 1988, which applies to public servants, deals with corruption basically in terms of 'taking gratification other than legal remuneration in respect of an official act'. The word 'gratification' is not restricted to pecuniary gratifications or to gratifications estimable in money. The offence consists of accepting, or agreeing to accept, or obtaining, or attempting to obtain, any such illegal gratification 'as a motive or reward for doing or forbearing to do any official act or showing or forbearing to show, in the exercise of his official functions, favour or disfavour to any person or for rendering or attempting to render any service or disservice to any person'[4]. Other offences under the Act include related misconduct, such as taking gratification in order to influence a public servant in the exercise of his official duties, acceptance of gifts by public servants, and possession of wealth disproportionate to known sources of income[5]. Thus, the various provisions of the Prevention of Corruption Act, 1988 add up to a reasonable working definition of corruption.

Characteristics of Corruption

Corruption can assume many forms, cover a wide variety of transactions, and operate at many levels. It can relate to acts of commission, omission or delay; involve the exercise of discretion; or the violation of rules, but not necessarily since illegal gratification can be taken even whilst technically conforming to rules.

The *quid pro quo* in corruption could relate to the past, present or future. Bribery can be in the form of cash, kind, services or other favours. At lower bureaucratic levels, it could take the form of 'speed money' to facilitate or expedite the issue of approvals or the delivery of public services or the fulfilment of rightful entitlements. Corruption may involve a voluntary or collusive relationship between the bribe-giver and the bribe-taker or it may be extortionate for rendering an entitlement, doing an undue favour or desisting from a harmful action.

Corruption can also reside in general policy decisions explicitly or implicitly aimed at benefiting special interest groups for a *quid pro quo* as well as in a wide gamut of specific transactions: public sector contracts for the purchase of goods and services; allocations of scarce materials; permits, licences, exemptions, and waivers; levy and collection of taxes; implementation of projects and programmes; delivery of public services; appointments, postings, transfers and promotions of public servants; different stages of the electoral process; conduct of legislators; and *so on*, for no list of this kind can be exhaustive.

In the public sphere, corruption operates at various levels of the political and bureaucratic hierarchies. It can do so independently among politicians and bureaucrats but, more commonly, there is a nexus between corrupt politicians and bureaucrats who are themselves corrupt or who passively collude with their political masters. In such a relationship of complicity, both gain and each protects the other. There is also a 'vertical integration' between different layers of the political and bureaucratic echelons: e.g., Minister-legislator-party functionary and Minister-higher bureaucracy - middle and lower bureaucracy. The lower levels operate as agents of the higher levels passing up to them shares in the bribes received at the operating level. Alternatively, the corrupt official may make an up front lump sum payment 'commuting' recurring payments of a share in the bribes. In such cases, government posts with lucrative potential for money-making are informally auctioned to the highest bidder from time to time. In this process of collusive corruption, appointments, postings and transfers play a prime role providing the bridge between corruption and political interference in administration[6].

Several characteristics of corruption make it difficult to track its course, expose it and effectively punish the culprits. Corrupt transactions take place in secret. In collusive corruption, the mutual interest between the recipient and the source of bribery make it difficult to unearth the evidence. In extortionate corruption, the victims are intimidated. Above all, corrupt politicians and officials who occupy high positions in government are in a position to suppress evidence or resort to threat or inducement because of their privileged access to government records. Furthermore, legal processes involved in tackling corruption — as is generally the case with the Indian legal system as a whole — are cumbersome, expensive, and time consuming.

Causes of Corruption

The extensive literature on the subject of corruption draws attention to political systems and practices, economic development, economic policies, sociological characteristics and the cultural milieu as the main factors which are relevant for a causal explanation of corruption[7]. For example, it has been argued that democracies and the costly electoral cycles associated with them are fertile grounds for political corruption. While in office, the political leadership and legislators, dependent on external sources of funding for their re-election campaigns, tend to be influenced by pressure groups. In poor developing countries, there is acute competition for the sharing of benefits. At the same time, inequality and expectations are both high. Such a situation provides an in-built impetus for corruption. Furthermore, economic policies based on administrative regulations — using devices like permits and licences for the allocation of investment approvals, scarce resources, welfare benefits and subsidies — create powerful incentives for bribery[8]. In terms of sociological factors, it has been argued that caste, kinship and patron-client relationships, especially in predominantly rural societies, generate and reproduce corruption through networks of nepotism, patronage and dependency. Cultural factors that have been relied upon to explain corruption include the custom of 'gift-giving' in traditional societies with the expectation of reciprocal rewards, something which tends to spill-over into institutionalised administration as well, especially, in Africa[9].

While there may be *prima facie* explanatory rationale in all these factors, none of them can be taken to be definitive or deterministic in explaining corruption in different societies at various times in their histories. Corruption, for instance, has been recorded at very high levels not just in democracies, but also in authoritarian regimes in Latin America, Africa and Asia[10]. Advanced economies, both socialist and market-oriented, are also prone to corruption (e.g., USA, the former USSR, Japan and countries in Western and Eastern Europe)[11]. Even sociological and cultural factors cannot be relied upon to systematically account for differential levels or trends in corruption. Accordingly, the conclusion that emerges on the basis of available empirical evidence is that it would be untenable to characterise democracies, developing countries or traditional societies as immutably condemned to a state of corruption. Within each such category there are less-corrupt and more-corrupt societies and also those which, over time, have been able to move to a lower level of corruption. In some societies, pervasive corruption has yielded to corruption which is more or less confined to certain sectors or types of activities. All that can be said is that while the various causal factors referred to have a bearing on the incidence of corruption, they cannot be taken — singly or jointly — to adequately account for it always and everywhere.

Consequences of Corruption

There is considerable agreement about the adverse effects of corruption on society, polity and the economy. Corruption corrodes the moral fibre of society. It undermines the legitimacy of governments because of the widespread cynicism bred on a mixture of facts and perceptions concerning the level of corruption. It has been pointed out that general impressions about corruption, circulated in public discussion and gossip, might be 'unfair and exaggerated but the very fact that such impressions are there causes damage to the social fabric'[12]. One result of such deterioration is political instability when one democratic regime after another is outvoted from office on the issue of corruption. More serious is the replacement of democratic governments with authoritarian or military rule. In a number of countries, such governments have come to power on the slogan of providing a clean administration but have themselves become highly corrupt in due course[13].

The adverse effects of corruption on the economy and on public administration are manifold. Government expenditures are inflated and wasteful projects and programmes are taken up in order to obtain kickbacks. Standards get diluted in investments (e.g., dams, roads, bridges and buildings), goods (e.g., drugs), and services (e.g., quality of doctors, engineers, teachers) causing hazards to safety, life and health. Government revenues get reduced on account of tax evasion. Subsidies and incentives are abused. The poor are the worst affected since they cannot pay bribes in order to obtain benefits to which they are legitimately entitled. Worse, they are denied basic justice in the hands of corrupt officials, such as the police and village officials. Corruption thus aggravates inequality in an already unequal society.

At the other end of the spectrum, it places a premium on directly unproductive rent-seeking activities on the part of officials and businessmen who seek to profit from, or utilise, opportunities for corruption in regulatory or tax administration[14]. The costs of bribery ultimately get loaded on to the consumer resulting in domestic inflation and non-competitive export prices. The rewarding of corrupt officials and penalisation of honest ones undermines morale and efficiency. In the course of time, corruption tends to cascade, deepen and spread and thus acquire a self-propelling momentum. It is clear that corruption can gravely undermine the public interest in terms of morality, economic development, equity and welfare.

While the foregoing is a summary of the mainstream view on corruption, there is also a revisionist standpoint that holds that corruption may be justified or actually be beneficial under certain circumstances. A bribe offered to escape from an unjust law or a repressive act, for instance, may not be morally reprehensible. If economic regulations are dysfunctional, corruption, by evading them, can result in greater efficiency. Speed-money can expedite decisions. Corruption may provide an opportunity for disadvantaged or minority groups to obtain benefits from which they might otherwise get excluded. Should the gains from corruption accrue to those who are able to invest them efficiently, the economy can benefit[15].

A number of reasons can be advanced for not acquiescing in these arguments relating to such purported 'benefits' of corruption. The first is the normative position that corruption is morally unacceptable regardless of any instrumental advantages it might bring. The second is the practical argument that it is not feasible to confine corruption to those areas or activities in which it might be marginally beneficial. And the third, the 'benefits' from corruption are argued on the assumption that corruption provides a safety-valve from repressive regimes, over-regulated economies, administrative delays, and discriminatory practices. There is no reason for taking this set of evils for granted. They also need to be tackled as part of the overall reforms for curbing corruption. Altogether, therefore, one should conclude that the costs of corruption are bound to overwhelm the benefits which might be associated with it on a superficial reckoning.

Corruption in India: The Current Context

In the background of the characteristics, causes and costs of corruption, we could move on to the specificities of corruption in the contemporary Indian context. It would appear that most of the political, economic, sociological and cultural factors that generally account for corruption operate in India to a greater rather than a lesser degree. India is a low-income developing country in which there is intense competition among both the affluent and the poor for scarce resources in an environment of rising expectations. It is an active democracy in which the high cost of electoral politics has been a major factor in fuelling corruption in the electoral process and, subsequently, governance. In recent decades, there has been a great deal of political instability as reflected in frequent elections and changes of government, especially in the States, which has accelerated corruption[16]. Divisions based on region, caste and language are the other factors that have promoted corruption, nepotism, and patronage.

India has not been free of corruption, whether in ancient times (at least as far back as the *Arthasastra*), the immediate pre-colonial period, British rule or the decades following Independence. Gandhiji was concerned with corruption in the provincial Congress Ministries formed after the 1935 Act. A number of cases of corruption in the States have been documented during the critical decades after Independence when Nehru was Prime Minister; nor were cases of corruption absent in the Centre itself[17]. It was in response to the concern expressed in Parliament on 'the growing menace of corruption in public administration' that the Government of India set up a Committee of MPs and officials, under the chairmanship of Sri K. Santhanam in the closing years of the Nehru period, to undertake a comprehensive inquiry into the problem[18].

A Crisis of Corruption

Neither the incidence of corruption in India nor the concern with it are, thus, new. However, the current state of corruption in the country is not just a linear continuation of the experience in the 1950s and 1960s. Beginning with the 1970s, changes in the level, trend, nature and spread of corruption in the 1980s and 1990s have been such as to suggest that corruption has assumed critical proportions. In other words, it might not be an exaggeration today to talk about corruption in terms of a crisis or a cancer endangering India's society, polity and economy.

Consider the following:

1. There has been a distinct increase — in terms of the number and amounts — in transactions in which the presence of corruption has been substantiated. At the Centre, these have included, but have not been confined to, defence contracts (e.g., Bofors, HDW submarines), civil contracts (e.g., railways), telecommunication contracts, commodity imports (e.g., fertiliser and sugar), privatization (e.g., Bailadilla mine), housing allotments, the financial sector (e.g., the Bank scam) and violations of the Foreign Exchange Regulation and Income Tax Acts (*Hawala* cases).

2. A number of Ministers and Governors of States have had to resign on account of being legally charged with corrupt transactions[19]. Leading politicians belonging to different political parties have been charged in the *Hawala* proceedings related to violations of the Foreign Exchange Regulation and Income Tax Acts[20]. In more than one instance Prime Ministers have been tainted with suspicion though investigations against them do not seem to have been expeditiously or effectively pursued[21]. In any event, it is not credible that widespread Ministerial corruption would have been possible without the acquiescence if not the involvement of the head of the government.

3. India has acquired the unenviable reputation of being among the most corrupt countries in the world. A careful poll taken among business interests and financial journalists by Transparency International (TI), the reputed anti-corruption non-governmental organization, placed India 9th from the bottom in its 1996 list of 54 countries. India scored 2.63 on a scale with a maximum of 10 for the totally corrupt-free country[22].

4. In a number of States, Chief Ministers and Ministers have been implicated in major corrupt transactions relating to liquor regulations, real estate approvals, large government contracts, allocation of scarce materials, transfers of public servants and so on. Similarly, on the basis of proven cases, well substantiated allegations and reliable internal information, it would appear that corruption among ministers in the States is widespread. This again cannot be the case unless it is countenanced by the heads of government in the States[23].

5. In both the Centre and States, evidence points to an increase of corruption in the higher bureaucracy. A sizeable proportion of higher level civil servants are believed to be either corrupt on their own and/or to be acting as accomplices, conduits or agents for corrupt Ministers. A larger proportion, while keeping themselves clean, have had to be silent witnesses to corruption among Ministers and their peers in the civil services. Some of them have been induced or intimidated into going along with financially irregular decisions and corrupt administrative practices. Yet, others have eased themselves out by taking early retirement. Many have paid the price for maintaining integrity by being exiled to posts which are not commensurate with their seniority or experience. Only very few have taken a principled stand in resigning from the civil service in a protest against corruption. Correspondingly, the transfer of civil servants in many States has been aimed at positioning pliable officials in posts with a high potential for corruption, moving out honest officials to innocuous post and frequently transferring those who have refused to oblige their political masters in corrupt transactions. The result of all this has been immense damage to morale, motivation and efficiency in the public services.

6. Concerning the lower levels of the bureaucracy, corruption mostly takes the form of speed money for expediting approvals and the demand for bribes for providing (or not withholding) legitimate services (e.g., in utilities such as telephones, electricity boards and civic services)[24]. Corruption is also rampant in the administration of welfare schemes, the public distribution system, the police, revenue, and irrigation departments and several other sectors in which the people come into daily contact with the administration. The higher bureaucracy seems to be unwilling or unable to tackle corruption at its subordinate levels.

7. Of grave concern is the interlocking or 'vertical integration' of corruption at various levels of the governmental hierarchy — elected politicians, higher bureaucracy and lower bureaucracy. The normal assumption is that the 'principals' at each of the higher levels would be committed to ensure that their 'agents' at respective lower levels would act according to standards and norms of probity[25]. In a situation in which the principals and agents collude with each other in corruption, the problem of tackling it becomes much more intractable.

8. In the public domain, corruption is not confined to the executive government. It has spread to legislatures, the judiciary, media and the

independent professions (such as lawyers, doctors, chartered accountants and contractors)[26]. Through mutual interaction, such a horizontal spread of corruption has entrenched it further in government and made its prevention and control much more difficult.

9. Mechanisms to prevent, monitor, and punish corruption are not adequate nor have they proved to be effective to the extent that they exist. At the national level, India still does not have an Ombudsman-type, Lok Pal legislation and machinery to deal with corruption among ministers and the higher bureaucracy. In general, governments at the Centre and in the States have been tardy, at best, and insincere, at worst, in investigating and pursuing corruption. Commissions of Inquiry established for the purpose over the years have not been able to effectively prove or punish corruption. Corruption has been politicised — just as politics has been corrupted — in the sense that cases of corruption have been used for partisan political purposes rather than with any serious intent to objectively tackle the problem[27]. As is to be expected, opposition parties in Parliament and State legislatures have played a role in agitating issues relating to corruption but, by and large, their efforts have not been effective[28]. Judicial processes under normal anti-corruption laws are dilatory although in recent times the Supreme Court, in response to public interest litigation, has intervened to enforce the law[29]. Investigative journalism has helped to expose corruption but, given its nature, media coverage has been episodic rather than sustained. A number of activist groups have taken up local issues of corruption[30]. However, their contributions have varied widely over different parts of the country and have not assumed the critical mass required to generate a popular movement against corruption.

The Response to Corruption

Despite the fact that corruption is pervasive and has gone largely unchecked and, indeed, perhaps because of it there is now a strong demand by the public for effective punitive and corrective measures to tackle the problem. That corruption is a national concern in the consciousness of the people has been demonstrated by the fact that it was the most important issue in the general elections to Parliament in 1989, 1996 and in several elections to State legislatures[31]. Essentially, the challenge that concerned citizens face is to translate the widespread public sentiment against corruption into effective public action.

What needs to be taken into account at the outset is that the very scale and spread of corruption has generated helplessness, at best, and apathy, at worst. These, in turn, tend to be rationalised in terms of cynicism or in arguments that tend to acquiesce in corruption. The first task is to generate the confidence that India is not doomed to live with corruption forever and that in India — as has happened in many other countries — it is possible to mobilise public pressure for reforms aimed at containing and rolling it back. As corruption intensifies and spreads its tentacles, it tends to reproduce and perpetuate itself on an increasing scale. No time should, therefore, be lost in undertaking all possible efforts to put a brake on the process. At the same time, there is a need for the sober recognition that it would not be feasible to eliminate corruption altogether. Tackling corruption is not achieved in one-stroke but through a continuous and cumulative endeavour. In addition, it carries its own costs. All that can be aimed at is to progressively move toward a state of affairs in which corruption is the exception rather than the rule.

It is possible and legitimate to approach the problem of tackling corruption from different angles. Generally speaking, four approaches can be distinguished. One consists of fundamental changes in the Constitution which would, like a Presidential system, insulate executive authority from legislatures and include appropriate checks and balances against the abuse of political power[32]. The second would emphasise thorough deregulation and privatisation of governmental activities so as to reduce the role of the state as much as possible along with reforms aimed at enhancing efficiency. The third would argue for an extensive decentralisation of governance so as to promote accountability and transparency at local levels in order to check corruption. The fourth would rely on an increased development of moral values among the people at large beginning with youth and focused on politicians and officials in particular.

Each of these approaches is doubtless germane to the problem of tackling corruption; they are necessary but not sufficient. They cannot be relied upon singly for each has its limitations. There can be much debate about the pros and cons of fundamental constitutional changes and, in any event, they would not appear to be readily feasible. Nor can there be the assurance that the replacement of parliamentary democracy with an executive government, notwithstanding the checks and balances that might be introduced, will not prove to be a remedy worse than the disease. Similarly, deregulation and decentralisation, for which there is already a wide consensus, cannot be a panacea. The state cannot be wished away, nor can it be expected to wither away. Corruption can continue under different forms in a largely privatized economy;[33] likewise, it can itself get decentralized, persisting in less visible ways under local authorities. The upgrading of moral values is of fundamental importance but a moral revolution cannot be expedited on the basis of rhetorical appeals that urge its necessity. It can be promoted and sustained only around a series of concrete incremental measures which demonstrate that reform is possible and can cumulate. This is the surest way to strengthen and channel the moral impetus for a more honest polity.

Focus of the Book

Compared to the macro policy approaches discussed above, the attempt in this volume is more modest and multi-faceted. The essays included in it concentrate on legal, institutional and systemic changes that would appear to hold the best promise for tackling corruption in the Indian context. On the basis of the research and thought that has gone into the issues involved, these essays offer prescriptive proposals which, when taken together, can add up to a strategic agenda for action. The intention has not been to cover all aspects of corruption or to say the last word on the topics covered. In planning this volume, the aim was no more than to make a beginning in the formulation of a coherent set of concrete proposals for tackling corruption.

The ten essays that follow aim at dealing with the problem of corruption against a broader canvas of political, economic and administrative reforms. Their specific focus on corruption is oriented towards three broad aspects: preventive, punitive, and promotional. Preventive aspects include curtailing corruption in the political process; insulating public servants from the abuse of political power; strengthening accountability in public administration; ensuring transparency in government; enabling access to and dissemination of information; promoting efficiency in the provision of public services; and measures to reduce the role of discretion in administrative law. These are themes of the contributions on *Corruption in the Political*

Process by K. Ganesan; *Corruption, Political Interference and the Civil Service* by Madhav Godbole; *The Role of Audit in Tackling Corruption* by Ramaswamy R. Iyer; *The Right to Information* by A.G. Noorani; *Corruption in Public Service Delivery* by Samuel Paul and Manubhai Shah and *Corruption and Administrative Discretion* by S.P. Sathe.

The two essays by A.G. Noorani, *Lok Pal and Lok Ayukt* and *Commissions of Inquiry*, and C.V. Narasimhan's essay, *Prevention of Corruption: Towards Effective Enforcement* are inter-related. They explore in detail various aspects related to the effective investigation and punishment of corruption at the ministerial and bureaucratic levels.

The volume concludes with a summary presentation by Samuel Paul of the specific proposals for tackling corruption contained in the individual essays. In cases where the authors have not come up with any single view, alternatives have been presented. In a few instances, proposals made in the thematic essays have been qualified or elaborated upon. In putting forward the proposals, an attempt has been to strike a balance between too much and too little detail. The aim has been to come up with an agenda which is reasonably specific and is, at the same time, sufficiently flexible so that it lends itself to being improved upon in further debate.

The bibliography includes the major contributions to theory, policy and international experience relating to corruption. Besides helping in a better understanding of the subject, we hope it will stimulate more policy-oriented research on various aspects of corruption in India.

Need for Public Action

While the proposals offered in this volume will be useful as an actionable initial agenda for tackling corruption in India, it is clear that no set of proposals, however well conceived, will themselves be able to bring about the necessary changes. They can only provide a basis for action. They will remain a dead letter unless public action is forthcoming at several levels for winning acceptance for the proposed reforms.

A very encouraging development is that the major Indian political parties — Bharatiya Janata Party, Indian National Congress, Janata Dal, Communist Party of India (Marxist) and the Communist Party of

India — included a number of proposals for tackling corruption in their manifestoes for the 1996 general elections to Parliament. Undoubtedly, this came about in response to the strong revulsion against corruption on the part of the electorate. The extracts reproduced in the Annexure from the party manifestoes on (a) the Lok Pal, (b) electoral reforms relating to probity of legislators and political parties and (c) other aspects, such as vigilance machinery, accountability, transparency, and preventing abuse of political power would indicate that there is a great deal of convergence as well as a high degree of specificity in the electoral promises relating to the control of corruption.

This opens up an excellent opportunity for public action in the form of a sustained and orchestrated campaign against corruption based on a concrete but evolving agenda. Such a campaign will have to be pursued by a wide alliance against corruption forged among politicians, administrators, legislators, jurists, academicians, journalists, industrialists and other sections of the concerned public. Meanwhile, citizen groups should be encouraged to tackle corruption at local levels on specific issues. Citizens should be made to feel that as tax payers and consumers of public services, they can demand administrative accountability as a matter of right and entitlement.

We shall feel rewarded if this volume were to help in contributing to such a process.

Notes

1. Tanzi (1994).
2. Senturia (1931).
3. For a discussion of definitions see Theobald (1990) Chapter 1.
4. Government of India (1988) Section 7.
5. Government of India (1988) Sections 8,9,11 and 13.
6. On the role of transfers, see Wade (1985 and 1989); Zwart (1994).
7. On causes of corruption, see Clarke (1983); Heidenheimer (1970); Myrdal (1968); Scott (1972); Theobald (1990).
8. See in this connection, Government of India (1978).
9. For critical assessments of the sociology of corruption, see Alatas (1980); Mauss (1990); Onoge (1982); Theobald (1990); Transparency International (1996).

10. For accounts of corruption in the developing countries of Africa, Asia and Latin America, see Andreski (1966; 1968); Carino (1986); Ekpo (1979); Harriss-White & Gordon White (1996); Klitgaard (1983; 1990); Le Vine (1975); Palmier (1985); Williams (1987); Wraith & Simkins (1963).
11. For corruption in developed countries, see Benson (1978); Doig (1984); Gardiner & Olson (1968); Levi & Nelken (1996); Tanzi (1982); Theobald (1990) Chapter 3. For interesting historical accounts, see Hurstfield (1973); MacMullen (1988); Noonan (1984).
12. Government of India (1964). On the 'folklore' of corruption see Baxi (1989); Myrdal (1968).
13. Notable examples are to be found in Brazil, Mexico, Ghana, Nigeria, Pakistan, Bangladesh and Indonesia.
14. For discussions of rent-seeking, see Bhagwati (1982); Buchanan et al (1980); Krueger (1974); Rose-Ackerman (1978); Tanzi (1994); Tullock (1987).
15. On this issue, see Leff (1964); Nye (1967); Rose-Ackerman (1978; 1987); Scott (1972); Theobald (1990) Chapter 5; Tullock (1987).
16. The frequent and mostly improper use of Art 356 of the Constitution to dismiss State governments has exacerbated instability at the State level. Shortlived governments at the Centre (e.g., the Chandrashekhar government in 1990-91) and in some of the States (e.g., the Mayawati government in Uttar Pradesh in 1995) have been associated with a high degree of corruption.
17. For an informative account of post-Independence corruption at the Centre and in the States, see A.G. Noorani (1973).
18. Government of India (1964).
19. During the P.V. Narasimha Rao government at the Centre (1991-96), as many as 14 Ministers in the Union Cabinet and three Governors of States had to resign on account of their alleged involvement in irregular financial transactions. See Noorani (1996).
20. Apart from politicians belonging to the then ruling Congress party, those belonging to major opposition parties such as the BJP (L.K.Advani), Janata Dal (Sharad Yadhav), INC (T) (Arjun Singh, N.D. Tiwari) were involved in the *Hawala* proceedings.
21. For cases involving Indira Gandhi, and Rajiv Gandhi see N.K. Singh (1996). P.V. Narasimha Rao has been alleged to be involved in the St. Kitts, *Hawala* and Jharkhand Mukti Morcha (JMM) bribery cases.
22. 1996 TI Corruption Index released in June 1996 by TI. India's score in the 1995 index was 2.78, higher than in 1996.

23. A.G. Noorani (1973). An updated version of this valuable book is forthcoming. See also Padhi and Muni (1987).
24. Samuel Paul (1995).
25. For a lucid discussion of corruption in the principal-agent framework, see Klitgaard (1988) Chapter 3. For theoretical contributions, Banfield (1979); Montias & Rose-Ackerman (1981); Rose-Ackerman (1978).
26. Numerous cases of the 'buying' and 'selling' of legislators have been reported, the J.M.M. bribery case in Parliament being a glaring recent example.
27. See Chapter 9 in this volume by A.G. Noorani.
28. This is borne out by the experience with the Joint Parliamentary Committees on the Bofors contract and the Bank scam.
29. The Antulay case, for instance, lasted for nearly seven years. In his study of it, Baxi (1989) comments: 'the temporality of the adjudication is inherently and irredeemably circular; the case against Antulay moves round and round in various forums with vertiginous speed and pace in a way which makes the calendar time virtually meaningless'.
30. For an impressive example, see Bunker Roy (1996).
31. A nation-wide poll conducted by *The Times of India* in April 1996 prior to the general elections to Parliament indicated that corruption was considered to be the single most important failure of the government with 33 per cent of the respondents citing to it. In Tamilnadu, the incumbent Jayalalitha (AIADMK) government suffered a massive defeat on account of its corrupt record.
32. For a cogent articulation of this thesis, see *'The Roots of Corruption'* and *'A Proposal for Constitutional Reform'* in Nehru (1986).
33. See Harriss-White & Gordon White (1996).

ANNEXURE

Extracts from 1996 Election Manifestoes of National Parties Relating to Controlling Corruption

1. Lok Pal

BJP

Appoint a Lok Pal to entertain complaints of corruption against anybody holding public office, including the Prime Minister.

INC(I)

Establish Lok Pal with jurisdiction over all political offices, including that of the Prime Minister and Chief Ministers.

JD

Lok Pal Bill will be adopted to enquire into complaints of corruption against Union Ministers including Chief Minister and Prime Minister and others holding high public office.

Multi-member Lok Pal will be appointed by the President in consultation with the Chief Justice of India, Speaker of Lok Sabha and Chairman of Rajya Sabha, and leaders of government and the opposition in the two Houses of Parliament.

CPI (M)

The immediate setting up of Lok Pal bringing in its purview the Prime Minister; to be appointed by an authority consisting of the executive, legislature and judiciary.

CPI

Lok Pal Bill, which includes within its scope legislators and also the Prime Minister, should be adopted.

Lok Pal institutions should be set up at the Centre and in the States to investigate corruption charges against ministers and bureaucrats.

2. Electoral Reforms relating to Probity of Legislators and Political Parties

BJP

Update and adopt the Goswami Committee report.

Make it obligatory on every elected representative to make public his entire income and wealth within 90 days of election.

Amend the antidefection law whereby a member of any Legislature who changes parties will lose his or her membership of the House.

Grant statutory status to the code of conduct drawn up by the Election Commission and give it teeth.

Take steps to curb expenditure on elections by imposing a ban on advertisements, cut-outs, etc.

Introduce electronic voting machines.

Introduce a scheme of State funding of candidates to all legislatures. Provide suitable incentives for open, official corporate funding to all recognized political parties.

Make it mandatory for political parties to submit audited accounts for public scrutiny annually.

INC (I)

All members of Parliament, legislatures and local bodies to declare their assets when assuming office and leaving office.

JD

Legislative initiatives will be taken to organise wide ranging reforms based on Dinesh Goswamy Committee Report.

Statutory provision will be made so that all those holding public offices and offices of political parties declare their assets annually which shall be scrutinised by an independent commission.

Janata Dal favours State funding of elections and legitimate activity of recognized political parties.

Public auditing of the accounts of political parties will be made a statutory requirement.

CPI (M)

Comprehensive electoral reforms to ensure the elimination of money and muscle power from elections on the basis of the Dinesh Goswami Report.

Amend Section 77 of the Representation of People Act to plug loopholes in enforcing ceiling on election expenditure of candidates.

Strict action against all manifestations of the criminalisation of politics.

CPI

The Representation of the People Act should be amended to (i) curb money and muscle power (ii) ensure State funding specially in the form of necessary election material

Persons with known criminal records should not be put up nor allowed to contest as candidates in elections.

3. Vigilance Machinery, Accountability, Transparency and Preventing Abuse of Political Power

BJP

The BJP will address itself to this challenge and task (of curbing corruption) by adopting measures that are mentioned hereunder. We do not claim that this is either the ultimate blue-print for the reduction of corruption or the last word on it. It is an expression of our commitment; a first step to setting right a very great wrong of many years' malignancy; a beginning and that, too, with ourselves.

A Government that intrudes the least, we hold, governs the best. We will endeavour to combine this with open and transparent governance.

Introduce extensive regulations and requirements upon those who hold public office so that no conflict of interest is ever permitted to influence a proper discharge of their duties.

Take measures to modify and reform the methodology of Government approval for contracts, schemes and large money value agreements so as to make them more transparent.

The powers of patronage, the right to say 'Yes' or 'No' to simple daily requirements of the citizens will be reduced drastically.

Expeditiously deal with cases of corruption unresolved and in which no action has been taken in the past 10 years.

INC(I)

Appoint a high-powered commission consisting of eminent jurists, parliamentarians and administrators to recommend legal, administrative and enforcement measures to control and contain corruption and implement these measures within 6 months.

Reduce the amount of discretion obtaining in administrative decision-making, including at Minister's level, so as to render them public, transparent and accountable.

Review the work of the enforcement agencies at the Centre and in the States with a view to accord adequate autonomy and insulation from interferences in discharging their duties.

Strengthening of internal vigilance and anti-corruption mechanisms for preventive and punitive vigilance in all Government, Quasi-Government and Public agencies/organisations.

Involvement of the public in vigilance and control of corruption through public hearings, access to information and promotion of voluntary organisations in this area.

JD

Honest civil servants at all levels will be protected from harassment and highhandedness.

Rules of business governing administrative work will be reviewed and role of peoples' representatives at all levels will be strengthened in relation to administrative processes.

Official Secrets Act will be drastically revised. Right of Information will be included in the list of Fundamental Rights of the Constitution.

Transparency will be introduced in all business dealings of government with foreigners and Indians including contracts of sale and purchase and granting of credit by public financial institutions.

The CBI will be freed from the control of the Department of Personnel and made autonomous. For investigation of white collar offences, a separate autonomous organization on the lines of the CBI will be set up.

CPI (M)

Streamline functioning of investigating agencies; protect them from political interference; ensure speedy disposal and appropriate action.

CPI

Transfers and postings which are a fertile source of corruption should be done by a committee of senior officials.

Citizens' Committees composed of personalities of well-known integrity to be set up at different levels for rousing public opinion and with right to initiate proceedings before Lok Pal institutions.

There should be more transparency in government, in all deals of contract and supply.

The Right to Information must be established so as to make administration more accountable to the people and their elected bodies.

Corruption in the Political Process
A Case for Electoral Reform

K. Ganesan

Some aspects of the Indian electoral system have given rise to corruption and other abuses necessitating urgent and comprehensive electoral reforms. It can be safely assumed that the springboard or source of all governmental corruption is present-day politics. Unless steps are taken quickly to reform the electoral process in India along proper lines, corruption will be uncontrollable. This paper seeks to deal with certain salient issues in the electoral process and the resultant corruption and proceeds to suggest some practical solutions. The discussions in this paper are divided into four broad themes. Theme I deals with the high cost of elections and places particular emphasis on the distortions of electoral law. The focus of Theme II is on the financing of elections and highlights existing loopholes and suggest some remedial measures. Elimination of malpractices during elections form the core of Theme III, and Theme IV articulates the need for regulating the operations of political parties. The paper concludes by summing up the major recommendations discussed under each theme.

Theme I: The High Cost of Elections

A number of factors account for the rising cost of elections. Some of these are:

(a) Large-sized parliamentary and assembly constituencies in terms of area and population coupled with the difficulties of terrain, etc., as compared to other democracies where the constituencies are of a manageable size. Quite a few of our parliamentary constituencies extend to the whole of a bigger administrative unit, i.e., a district. This entails higher election costs to political parties and candidates in reaching out to the voters.

(b) Because of the federal system, repeated elections to Parliament and State Legislatures become unavoidable adding enormously to the high costs; multiplication of election processes at different periods to Lok Sabha and State Assemblies involves more or less twice the cost.

(c) Because of the galloping increase in the prices of essential materials, election campaigns and other inputs have become costly.

(d) The existence of high levels of illiteracy limits the methods adopted in other developed modern democracies like the distribution of printed materials to voters; this, in turn, necessitates the use of other expensive methods of campaigning, such as public meetings, rallies, processions and posters.

(e) Radio and television — two potential sources which can be successfully and effectively used for election campaigns in wider areas — are used to a lesser degree in India. While radio is solely owned by the Central Government, and so a state monopoly exists, the reach of the private television channels is limited and their use by private persons involves prohibitive costs. The television channels owned by the Union offer limited scope and that also is denied for political purposes.

(f) There is an increasing trend of depending too much on vote banks, communal politics and caste feelings.

(g) There is a show of one's financial strength and lavish spending on elections by more affluent contestants and political parties.

(h) There is a non-nurturing of the constituencies by political parties over a longer period and resorting to rough and ready short-cut methods when elections are near, expecting quick success.

The resultant consequences are many. To list a few:

(a) These factors violate free and fair elections and places a premium on the money power of political parties. Candidates and irrespective of their questionable character and honesty, jump into the election fray by successfully securing party sponsorship. The result has been that more honest and upright persons, but less affluent, are discouraged from contesting Indian elections.

(b) Because of the heavy expenses on elections, candidates extract free loans and collect and accumulate large funds under questionable means. Administrative corruption in every major organ of the Government is rampant because successful parties and candidates, especially the ruling party, try to recover the costs of elections.

(c) Realising the role money plays in elections, scope is created for enriching private pockets and accumulating funds and financial resources to fight future elections.

Unless the quantum of election expenditure is kept within a reasonable limit, the fairness of elections would be affected, opening up an opportunity for the pernicious role and adverse influence of big money in the election process, and catalysing a progressive generation of a black money economy.

Election Law: Distortions and Remedies

In most countries, the law regulates the election expenses of all candidates. In India which drew guidance from the UK for shaping its electoral law, the ceilings of election expenses are fixed under the law. The present ceiling, fixed in 1994, is Rs. 4.50 lakh per parliamentary constituency and Rs. 1.50 lakh per assembly constituency[1].

It is reported that the Election Commission has recently recommended *inter alia* to the Government an upward revision of the ceiling per parliamentary constituency from Rs. 4.5 lakh to 15 lakh on condition that the political parties which set up candidates should spend the money and show the spent amounts in the candidate's accounts. In other words, Explanation I, Section 77 of the relevant Act (see reference No. 1) should be deleted. The recommendations have yet to be accepted by the Government.

It is generally conceded that the statutory ceilings on election expenses are seldom observed in practice, and the actual expenditure incurred by a contestant does not bear any relation to the maximum laid down by the law. The ground reality in this respect is always that candidates usually spend much more money than the ceilings fixed by the law.

Serious inroads in this regard were made both in 1956 and 1974. The changes in the law relating to the return of election expenses effected in 1956 are along the following lines and without any regard to the fairness of elections[2]:

(a) The law, as amended, has narrowed down the period of accounting election expenses between the date of notification and the date of declaration of results as against the expanded period prevalent earlier, i.e., either before, during or after the elections.

(b) While the earlier provision provided for the return of all election expenses, the amended provision limited the accountability only to expenses in connection with the election "incurred or authorised by the candidate or his election agent."

(c) The declaration by a candidate and his election agent on solemn oath or affirmation which formed part of the return of election expenses itself under the earlier law has been eliminated.
(d) The disqualification period has been reduced from 5 years to 3 years.

These amendments have facilitated lavish spending by members of the party in power whose resources are multiform and enormous; also they help big money interests to influence the elections. However, it is disputable whether monetary power alone can win the elections.

The second serious amendment was made in 1974 to Section 77 by inserting an Explanation to Subsection (1) thereof after the decision by the Supreme Court in Amarnath Chawla's appeal and before the decision on the election appeal in the Supreme Court filed by Smt. Indira Gandhi against the order of the Allahabad High Court setting aside her election to the Lok Sabha. The correct rationale of the judgement of the Supreme Court in Amarnath Chawla's case was as follows[3]:

> "When the political party sponsoring a candidate incurs expenditure in connection with his election, as distinguished from expenditure on general party propaganda, and the candidate knowingly takes advantage of it or participates in the programme or activity or fails to disavow the expenditure or consents to it or acquiesces in it, it would be reasonable to infer, save in special circumstances, that he implicitly authorised the political party to incur such expenditure and he cannot escape the rigour of the ceiling by saying that he has not incurred the expenditure, but his political party has done so."

Firstly, the preposterous amendment by the insertion of Explanation I to Section 77(1) of the Act was made. The amendment is as follows[4]:

> "Notwithstanding any judgement, order or decision of any court to the contrary, any expenditure incurred or authorised in connection with the election of a candidate by a political party or by any other association or body of persons or by any individual (other than the candidate or his election agent) shall not be, and shall not ever be deemed to have been, expenditure in connection with the election incurred or authorised by the candidate or by his election agent."

Secondly, the R. P. Acts were included in the Ninth Schedule to the Constitution which is mainly intended to save the Land Acquisition Acts from attack based on Article 31A. For this purpose, the

Constitution was amended in 1975, passed by both the Houses of Parliament in record time and ratified by the States with undue haste[5]. There was no precedent anywhere in the world for such a patently and grossly objectionable legislative measure dealing with the basic law, the Constitution of India. The whole exercise came to be considered as one of the aberrations of the Emergency period and a blot on Indian political history; such misadventures should not be allowed in the future.

This enactment, was later repealed by the Constitutional Amendment in 1979[6]. However, the Constitution Bench of the Supreme Court which examined the provisions of the Constitution amended in Indira Gandhi's appeal, struck down the provisions in Clauses (4) and (5) thereof which took away the right of the judicial forum to determine election disputes (majority in the Bench), holding them as unconstitutional[7].

Previously, there was a statutory provision in Section 79 (b) of the R. P. Act, 1951, to give expression to the theory of 'holding out,' a close relevance to the incurring or authorising and accounting of election expenses through the definition of a 'candidate.' This theory of 'holding out' has been given a complete go-by through the amendment of 1975 which had also been given retrospective effect[8].

It is most unfortunate that the salutary provisions of law regarding election expenses borrowed originally from the UK law have been mutilated and destroyed beyond recognition. The provisions have been made nugatory in their effect.

In the UK, the revision of the ceiling of election expenses takes place frequently after due review on the basis of changes in the value of money or other justifiable grounds through the Secretary of State. There is no such provision under our law for periodical review at all. In the UK, the draft form of the revised ceiling is laid before and approved by each House of Parliament[9]. The present ceiling in the UK was fixed in 1994[10].

The law pertaining to election expenses should be put back to the old pristine position and follow the UK law in respect to election expenses, and the periodical review of the ceilings should be undertaken by the Commission if the ceilings on election expenses are to be kept at a reasonable level.

In 1985, the Constitution Bench of the Supreme Court observed[11]:

> "The candidate is not allowed to place his own funds in the power or possession of his political party or a trade union and then plead protection of Explanation I. That would be only a mere facade or subterfuge for evading the restraint imposed by main Section 77 (1). The deciding factor and essence of the matter is whose money it is and not whose hands it is that spends the money. It is only if the money expended by a political party is not laid at its disposal by the candidate or his election agent, that Explanation 1 would apply."

Recently, the Supreme Court pronounced a landmark judgement recognising the power of the income tax authorities to resort to remedial steps if a political party fails to submit its accounts under the law, the power of the Election Commission to issue directions to a party to render its expenditure account, etc.[12].

Theme II: Financing of Elections

(a) Banning or Regulation of Political Donations and Contributions

Politics has now been perfected into a well-organised profession or business where the investment brings forth manifold and profitable returns. Firstly, most of the recognised national and State parties are non-cadre based and unorganised at all levels. The organisational side of these parties is fragile and lacks cohesion and durable loyalty among their adherents and workers. Secondly, these parties do not enjoy the raising of funds through small subscriptions from their members.

In the regimented and control-oriented economy prevalent in India, the ruling party at the Centre and, to some extent, at the State level is able to coerce any business house at any time to part with large sums of money and, for this purpose, its administrative power of granting favours through the control of imports, exports and other licences becomes very useful. The ruling party could annoy, intimidate, delay and ruin business and, on the strength of coercive means, collect fat sums from those in charge of the management of companies and industries. Of late, corruption has increased manifold primarily because of the extension of controls, the proliferation of officers administering a multiplicity of regulations in which there is a large element of discretionary power, 'mutual benefit connection' built between the bureaucracy at higher levels and political leaders in power and the lack of a real decentralisation in these matters.

Donations or contributions to the ruling party should not be taken as voluntary, but as an extortion since no businessman or industrialist would readily part with huge sums of money unless he has a clear understanding that the political contributions made would bring him rich returns. As the late C. Rajagopalachari (Rajaji, as he was fondly called) summed up in his own inimitable way "contributions to the party in power would be impossible but for the wide element of discretionary power exercised in the administration of the 'licence-permit-raj'[13]."

A less debatable objective of regulating campaign funds is the elimination of dangerous financial pressures on elected representatives. Even if contributions are not motivated by an expected return of political favours, the legislator cannot overlook the effects of his decision in choosing the sources of campaign funds. Many politicians do not realise that they are mere spokesmen of their financial supporters. Quite often, they are not able to change their belief that what is good for their supporters is good for the country.

The Santhanam Committee, appointed to suggest measures for prevention of corruption, felt that if one family in three pays one rupee a year to a political party, the total annual contribution will be more than what is needed for all legitimate purposes of political parties in India. It is the reluctance and inability of these parties to make small collections on a wide basis and the desire to resort to short cuts through large donations that constitute the major source of corruption or a basis for suspicion of corruption. Though various other committees have given in their recommendations, no serious effort has been subsequently taken to implement them.

At present, the relevant law allows 5% of a business company's average net profits made in the preceding three years, as political contributions or for political purposes if a resolution is passed at a meeting of the Board of Directors. It should, however, be disclosed in the company's profit and loss account. Of course, there is a complete ban on government companies in this respect[14].

The most unfortunate part of unaccounted contributions that strikes one is that a substantial portion of it easily finds its way to private pockets without any enforceable compulsion or obligation of remitting it in full to the coffers of the party for which it is meant. This phenomenon is unavoidable as long as unaccounted black money is a means of contribution to political parties.

The flaws in the provisions of the relevant Section of the Companies Act were perhaps intentionally left unplugged — not defining either of the expressions used in the law, viz. "legitimate role" and "political purpose." In the UK, the law defines "political purpose" which discourages gross abuse of the practice of political contributions[15]. The loophole in the Indian law gives impetus to the corrupting influence of money power in politics. Secondly, the shareholders of a company have no say in the matter even if they hold different political views. It is left to the Board of Directors to decide the vital matter of contributions to political parties and the quantum thereof. When the situation is considered in juxtaposition to the restrictions of the Trade Union Act under which no member would be compelled to contribute to the political funds of the Union, the defect in the Companies Act would appear pronounced. Thirdly, the present provision permits contributions up to 5%, removing any reference to any specified amount, i.e. Rs. 25,000 or Rs. 50,000.

It is, therefore, suggested that instead of the Board of Directors the shareholders should consciously decide the matter at a general body meeting.

It has also been suggested that the stipulation that contributions should not exceed 5% of the average net profit might actually work out to be a very large amount in the case of major companies, at times exceeding even a crore of rupees[16]. As in other democratic countries, the limit under the law should be laid down in specific figures and not in terms of a percentage of net profit. Another suggestion is that the prohibition should extend to non-governmental companies in which the government or its financial institutions hold one-third, or even one-fourth (25%), of the shares.

Despite all restrictive measures, clandestine financial contributions to political parties would still be possible by government companies circumventing the ban through indirect methods. For instance, a company could ask its large sub-contractors to contribute liberally to the political party in power by promising them substantial compensation by way of favourable and generous terms in their contracts. It is difficult to prevent the abuse at the donors' end unless the entire strategy somehow changes and also makes the donees accountable and criminal action is initiated against both donors and donees for any violation.

The Tarkunde Committee studied the matter in detail and recommended that there should be a complete ban on political donations and contributions to political parties[17]. However, even if such a ban is imposed, the caravan of such donations and contributions would continue and the attitude of the contestants and their dishonest political parties would not change drastically if general honesty and rectitude were not to prevail. A strong public opinion should prevail for this purpose. Besides the imposition of severe criminal punishments on both the receivers and givers of donations and contributions, derecognition of recalcitrant political parties for the violation of any ban should be a part of the law.

(b) Income Tax Exemptions to Political Parties

The relevant provisions of the Income Tax Act, 1961 and those of Wealth Tax Act, 1957[18] provide for the exemption of political parties from the taxing of contributions made to them by industrialists, companies and individuals provided they maintain proper accounts for the same. Though there are adequate provisions in this law for punitive action against recalcitrant parties[19], no action has so far been initiated by the Income Tax Authorities against any political party even though they may have flouted this provision. However, the Supreme Court judgement referred to in an earlier section should set a healthy trend in this regard.

A stringent provision in the Election Law should be inserted with a view to derecognising a party for a violation of the Income Tax Act, taking criminal action against the concerned income tax authorities for their failure to take any action, and also against the concerned political parties for their failure to lodge correct and accurate returns every year. In view of the recent judgement of the Supreme Court referred to above, after giving notice to the Government to amend the election law for this purpose, waiting for a reasonable period and consulting representatives of the recognised political parties, the Commission should undertake the amendment of its Symbols Order, 1968[20].

(c) State Funding

"Elections now are largely, so to say, private enterprise whereas this is the one thing that should first be nationalised. The pluralist party structure is absolutely essential for a free democracy to function on sound lines. The expensive nature of the election is a big block in the way of a good and strong opposition party". (C. Rajagopalachari)

At present, great disparities exist in the amount of money available at the disposal of different political parties and candidates for election campaigns. This has a significant bearing on the outcome of elections, all other things being equal; the less fortunate but otherwise more deserving candidates, are placed at the greatest disadvantage. These factors induce the contestants to lean heavily on wealthy donors and interest groups to provide the necessary financial support howsoever dubious and suspect the sources of money may be. This reliance on 'fat cats' and interest groups for financial support has the effect of grossly tainting the election process.

In order to preserve the integrity and purity of the election process, it is necessary to enact legislation designed to equalise the finances of major party candidates and eliminate the possibility of contributions from wealthy individuals and interest groups influencing the election outcome. The role of wealthy contributors and interest groups, and their adverse influence on government policies and actions, can be effectively reduced by the government enacting electoral reforms providing for financing of the election campaigns. It would also have the effect of enabling competent men of integrity and public spirit, who are otherwise unable to contest the elections because they lack the necessary financial support, to wage an effective election campaign, and thereby vitalise the democratic system of the country. In other words, though State funding of elections may not fully eliminate the role of money power at the elections, it would certainly open up chances of encouraging many otherwise qualified persons to contest elections.

At present, recognised political parties at the national and State levels are entitled only to a specified number of electoral rolls free of cost. They are also entitled to two rounds of electioneering broadcasts and telecasts through All India Radio and Doordarshan, free of cost, under a restricted scheme drawn up by the Election Commission. At election time, they are also entitled to copies of the list of polling stations in the contesting constituencies and other minor items free of cost. There are still problems like defraying the heavy expenses on several items like the printing of posters, holding of public meetings, employing polling agents and counting agents, hiring of transport vehicles and distribution of voters' identity slips.

An overview of the practices followed in other democracies would place the issue in a better perspective.

In the United States of America, there is a scheme started in 1974, for providing federal matching funds to the candidates contesting elections to the federal offices of the President and Vice President. This law was enacted on strong public demand subsequent to the Watergate scandal which led to the disclosure of dubious and illegal campaign finance practices[21]. Besides public disclosure of contributions and expenditure for election purposes and setting contribution limits, this enactment provides for public funding.

The Federal Law of West Germany provides for the reimbursement of election costs under certain conditions.

In the United Kingdom[22], the candidates are entitled to:
(i) Free use of public schools and voluntary schools to hold public meetings for the furtherance of their candidature at reasonable times during the election campaign period.
(ii) Sending free of postage, subject to post office regulations, one poll communication relating to elections, addressed to each elector.
(iii) Certain broadcasting and telecasting facilities through the BBC with stipulated conditions.
(iv) Arrangements for party election broadcasts on radio and television during the general elections made by a committee comprising of representatives of the political parties, BBC, Independent Television Commission (ITC) and the radio authority.

France, Sweden, Italy, Austria, Finland, Netherlands, Norway and Denmark are some of the other countries where political parties receive substantial public subsidies.

Table I has been prepared with a view to highlighting the election expenses on major items to suit our conditions.

Table I

Parliamentary Constituencies

Average electorate per parliamentary constituency	10,00,000
Average polling stations per parliamentary constituency	1,140
Average assembly segments in a parliamentary constituency	8
Average number of contestants set up by recognised political parties in a parliamentary constituency	5

I. Transport and Fuel

(a) One vehicle for use by workers — for 10 days — for every assembly segment. The total number of such segments for parliamentary constituency is taken as 8 — hire charges for a vehicle with fuel — Rs. 1,500 a day. Total cost: 10 x 8 x 1,500 =   Rs. 1,20,000
(b) One vehicle for the candidate   Rs. 15,000
(c) One vehicle for the election agent 10 x 1,500 =   Rs. 15,000
(d) One vehicle on poll day extra   Rs. 10,000

Total   Rs. 1,60,000

II. Paid Workers

(a) For a polling area of 2,000 electors (2 polling stations) for 7 days — remuneration at Rs. 50 per day for campaigning: 600 x 7 x Rs. 50 =   Rs. 2,10,000
(b) On poll day, two polling agents employed per polling station at Rs. 40 each: 1,140 x 2 x Rs. 40 =   Rs. 91,200
(c) Two agents per polling station deployed outside polling stations to issue identity slips. Also, hire charges for furniture: 1,140 x 2 x Rs. 40 =   Rs. 91,200
(d) Agents for counting of votes (15 tables) for each assembly segment. Total - 120 tables + 8 counting tables and the table of the R. O. or Asst. R. O. Total agents involved at the rate of 2 per table 128 x 2 = 256
Remuneration at Rs. 40 per worker:
128 x 2 x 40 =   Rs. 10,240

Total   Rs. 4,02,640

Table I *(Contd...)*

III. Election Materials and Electioneering

(a) Distribution of identity slips to each elector (10 lakh electors in a parliamentary constituency, printing paper, writing charges, etc. at 5 paise per slip)
10,00,000 x .05 paise =   Rs. 50,000
(Ultimately, this task should be taken up by the electoral authorities.)

(b) Posters (3 multi-colour posters and others for each polling area: Rs. 9 per poster + Re. 1 for pasting or distribution) 1,140 x 3 x 10 =   Rs. 34,200

(c) Pamphlets, badges, banners, leaf-lets, cut-outs, etc. - Rs. 225 for each polling area 1,140 x 225 =   Rs. 2,56,500

(d) Public meetings, processions, etc. (mikes, posters, chairs, etc.) — 3 per each assembly segment — Total 8 x 3 = 24 meetings: Rs. 3,000 per meeting
3,000 x 24 =   Rs. 72,000

(e) One meeting addressed by a national leader or a State leader   Rs. 10,000

Total   Rs. 4,22,700

IV. Stationery, Voters' Lists, Books, etc.   Rs. 60,000

V. Miscellaneous Expenses   Rs. 30,000

Progressive total: Item I   Rs. 1,60,000
Item II   Rs. 4,02,640
Item III   Rs. 4,22,700
Item IV   Rs. 60,000
Item V   Rs. 30,000

    Rs. 10,75,340

Rounded off to   Rs. 10,75,000.

(a) Bigger parliamentary constituencies may be 520 out of the total of 543 constituencies: 520 x 10,75,000 = Rs. 55.91 crore.
(b) For the remaining 23 small constituencies, the total election costs, at the rate of Rs. 7,00,000 work out to: 23 x 7,00,000 = Rs. 1.61 crore.
(c) If the average number of contestants set up by recognised political parties is taken as 5 per constituency, the total cost of public funding on this basis works out to: 5 x Rs. 57.52 crore = Rs. 287.60 crore (rounded off to Rs. 288 crore). It may not exceed Rs. 300 crore in a five-year slot.

State Assembly

The total number of elective assembly seats vary from State to State depending on the multiple of assembly constituencies for a parliamentary constituency. For example, Uttar Pradesh has at present a multiple of 5 assembly seats for each parliamentary constituency (the total number of parliamentary constituencies in that State is 85 and the total number of assembly constituencies is 425); Tamil Nadu has at present a multiple of 6 assembly seats for each parliamentary constituency (the total number of parliamentary constituencies in that State is 39 and the total number of assembly constituencies is 234); and Karnataka has at present a multiple of 8 assembly seats for each parliamentary constituency (the total number of parliamentary constituencies is 28 and the total number of assembly constituencies is 224).

Applying only a rough and ready method — It is not feasible to apply the above formula in respect of parliamentary elections — the average total number of electors works out to 2,00,000 and on the basis of an election expense of Rs. 1.5 per elector, the total amount works out to Rs. 3 lakh. On the basis of an average of 7 contestants, the total amount for a constituency comes to Rs. 21 lakh. The total amount required for State funding in respect of assembly elections is not calculated since the total number of elective seats vary from State to State.

When State funding is adopted, there may not be any need for private election expenses, or only a nominal amount may be required for a ceiling. If a ceiling is provided under the law, the amount may be fixed at Rs. 50,000 per parliamentary constituency per candidate and Rs. 10,000 per assembly constituency per candidate in a bigger State.

The matter, no doubt, requires detailed discussions by the Election Commission with the representatives of recognised political parties. The discussions may also be on various items relating to election expenses and State funding like accounting method, lodging of election accounts with the concerned authorities and donations and contributions, if any, received by political parties and contestants from companies and industrial houses.

If each income tax payer in India pays a graded contribution, i.e. Rs. 25, Rs. 50, Rs. 100 or Rs. 200, through his income tax returns as in the USA, where the scheme is a $ 1 lay off check-off by each income tax payer to be paid over to the Presidential Election Campaign Fund[23], the total contribution may fully meet the Rs. 300 crore incurred in the State funding of elections besides meeting the legitimate annual expenses of recognised political parties on political purposes. As in the USA, the Government of India, State Governments and political parties should not have any say in the collection and distribution of the funds raised in the above manner.

While considering the scheme of State funding, certain basic and relevant postulates should not be lost sight of. They are:

(i) Since a very large number of non-serious candidates jump into the election fray, State assistance should be made available only to candidates set up by recognised political parties. Otherwise, the scheme would be self-defeating as it would become quite unmanageable and also a heavy drain on the public exchequer. However, if any candidate other than one set up by a recognised political party wins the election, legal reimbursement may be provided to him.

(ii) There is much force in advocating State assistance only *in kind* and not in cash. If, as in other advanced countries, cash assistance is provided, State funding is likely to flounder as no effective means could be worked out to prevent affluent candidates from lavishly spending from their own resources in addition to the amounts provided by the State. If, on the other hand, assistance is granted only in kind with respect to such items as can be brought under the complete and effective control of the authorities by imposing a total ban on private expenses, then the scheme would have a greater measure of success.

(iii) State assistance in kind should be given only with respect to areas where the application of legal provisions imposing a total ban on private expenses is full, effective and meaningful. There are certain specific and major areas of expenditure on which such a ban is quite feasible.

State assistance is possible in respect of (i) a limited number of transport vehicles to be used by the contestants only on permits issued by the returning officer concerned and the grant of fuel coupons, the cost of which must be borne entirely by the Government; (ii) the preparation and issue of voters' identity slips to voters by the electoral authorities (the entire work would go away with the introduction of a multi-purpose heliographed identity cards to every citizen); (iii) paid workers for campaigning and as polling and counting agents, the costs to be borne by the Government; (iv) posters, banners, etc., these items which are currently attended to by the contestants can be eliminated and private expenditure totally banned. The Election Commission could restrict the numbers, fix printing presses and bear the entire cost.

The above items have been chosen as they cannot be done stealthily. The proposed law could impose a total ban on these items or easily control them. In respect of some items, like polling and counting agents, the law has already laid down the numbers. Further, the rivals could detect the infraction of the proposed law and the Election Commission, as is already done, could send out monitoring agencies to supervise and regulate their working. It is also easier to penalise the recalcitrant offenders of the law after enquiry.

Besides the above items to be regulated by law, the following measures would reduce election expenses considerably:

(i) Selection of common places for holding public meetings by all contestants with public address systems like loudspeakers fixed.

(ii) Use of electronic voting machines.

(iii) Holding simultaneous elections to the Lok Sabha and State assemblies only at the end of a five-year term.

To achieve what is mentioned in item (iii) the Constitution should be amended for the imposition of President's rule at the Centre as well. In the event of a constitutional breakdown of the Government machinery, like in Article 356, the Centre should be brought under President's rule for the full period of the remaining term of the five years so as to enable the holding of the General Elections to the Lok Sabha and State assemblies simultaneously.

In that event, the Central Government would be ruled by the President with experts appointed to man the ministries and implement all the necessary legislative measures passed by the Rajya Sabha. This would drastically reduce election expenses.

(iv) Appointment of watch-dog committees at polling stations and constituencies to monitor the election arrangements and supervise them effectively. The committees should consist of only non-political persons, drawn locally from eminent jurists and other public spirited persons.

(v) Implementation of heliographed multipurpose photo identity cards for every citizen so that progressively the revision of electoral rolls could be totally eliminated.

(vi) Discouraging of non-serious candidates from contesting elections by the imposition of acceptable measures of restrictions on them.

(vi) Throwing open to the contestants (for electioneering) a separate channel in the official and private television channels and All India Radio, free of cost.

Theme III: Eliminating Malpractices during Elections

A. The Role of Civil Servants and Police

In India, there is no clear division of the roles between top-level bureaucrats on the one hand and the executive political bosses on the other hand. In a democracy, it is the duty and responsibility of the political set-up to lay down Government policies and aims, and it is left to the administrative set-up at the various concerned levels i.e., bureaucrats, to faithfully implement those policies. In India, there is an intermixing or overlapping of these duties and responsibilities most of the time. Bureaucrats at the higher levels often actively assist their political bosses in the Government to decide on policies and to carry them out. Quite often, loopholes are purposely left unplugged, giving enormous scope for corruption and bribery all around. This does not augur well for the effective functioning of democracy. It is virtually against the principles of democracy. This has given bureaucrats and the ruling political set-up, acting as the executive government bosses, to build up close links and relations between them. Unfortunately, quite often, there is a sharing of booties emerging from these policies and their implementations. And, at election time, these administrative forces are often found to assist the ruling party, directly or indirectly, in many ways.

The existing provisions of the law placing these staff on deputation with the Election Commission do not discourage them from assisting the contestants. The legal provisions, therefore, require strengthening in many respects by plugging the loopholes in existing provisions. The Election Commission should be the ultimate authority in all such cases to initiate criminal and other disciplinary actions.

In the UK, there are clear rules and regulations governing the role of civil servants during elections. The Conduct Rules in India also govern the role of civil servants during elections and ban any indulgence in politics[24].

The Code of Conduct evolved by the Election Commission for observation by the ruling party prescribes elaborate details on the role of civil servants which should form part of the legal provisions in the election law as recommended by the Dinesh Goswami Committee. Any violation of the same should be made a penal offence. Besides conviction and sentence, the violators should be debarred from standing for elections for 10 years.

In regard to the disciplining, appointing and potentially vindictive transfers of civil servants, there is need to constitute some sort of ombudsmen composed of eminent jurists. In this way, the scope for civil servants to depend on and obtain favours from political bosses could be effectively reduced.

There is a case for strengthening the existing provisions in the election laws[25] for taking disciplinary action against recalcitrant civil and police forces employed for election purposes exclusively by the Election Commission, and also making them more stringent.

In fact, nothing is more deterrent than the fear of prompt disciplinary action, and this would inculcate in them the right approach and absolutely impartial conduct. It is now left to the appointing authority to take action on the basis of the report of the Election Commission. On the prompting of political bosses and parties, the recommendations of the Election Commission are quite often ignored or delayed.

The election law describes the items of corrupt practices as illegal gratification, corruption and bribe to vote, and these are prohibited. These are described under different clauses of Section 123 as the details would show[26].

The police force is being misused for sundry purposes, particularly at State levels. During elections in India, the police quite often plays a role advantageous to the ruling party and not in an impartial manner. The police force's primary duty at election times is to create ideal conditions of peace so that free and fair democratic elections are possible. Unfortunately, its services are utilised to further the political fortunes of its bosses. The police looks after the interests of its 'political bosses' with all the means at its disposal. Elections provide a golden opportunity to prove and demonstrate loyalties. The career path of an upright and duty-conscious police officer is strewn with perils.

Appointments, transfers and comfortable postings are decided upon factors other than merit and competence. All these developments give scope for corruption and bribery.

The provisions of the Prevention of Corruption Act[27] appear to be ineffective in the sense that the law does not touch even the fringe of the problems. As already stated, the Election Commission should be armed with powers to initiate criminal action under the law.

There is an urgent need to make the police forces in a State totally independent from the political administration to enable them to function without fear or favour. For this purpose, the first essential requirement is to implement the National Police Commission's recommendations fully — at least in regard to the appointment of higher police officers, etc.[28]

B. Use of Electronic Voting Machines

It is a sad reflection on our electoral system that most of the current political parties do not countenance any desirable improvements in the electoral process. This is true at least with respect to the use of electronic voting machines (EVMs) in our elections. This scheme has been put off because of the unreasonable reluctance of political parties to accept it. The ultimate masters, i.e. the electorate, are helplessly caught in a vicious circle and are not in a position to force the issue.

The advantages of the electronic voting machine are manifold; to name a few:

(i) Counting can be done in a few minutes. No storage is necessary. As soon as the polled machines are taken to counting centres from the polling stations and operated by connecting them to a master computer, the mixing of votes could be done and the results displayed automatically. Such a procedure considerably reduces the burden and expenses of the contestants.

(ii) The pace of polling will be faster, easier and smoother.

(iii) The machines, through a suitable built-in-procedure, eliminate the possibility of large-scale impersonation.

(iv) A single EVM can record up to 4,000 votes with the result that up to three polling stations housed in the same premises could be combined.

(v) Only a few items like a register for signature or thumb impression, sealing materials, etc., are required.

(vi) The numbers of polling personnel could be reduced considerably.

(vii) The cost of printing ballot papers is almost eliminated as only one sheet of ballot paper is required to be pasted on each balloting unit.

(viii) No invalid votes.

(ix) Counterfoil of the ballot paper need not be printed.

(x) An EVM can be fitted in a small transport vehicle and stationed at the door-step of electors. Large-scale impersonation and booth-capturing are eliminated. Such a procedure can reduce the loss of innocent lives in large numbers as in the case of elections in 1989, 1991 and 1996.

The savings on expenditure both for the candidates and the exchequer are so enormous that any authority who has financial concern or prudence would welcome the move for the immediate use of EVMs. The use of EVMs at Indian elections has the potential of reducing cost of elections considerably. Consequently, it is possible to contain the use of monetary power; for this reason alone, the scheme should be introduced without any further delay.

C. Photo Identity Card for Each Adult Citizen

The provision of a photo identity card for every elector only for elections may not fully serve the purpose. More than Rs. 500 crores may have been spent so far to push through the scheme in haste without understanding the related basic realities. In fact, such a system may not be successful as has been proven in the case of some States in the past. Given this experience there would be reluctance on the part of the electors to own such cards. On the other hand, the scheme may succeed if these cards are made compulsory for (a) drawing rations; (b) admission of wards to schools and colleges; (c) driving licences for vehicles; (d) transfer of property; (e) elimination of caste certificates which are now granted by Government authorities (since a photo identity card would indicate the caste of the holder); (f) granting of passport, etc. Only then would they prove to be useful.

The preparation and distribution of photo identity cards nationwide would dispense with the annual preparation of electoral rolls. This would, in turn, eliminate, to a large extent, impersonation and bogus voting at the elections. The scheme would result in considerable savings to the exchequer and the contestants in many ways.

Of course, by spending money on a large scale to cover the entire country by this elaborate exercise, on the basis of Rs. 15 per heliographed photo identity card in duplicate, the total cost would come to around Rs. 1,500 crore for 100 crore citizens. This expenditure can be shared between the Union and the States on a 50:50 basis. If the expenses are spread over six years, only Rs. 225 crore need be provided annually in the Union Budget, and the balance Rs. 225 crore could be recovered from the States.

D. Creation of a Watchdog Committee for Every Assembly Constituency to Supervise the Conduct of Elections

There is no substitute for building up confidence in the electoral machinery charged with the duty and responsibility of conducting free and fair elections. This could be achieved by the creation of a watchdog committee for every assembly constituency or assembly segment in a parliamentary constituency and the association of each such committee with the concerned electoral machinery and process. These committees should consist only of non-political local persons drawn from eminent retired civil servants and citizens who are not in any way affiliated to a particular political ideology or party. The members should be scrupulously honest and of sterling character and rectitude.

Their main duty would be to oversee the actual conduct of elections in the assembly constituency or assembly segment under their charge. In an assembly constituency or segment, there are about 200 polling stations. For each polling area, about five local persons with the utmost dedication, honesty and moral rectitude should be associated with every activity, inside and outside a polling station to supervise and monitor, so as to facilitate free and fair elections.

Specific norms should be laid down for the above purposes. Each committee should consolidate the reports from its teams deployed at the polling stations and submit a report immediately after the elections to the returning officer, the chief electoral officer of the State concerned and the Election Commission in New Delhi. This report should receive due and quick consideration by the authorities. In case of any adverse report or comment in a particular report, the authority should take the necessary remedial action including postponing counting and repolling. Again, on the basis of the report, the Election Commission should have the power of setting aside an election, disqualify the guilty contestants from contesting any election for 10 years, and to initiate criminal action.

Theme IV: Regulating the Functioning of Political Parties

"Party divisions, whether on the whole operating for good or not, are things inseparable from free government. This is a truth, which, I believe, admits little dispute having been established by the uniform experience of all ages." (Edmund Burke)

A. Need for a Constitutional Provision

The prime goal of all political parties is to seek the control of the government and assume the exclusive responsibility for governance of the country. Neither the ruling party nor the parties in the opposition can afford to function irresponsibly without any sense of concern for the national welfare or common good. In view of the manifold drawbacks in the set-up and functioning of political parties in India, there is a need for immediate rectification.

In Great Britain, the major political parties active on the political scene are only a few with clear-cut policies and aims. All the three major parties i.e., Conservatives, Labour and Liberals, follow their party constitutions to the last word, both in letter and spirit. Their party organisations never face disarray in the sense that they do not give up organisational elections for any reason whatsoever as easily as in India. They always remain in a state of preparedness to face the challenge of elections at any time. Their process of selection of candidates proceed on well-defined principles and procedures which always keep in view the basic element of primacy to the party. There is no question of there being parties carrying on their activities, at any level, on an *ad hoc* basis. Their sense of commitment and adherence to the principles of democracy are so firmly rooted in their working that they consciously observe these principles.

After the traumatic experience of the Nazi regime, the Constitution of West Germany specifically invests the political parties with the status of institutions under the country's basic law (Article 21).

In the USA, the process of evolution in political history reached its peak when two competing parties, the Republican and Democrats, emerged firmly on the political horizon. The working of political institutions is thus made easy by limiting the people's choice to candidates set up by any one of these parties. Both are so well organised that any one of them can easily transform itself into the ruling party or sit in the opposition without any disturbance.

However, in India, there are at present a plethora of political parties — eight recognised national parties, about 35 recognised State parties and about 350 registered parties. Strangely enough, they are allowed to participate in democratic elections to the Lok Sabha and Assemblies of States without observing democratic principles in the day-to-day working of their constitution and the Party's internal matters.

Against this backdrop, a special law should be enacted on the following lines:

- The parties should strictly adhere to their constitution in regard to the holding of organisational elections at all levels.
- Each party should maintain day-to-day accounts which should be opened for inspection and independent audit by auditors named by the Election Commission.
- The audited accounts should be submitted annually to the Election Commission together with a declaration that elections to the party organs have been held periodically.
- The Election Commission should be armed with powers to derecognise a party in the event of a failure to observe the proposed law.
- The Election Commission, in turn, should forward an yearly consolidated report together with a copy of the audited accounts of each Party to the Speaker of the Lok Sabha in the case of recognised national parties and to the Speaker of the State Assembly in the case of recognised State parties.

B. Code of Conduct for Elected Representatives

The author suggests that a Conduct Committee be formed for this purpose with the Speaker or the Chairman of the House concerned at the top and consisting of members drawn from the parties represented in the House. A parliamentary law should be made regulating the conduct of the members and the punishment to be awarded to the violators of the Conduct provisions including expulsion of the member concerned from the House. The Supreme Court should be given the power to finally decide on the appeal, if any, filed against the Conduct Committee's decision. The Court should also be invested with the power to pass interim orders including a stay of the Committee's adverse orders.

The following guidelines spelt out by G. Durgabai Deshmukh should come in handy in such an exercise[29]:

(i) A member should not try to secure business from the government for a firm, company or organisation with which he is directly or indirectly concerned.

(ii) A member should not give certificates which are not based on facts.

(iii) A member should not make profit out of a government residence allotted to him by subletting the premises.

(iv) A member should not unduly influence government officers or the ministers in a case in which he is interested financially either directly or indirectly.

(v) A member should not receive hospitality of any kind for any work that he desires or proposes to do from a person or organisation on whose behalf the work is to be done by him.

(vi) A member should not proceed to take action on behalf of his constituents on some insufficient or baseless facts.

(vii) A member should not permit himself to be used as a ready supporter of anybody's grievances or complaints.

(viii) A member should not endorse incorrect certificates on bills claiming amounts due to him.

(ix) A member should not write recommendatory letters or speak to government officials for employment or business contacts for any of his relations or other persons in whom he is directly or indirectly interested.

C. Benefits, Privileges and Powers of Elected Representatives

Of course, MPs should enjoy very legitimate privileges if they are meant to carry out faithfully the responsibilities and tasks entrusted to them. But they quite often misuse their position. Each MP enjoys certain benefits which, even if they are scrapped, would not matter much to the welfare of the country as a whole. Some of the benefits enjoyed by each MP are[30]:

- Emergency quotas in respect of railways for travel which can be operated by MPs.
- Special quota of 100 gas connections per year allotted to each MP which is operated upon by him.
- A quota of 25 telephone connections.
- Recommendation for admission of two students to central schools every academic year.
- Allocation of a development fund of Rs. 2 crore per annum per MP for constituency development.
- Free accommodation at New Delhi and free telephone calls.
- Allotment, on a priority basis, of petrol pumps, etc. on the recommendation of an MP.

These benefits are in addition to the monthly salary, pension and free travel by rail or air to attend Parliament. They make the MPs demi-gods and place them in a special category. All these change the representative character of MPs and make them behave in a most irresponsible manner to even the legitimate pleas of their constituents.

D. Regulation of the Role of Cabinet Ministers, etc.

Many Cabinet Ministers enjoy enormous status, which could be traced to their powers to grant favours to selected persons. Many of them are not above board in regard to accumulating wealth, for themselves or their party, through illegal and questionable means. As they are in power, they could quite successfully hide their corrupt activities and escape the public and media notice. Otherwise, the Bank Security Scam, the Bofors case, the Hawala Case and the Enron problem would not have arisen. The entire administrative set-up including the CBI are under their control and the truth would not come out easily. The only effective remedy and hope now available is the activist attitude the Supreme Court has begun to adopt of late with respect to public interest litigation.

There is also justification to make it compulsory for every elected candidate to declare his assets and wealth every year and before he is allowed to take oath as a member of the legislature.

E. Misuse of Anti-defection Law[29]

The anti-defection law which is in operation now seeks to outlaw defections. However, the legal provisions have so far led the authorities i.e. Presiding Officer of the House in various States, to offer different interpretations in regard to cases presented before him for his determination, resulting in unchecked spread of the evil of defection. The general phenomenon increasingly noticed has been that more than one-third of the members of a party represented in legislative bodies stage defections on the specious ground of a 'split' which is legally exempt from incurring disqualification.

This sad phenomenon had been increasingly noticed after the 1967 general elections to the Lok Sabha when the political picture of a monolithic party ruling the Centre and a number of States changed, with no political party securing absolute majority, and resulting in coalition governments of parties. Ministries fell because of large scale defections and new ministries were formed with the support of fresh defectors. It was also estimated that after the 1967 general elections during one year period, 175 Congressmen defected to other parties and the Congress Party gained 139 members by way of defections from other parties. It was estimated that after the said general elections, 800 MLAs defected between 1967 and 1970. We have now the sorry spectacle of the entire block of our elected representatives in one State led by their shrewd leader shifting loyalty and changing colours.

The act of defection was known in British House of Commons as 'floor crossing'. Even Sir Winston Churchill and Lloyd George had at least at one time or the other staged 'floor crossing'. Of course in that country, floor crossing was quite often the outcome of honest differences of opinion with others in their original parties unlike in our country. The underlying principles of the Tenth Schedule to the Constitution, otherwise termed as Anti-Defection Law, is quite laudable. But putting the legal provisions thereof to actual practice produced ill effects.

The provisions urgently require drastic changes in the following manner to make the law more effective:
(i) Firstly, the Speaker or Chairman (vide paragraph 6 of the Tenth Schedule) is made the final arbiter in determining the disqualification cases under the Anti-Defection Law. Paragraph 7 of that Schedule barring the jurisdiction of the courts has been

struck down and the decision of the Presiding Officer is now made subject to the judicial review by the High and Supreme Courts. Still making the Presiding Officers the deciding authorities in this important matter passes one's comprehension since every Speaker in our country is elected every time in a contest with support of the majority party in the House, namely the Ruling Party unlike in the UK and elsewhere where the principle of 'once a Speaker always the Speaker' normally applies.

(ii) The Election Commission should be made the deciding authority in the matter of disqualification under the Constitution. If grounds for disqualification are established, the seat should be declared by the Election Commission as vacant. In other words, the member should not be entitled to continue as such member once a declaration is made by the Election Commission. Of course, the rule of law and principles of natural justice should be applied before the Election Commission takes a final decision in a given case. The Election Commission should also be clothed with the power of giving interim orders before a final decision is given by it.

(iii) Until the Commission decides legal issues based on evidence, there is scope also for an interim order passed either by it or by the Presiding Officer of the House concerned disqualifying the concerned member from holding 'any office' under the Government or participating in any debate or voting in the House.

(iv) A reasonable time limit, say 3 or 6 months, should be fixed in the law, for the final disposal by the Election Commission of a disqualification case.

(v) Having regard to the sacred principles of democracy, there is absolutely no justification for differential treatment of members. For example, independent and nominated members should not be treated differently.

Summary of Recommendations

- The provisions of law as to election expenses should be put back fully to their pristine position and should be along the lines of the UK provisions in this respect. As in the UK, periodical review of

the ceilings of election expenses must be undertaken by the Election Commission and its recommendations in that behalf should be made binding.
- There should be a complete ban (Section 293A of the Companies Act) on contributions to political parties by business houses and companies. In the alternative, the contributions could strictly be regulated by taking remedial measures; as regards state funding of elections, the items chosen should be such as may easily eliminate or contain wasteful election expenditure; the state subsidy should be in the form of kind only and not in cash (in terms of cost, one round of parliamentary elections would be about Rs. 10.75 lakh for a bigger constituency and Rs. 7 lakh for a smaller constituency; only candidates of recognised political parties should be made eligible with the provision for later reimbursement if any other candidate is elected to raise necessary funds (about Rs. 300 crore in total for parliamentary elections); and graded amounts should be laid down in the Indian income tax law as in the USA which may be deducted from specified income taxpayers. Except Election Commission, no other authority should have any control over the funds and their distribution. Similarly for State Funding for State assemblies' elections, deductions should be made from sales tax payers and necessary funds raised; if a ceiling on expenses is still required after the scheme of the state funding of elections is put into operation, it should be kept low.
- The elections to the Lok Sabha and State assemblies should be held simultaneously only after a period of 5 years from the constitution of the house. In these matters, a referendum may advisedly be held.
- Apart from simultaneous elections, there should be selection of common places for holding public meetings by all parties; use of electronic machines in elections; use of the scheme of multi purpose heliographed photo identity cards for citizens; appointment of watchdog committees at various levels in the constituency; elimination or strict restriction on non-serious candidates; throwing open a separate TV channel, free of cost, for carrying on electioneering campaign by candidates of recognised political parties.

- There should be regulation of the functions of political parties on proper lines.
- The provisions in the model code of conduct evolved by the Election Commission (the present provisions of Para VII of the Code) should form part of the election law;
- There should be strengthening of the existing provisions of the R.P. Acts, 1950 and 1951 regarding the deputation of officials connected with elections and by inserting stringent punishment on the officials;
- The Election Commission should be clothed with power to:
    (i) initiate criminal action against recalcitrant officials (at present, only the appointing authority is clothed with such power);
    (ii) constitute a special court for the purpose;
    (iii) take disciplinary proceedings on its own. In other words, for any violation of the rules relating to the Code or rules of the game of elections, the Election Commission should be the ultimate authority for initiating disciplinary proceedings and impose punishment; and
    (iv) impose severe punishment on the recalcitrant servants.
- Regarding police officers in the higher ranks, the recommendations of the National Police Commission should be implemented.
- There should be a separate judicial agency, i.e., Ombudsman, to enquire into the conduct of civil and police officers at the time of elections on a complaint by any of the political parties or public men.
- A code of conduct should be laid down by law and a Conduct Committee under the head of the Speaker or Chairman and consisting of members of the House drawn from the parties represented in the House concerned should be formed and punishment should be given for violators. An appeal should lie to the Supreme Court to finally decide the issue and with powers to give interim orders including stay of the adverse decision by the Speaker.
- Elected representative should also file their accounts of assets every year.
- The proposed Committee should be allowed to scrutinise members' annual return of assets, etc.

- The Lok Ayukt under the Lok Pal enactment should cover not only all the Ministers but also the PM, CMs and the elected members. The law in this respect should be made without any delay.

Notes and References

1. The Table under Rule 90 of the Conduct of Elections Rules, 1961.
2. The Representation of the People (Amendment) Act, 1956 (Act No. 270 of 1956).
3. Kanwarlal Gupta v. Amar Nath Chawla and Others (AIR 1975 S.C. 308).
4. The Representation of the People (Amendment) Act, 1974 (Act No.50 of 1974).
5. The Constitution (Thirty-Ninth Amendment) Act, 1975.
6. The Constitution (Forty-Fourth Amendment) Act, 1979.
7. 1975 [SUPP] S.C.C. 1.
8. The Representation of the People (Amendment) Act, 1975 (Act No.40 of 1975).
9. Section 76 (2) of the U.K. Representation of the People Act, 1983.
10. U.K. Representation of the People (Variation of limits of Candidates Election Expenses) Order 1992 (came into force on the 11th March, 1993).
11. Dr. Nalla Thamby Terah v. Union of India (AIR 1985 S.C. 1133).
12. Common Causes Society (Mr. H.D. Shourie, Director & Others v. Union of India-JT 1996(3) 706 (SC).
13. C. Rajagopalachari, *Rescue Democracy,* Bharatiya Vidya Bhawan.
14. Section 293A of the Companies Act, 1956 (Act No.1 of 1956).
15. Section 19(3) of the U.K. Companies Act, 1967.
16. L.P. Singh, *Electoral Reforms,* Centre for Policy Research, New Delhi.
17. The Report of the Committee (CFD) set up by Shri Jaya Prakash Narain under the Chairmanship of Justice Tarkunde in August, 1974 Popularly known as "Tarkunde Committee Report".
18. Section 13A, of the Income Tax Act, 1961 (Act No.43 of 1961) and Section 45(1) of the Wealth Tax Act, 1957.
19. Sections 142 and 276CC Income Tax Act, 1957.
20. The Election Symbols (Reservation and Allotment) Order, 1968 made by the Election Commission in exercise of its powers under Article 324 read with the rules 5 and 10 of the Conduct of Elections Rules, 1967.

21. The U.S. Federal Campaign Act, 1975.
22. Section 91 of the Representation of the People Act, 1983.
23. U.S.A. voluntary checked off (one U.S. dollar by income tax payer — See part VIII — Designation of Income Tax payments to Presidential Election Campaign Fund — see section 9006(a) 'Bibliography' a book entitled *Federal Election Campaign Laws, Compiled by the US Federal Election Commission*.
24. Rule 5 of The Central Services (CONDUCT).
25. The Representation of The Peoples Acts, 1950 and 1951.
26. Section 123 of the Representation of the People Acts, and 1951.
27. The Prevention of Corruption Act.
28. National Police Commission's Report.
29. A. Surya Prakash, *What Ails Indian Parliament*, p. 263.
30. The Constitution (Fifty Second Amendment) Act, 1985.

3

Corruption, Political Interference and the Civil Service

Madhav Godbole

With rampant corruption and sharp deterioration in the standards of public morality it is not surprising that India is now categorised as one of the most corrupt countries in the world. Recently, this was reaffirmed in a statistical index drawn up by a German non-governmental organisation, Transparency International, which measured perceptions of corruption in 41 countries by polling international businessmen and financial journalists. The survey placed India among the seven most corrupt countries. In such an alarming situation, the role of the civil service is justifiably coming under increasingly closer scrutiny and evaluation.

As the title indicates, this paper deals with two facets of abuse of political power — abuse through the civil service, and the abuse of political power by politicians to harass, demoralise and subjugate the civil service into the role of a hand-maiden for the political party in power. This paper deals mostly with the higher civil services, particularly the All India Services, as they occupy a pre-eminent position in both the States and the Centre. If these services are corrupt, integrity cannot be promoted or enforced in the other services. Further, the abuse of political power is largely found in the higher civil services. However, corruption has permeated the administration at all levels in the local self-government institutions, State governments and the Centre. While institution-specific and work-related solutions will have to be found to deal effectively with each of these areas, the broad conclusions of this paper, with suitable modifications, will hold true for many areas of administration. This paper suggests a number of changes in the institutional, legal and policy framework governing the civil services while raising some awkward, inescapable and difficult questions. For example, should a civil servant be a silent spectator when a palpably wro decision is made for corrupt motives, or should he consider it his public duty to come out against such a decision? An equally important issue is whether the civil servant in such a situation should be provided any statutory protection against harassment by the government. This paper also looks at the oft-mentioned strategies of enforcing accountability, transparency, timely and effective investigation of cases under the Prevention of Corruption Act, putting the investigating agencies such as the Central Bureau of Investigation (CBI) under statutory authorities established both in the States and the Centre, redefining the ambit of the Official Secrets Act and passing a law which confers on citizens the right to information.

Ideally, the civil service should represent the highest standards of efficiency, public service, integrity and political neutrality. It should enjoy freedom to give objective, dispassionate and frank advice. If its advice is disregarded, it should have the freedom to resubmit the matter to the political executive for a reconsideration of his decision. The political executive should clearly indicate in writing the reasons for disregarding the advice tendered to him. All oral orders of the superiors, whether in the civil service or political hierarchy, should always be faithfully and promptly reproduced in writing as has been suggested by the Transaction of Business Rules. Civil servants should not be allowed to hide behind oral orders; they will have to be personally culpable for irregular actions purportedly based on oral orders. There should be no direct or indirect pressure exerted on a civil servant to record a note or to take action in any particular way. The political executive should have the moral courage to stand up and take responsibility for his decision and to defend it in the legislature and outside. These ground rules are sensible and easy to understand. But in recent years, they are being increasingly ignored which will lead to a total collapse of the foundation on which the super-structure of the civil service was erected.

It must be underlined at the very outset that the civil service is not a paragon of virtue. It will be wrong to proceed on the assumption that it is only the political system which is to be blamed or found faulty. The civil service is equally remiss in discharging the responsibilities entrusted to it. Today, it is marked by corruption, subservience, venality, misuse of power and position, nepotism, and favouritism. Members of the service often take pride in being identified with one political party or a particular political leader or ruling family, which is against the basic norms governing the civil service. It is not uncommon to find officers flaunting political affiliations, caste and religion to derive maximum benefits from the system. Convictions of several senior officers in addition to severe criticism for non-implementation of the orders of the high courts and the Supreme Court have lowered the image of the civil service and cast doubts on its commitment to uphold the rule of law. In every sense, the civil service has come a long way from the initial euphoria at the time of its creation.

While some of these observations apply with equal force to the Indian Police Service (IPS), there are some concerns which are specific to this service. These include widespread violation of human rights, large-scale abuses of office and authority by a number of unscrupulous officers, close connections among the police, criminals and the politicians, undue lenience in criminal and other cases against industrialists, business persons, politicians and others, and so on. The unsympathetic attitude to the economically and socially weaker sections of society and minorities has led to a further lowering of the image of the police in society. Meanwhile, reports of major commissions and committees to reform the system are gathering dust.

It is interesting to recall that in his letter to the Constituent Assembly dated 15 October 1948, Deputy Prime Minister, Vallabhbhai Patel wrote:

"I need hardly emphasise that an efficient, disciplined and contented service assured of its prospects as a result of diligent and honest work, is a *sine qua non* of sound administration under a democratic regime... The [civil] service must be above party and we should ensure that political considerations, either in its recruitment or in its discipline and control, are reduced to the minimum, if not eliminated altogether."[1]

Defending the civil service, he emphasised:

"Today, my Secretary can write a note opposed to my views. I have given that freedom to all my Secretaries. I have told them, 'If you do not give your honest opinion for fear that it will displease your Minister, please then you had better go. I will bring another Secretary.' I will never be displeased over a frank expression of opinion."[2]

Corruption, Political Interference and the Civil Service 63

The need for the All India Services was reiterated in the 1980s by the Commission on Centre-State Relations which was equally emphatic in its recommendations. The Commission wrote:

> "The All India Services are as much necessary today as they were when the Constitution was framed and continue to be one of the premier institutions for maintaining the unity of the country. Undoubtedly, the members of the All India Services have shown themselves capable of discharging the roles that the framers of the Constitution envisaged for them. Any move to disband the All India Services or to permit a State government to opt out of the scheme must be regarded as retrograde and harmful to the larger interests of the country. Such a step is sure to encourage parochial tendencies and undermine the integrity, cohesion, efficiency and co-ordination in administration of the country as a whole."

The Commission went on to add that the All India Services should be further strengthened and greater emphasis laid on the role, they are expected to play. This can be achieved, it said, through well planned improvements in selection, training, deployment and promotion policies. The Commission also cautioned, "The Union Government may dissuade State governments from misusing powers of transfer, promotion, posting and suspension of All India Service officers in order to discipline them."[3]

The civil service has gone through a number of upheavals. Over the years, a concept which caused havoc in the civil service was to the so-called "committed civil service" which was propagated by the ruling Congress (I) party in the early 1970s. This concept drew serious criticism as it questioned the very precept of political neutrality on which the edifice of the civil service is built. A new breed of civil servants who were ambitious and wanted to go places fast, quickly came into prominence. "Be committed or get omitted" became the slogan in the rat race. Fortunately, a large number of people saw the dangers in the new system and raised their voices against it. As a result, Prime Minister Indira Gandhi hastily backtracked and clarified:

> "I do not want politically convenient or servile civil servants. Their job is to give frank advice, but they should feel committed to the objectives of the state which have been approved by Parliament. They should have unreserved faith in the programmes which they administer."

This window-dressing hid the truth; an era of politically-pliable and flexible civil servants was ushered in. This was clearly a turning point in the post-Independence history of the civil service. The new success stories passed among civil servants were largely of those who were committed to the ruling party and, better still, to the person in charge.

The worst manifestation of this trend was found during the Emergency in 1975-77 when many excesses were attributed to those who were keen on pleasing their political bosses. The Shah Commission, which inquired into Emergency excesses, divided the public servants into three broad categories:

(i) those who may have simply acted in compliance with the orders or instructions given to them;

(ii) those who may have carried out the instructions a little more zealously than others; and

(iii) those who had exceeded or misused or abused their powers or authority for securing personal gain or for securing advantage to other individual(s) and/or organisations.

The Commission also observed that a calculated effort was made by the then-ruling party, Congress (I), to place in vital positions such persons who were willing to further the interests of those in power in gross violation of established administrative norms and practices. The Commission further stressed that "it is necessary to face the situation squarely that not all the excesses and improprieties committed during the Emergency originated at the political level. In a large number of cases, it appears that unscrupulous and over-ambitious officers were prepared to curry favour with the seats of power and position by doing what they thought the people in authority desired".

With different political parties ruling in the various States, and with the quick changes in governments in some States, a "committed" or politically aligned bureaucracy can be a major debilitating influence on administration leading to a loss of public confidence and serious divisions in the civil service itself.

During the initial euphoric days of the Rajiv Gandhi regime in the mid-1980s when there was talk of chalking out strategies to take India into the twenty-first century, the coterie of civil servants around him had started advocating the "Japan Incorporated" model and the importance of building a close nexus between the bureaucracy and business. Apparently, a series of informal meetings over cocktails and dinners were held at which businessmen and top bureaucrats in the

Central Government established new bonds by addressing each other by their first names. As the Japanese experience shows, once the long rule of the Liberal Democratic Party ended, the systems and practices governing political life and the bureaucracy, with their corrupting influences, came under considerable pressure. Bureaucracy had fully or almost completely identified itself with one political party.

In any case, a nexus between bureaucracy and business houses would hardly find acceptance in the new political, social and administrative culture in India. This is particularly relevant in the contemporary situation in which every decision of the previous government is reopened by the succeeding government which attributes motives of corruption and kick-backs to the previous regime and bureaucrats.

The debate about a generalist civil service *versus* the current regime of technocrats and specialists is as old as the All India Services themselves. The thinking in the Western world itself has undergone a radical change from one end of the spectrum to the other, and those used to looking to the West for solutions to all of the problems at home have often been disappointed. As the experience in various fields has shown, home-grown solutions keeping with the local ethos and circumstances will finally succeed. This is particularly true in the field of public administration. No foreign expert can give ready-made solutions to the governance of a socially and politically fractured society like India.

In recent years, a number of issues concerning the problems and challenges of the civil service have come to the fore. The first relates to the emoluments for the civil servants. While high pay scales and perquisites may not necessarily be a guarantee against corruption in the civil service, it has to be accepted that the differential between the emoluments in the private sector and in the government has perceptibly widened. Continuance of this phenomenon, leave aside its widening in the future, will have serious implications for attracting meritorious candidates to the civil service. It will also be a contributory factor for a further increase of corruption in the civil service. It is not unreasonable to expect that civil servants should need to be paid a decent salary which would enable them to live comfortably and look after the well-being of their family members. To expect only civil servants to make sacrifices when all other sections of the society are trying to get the best for themselves is futile.

For many years, the age limit for recruitment to the civil service continued to be 21 years (minimum) and 24 years (maximum). Over time it has been stepped up to a maximum age limit of 28 years with further relaxation for candidates belonging to the Scheduled Castes (SCs), Scheduled Tribes (STs) and Other Backward Classes (OBCs). By the time a person enters an All India Service at such an advanced age, he is no longer amenable to healthy influence, and often has set ideas on a number of issues. It is also difficult to build a feeling of *esprit de corps* in a group of older trainees. Furthermore, the qualities of idealism and zeal which were the hallmark of the young direct recruits in the olden days is often missing, particularly in the recruits belonging to older age groups. Such new entrants are often married, have children, and are averse to throwing themselves into their work with as much passion and dedication as their younger batch mates.

A related question is whether a person should be permitted to avail of innumerable chances for appearing for the competitive examinations. The earlier practice of permitting not more than three chances needs to be restored to improve the standards of recruitment to the services. All available evidence shows that those candidates who pass with each succeeding chance contribute increasingly to the erosion of standards in the services.

An interesting feature in recent years is the decline in popularity of the Indian Administrative Service (IAS) among the new recruits. It is no longer the most coveted service among the several services for which competitive examinations are held each year. Apparently, the Customs & Excise and the Income Tax Services now attract many more higher ranking candidates. The fact that these services offer more opportunities to make easy money is only one explanation, but it is wrong to proceed on the assumption that this is the only or even the most over-riding explanation. More specific answers to this phenomenon can be found in the many difficulties, particularly increased political interference and corruption, faced by the Indian Administrative Service (IAS) and Indian Police Service (IPS) officers throughout their working lives. The officers are faced with the prospect of making difficult choices involving personal honesty, integrity and moral rectitude early in life.

It must be admitted that the training imparted to the new recruits does not equip them adequately to face the difficult reality. The training programmes do not place adequate emphasis on building strong morals and a value system which can see them through the unimaginable rot which has afflicted society. Unless the training academies can instil these values and produce civil servants who are totally incorruptible and fearless in putting down corruption, not just with a heavy hand but by their own personal example, there is clearly no hope either for the administration or the society at large.

One of the factors which has made the IAS and IPS unpopular among the new entrants is the roster system by which the State allotment is made. This system is based on the objective of allotting meritorious candidates by rotation to all States, including those which are "unpopular" or remote and inaccessible. But this results in a candidate getting allotted to a State in which he may not like to spend most of his working life. The earlier system gave a choice to the candidates regarding the States in which they would like to serve and this system had much to commend to itself. Addressing this issue is particularly relevant if the present arrangement leads to driving away meritorious candidates from the two most crucial services in the country.

The unduly large intake in the IAS during the 1970s and early 1980s has resulted in a number of problems. Apart from considerably diluting the standards, large batches have led to a serious problem of stagnation leading to a feeling of frustration and despondency. A number of officers are occupying sinecure posts which dilute the very image of the civil services. A number of States, as also the Centre, have taken recourse to upgrading a number of posts thereby raising serious questions of propriety and efficacy in the manning of such posts by senior officers. The number of secretaries and special secretaries in the Government of India and the States is now a scandal. Clearly, it is time that the very basis of recruitment to the services be re-examined.

Also, there is need for greater selectivity in deciding which posts should be manned by the All India Service officers. Far too many posts have been encadred over the years, leaving little scope for the other services at the State and Central levels to man such posts. This has created a legitimate feeling of grievance, frustration and neglect among those services. There is a seething resentment among them against the higher civil service. It prominently comes to the fore before every Central Pay Commission, and all these grievances are forcefully presented before it. While these issues are important and need urgent attention, one can legitimately ask a question whether the Pay

Commission is the most appropriate forum to make recommendations on these basic issues underlying the future of the civil services.

The sanctity and rationale of rules, regulations and procedures governing the selection of officers for promotion to higher posts have become increasingly important in view of the perceptible politicisation of the civil services on the one hand and the large stagnation at higher levels on the other. The system of empanelment for the posts of Joint Secretary and above in the Government of India has resulted in a large number of officers in each batch being left out of the panels. There is justifiable anger and resentment against some officers who exert political pressures to get themselves empanelled for senior duty posts. Cases are not unknown where an officer who had not even been empanelled for the post of Joint Secretary was appointed as Secretary to the Government of India. Even officers of doubtful integrity have often made the grade while several others of impeccable honesty and integrity have been left out. In this rat race, officers have not thought twice about making use of power brokers, godmen, astrologers, politicians and business and industry tycoons to further their own prospects. As can be imagined, such support comes neither cheaply nor without suitable *quid pro quo*.

In spite of this highly-disturbing situation, the Government of India made strenuous efforts to ensure that the judgement of the Central Administrative Tribunal (CAT) in the case of Jagdish Chander Jetli, which laid down that clear criteria, procedures and guidelines must be prescribed for the selection of officers, was reversed in the Supreme Court. In its anxiety to retain unlimited powers with the Appointments Committee of the Cabinet, in the selection of officers, for appointment at the level of secretaries to the Government, the Government did not hesitate to put forth arguments which undercut the very basis of the All India Services.

An interesting but highly undesirable fall-out of the case was an observation made by the Supreme Court judge during the course of the hearing which received wide publicity throughout the country. The judge observed:

> "The appointment of the Secretary to Government of India is not on the basis of a competitive examination where a candidate who secures 99 per cent of marks has to be appointed. Even when a person appoints a cook or a watchman, he looks for a person in whom he has faith. How

can Government of India appoint any person as Secretary in whom it has no faith?"

In the public mind, and particularly in the minds of politicians, an impression was created that making appointments to senior posts in the Government was like appointing one's own private servants. Acceptability to the political executive rather than merit and competence became the deciding factor in the selection of officers. The appeals filed in the Supreme Court by both the Government and Jetli were dismissed because, in the meantime, Jetli had been promoted as a Secretary to the Government of India. But in the process, the salutary judgement of CAT that there must be properly specified criteria for the selection of officers as Secretaries was also set aside by the Supreme Court without going into the merits of the case. An important issue of vital concern to the morale, strength and image of the civil services thus continues to cause problems.

Another highly disturbing development in recent years is the misuse of power to transfer officers. A stage has come when a question has to be asked and answered as to when a transfer becomes a punishment, and when it should not be treated as such.

Prime Minister Morarji Desai had written to all Chief Ministers in 1977 expressing his concern on the subject and urged:

"If officers are to be responsible for producing results, particularly in the developmental sectors, they must have a measure of continuity in their jobs. Over the years, a tendency to transfer officers on comparatively minor issues has developed and this has led to short tenures for incumbents of important jobs. Frequent transfers, particularly of secretaries, heads of departments, district magistrates and other district level officers only create a feeling of demoralisation and diffidence amongst them, and inhibit initiative and creative effort."

Over the years, the situation has deteriorated considerably in the Government of India itself. It is widely known that large industrial and business houses continue to wield considerable influence in the transfers and placement of officers of their choice in important positions in the Central Government. Even transfers of officers at the level of Secretary to the Government of India have been effected at the behest of these power brokers. But businessmen alone cannot be blamed for this situation. Without the active role of senior civil servants in soliciting favours from such persons, they would not have so much power. It is indeed a sad commentary that the support of such business lobbies, astrologers and godmen is feverishly sought by a number of civil servants to further their prospects. Each change of government at the Centre has seen large-scale reshuffling of Secretaries to the Government. This is most unfortunate. With such a record of performance, the Government of India has no moral authority left to tell the State governments how they ought to conduct themselves in this matter. For instance, it is doubtful if a letter written by the Minister of State for Personnel to the chief ministers asking their governments to desist from resorting to mass and frequent transfers of officers of All India Services would carry any weight. Further, if the Government of India were serious, the Prime Minister himself could have taken the trouble to address the chief ministers thus underlining the importance of the subject.

The State governments seem to have thrown to the winds all sagacity and political maturity in exercising their power to transfer officers. Irrespective of the political party in power, the hallmark of a political executive's authority is seen to be established in transferring, mindlessly and in utter disregard of rules and regulations, the host of civil servants under it. Each change of government in a State, even when the political party in power continues to be the same, leads to the large-scale transfers of civil servants. Such transfers can run into numbers exceeding 30,000. Allegations are made of corruption on a large scale both in effecting a transfer or getting a transfer stayed. After the change of government in early 1995, a minister in Maharashtra stayed all transfers in his department on the ground that over 10 to 15 crore rupees had changed hands in these transactions and publicly quoted the rates charged for transfers at various levels. The transfer *mela* gets converted into a wholesale market where posts often go to the highest bidders.

Even the higher civil service is no longer immune from these influences in several States. Caste is a new element which has recently come into prominence. An outstanding example of this was the replacement of the Chief Secretary of Uttar Pradesh on the ground that he was a Brahmin — something which would have been unthinkable only a few years ago.

The average tenure of incumbents in various posts has decreased sharply. In Uttar Pradesh, by December 1990, the average tenure of a district magistrate was only 9.41 months; that of commissioners of the divisions 10 months; and secretaries to the Government 9.93 months. Successive chief ministers — Kalyan Singh, Mulayam Singh Yadav and Mayawati — tried to outdo the predecessor in transferring IAS and IPS officers. Chief Minister Mayawati set an all-time record by transferring as many as 270 of the 405 IAS officers and 250 of the 310 IPS officers in the State in the short span of 100 days. Some officers were transferred as many as six times in this period. This was indeed the nadir of administration and is a clear warning of what can happen to any administration if the political party in power behaves irresponsibly.

Another disturbing feature is that this kind of havoc is being played with the civil services in almost every State. Each political party has acted as recklessly as the other while in power, despite whatever pronouncements it might have made while in the opposition. Against this background, it was hoped that the public interest litigation filed by Common Cause, a non-governmental organisation, in the Supreme Court against the transfer mania sweeping the country would bring some relief to this totally unsustainable and indefensible situation.

The petition, *inter alia*, submitted that while rules have been framed by the government on a number of subjects such as appointments, promotions and imposition of penalties in departmental actions, there are no rules on the subject of transfers. The petition prayed that the Government of India and the State governments should be directed to lay down specific guidelines and regulations for transfers as well. It was suggested that the following rules could be adopted for the purpose:

(i) No official posted to a transferable post should be transferred from the post before the completion of a period of three years which should be considered the normal period of posting; and

(ii) If any transfer of an official posted to a transferable post is necessitated by exigencies of service, it should be effected only after the matter has been examined by two officers, one immediately superior to the concerned officer and another either of an equivalent rank or holding the next higher post. They should then confer to see if they concur with the proposed transfer on the basis of the supposed exigency of service. It was suggested that the reasons for the transfer must be recorded and communicated in writing to the concerned official and should be open to appeal.

Unfortunately, the Supreme Court declined to interfere and stated, "We do not consider it necessary to entertain this writ petition...since the guidelines for taking such administrative decisions are well settled and it is obvious that all administrative decisions should satisfy the rule of non-arbitrariness and be honest and fair. Individual cases in which the decision-making process is vitiated for any such reason can always be challenged in a suitable manner."

A Review Petition was filed by Common Cause stating once again that transfers these days can become a punishment resulting in the disruption of the family life, dislocation of the children's education, problems of finding alternative accommodation, and more importantly, causing humiliation to the officers. It has also been emphasised that it has become impossible to secure redress against indiscriminate and unjustified transfers because the basis of decisions are not generally recorded.

The response of the Supreme Court is indeed disheartening in view of the fact that approaching the CAT against the totally unjustified transfers of a former Chief Secretary of Karnataka and a Joint Director of the CBI who was investigating the notorious St. Kitts case — transfers clearly based on politically-motivated and extraneous considerations proved futile. In fact, the CAT went a step further and held that the Government had unrestricted powers to transfer officers. It is impossible for thousands of individual officers to approach the administrative tribunals to seek redress against repeated, politically-oriented or unjustified transfers, particularly when the outcome is so uncertain. Further, the only recourse against the orders of the CAT is the Supreme Court. Most of the aggrieved persons simply cannot afford to incur the huge expenses of such litigation. Yet, it is no longer a question of injustice suffered by individual officers. At stake is the morale of the civil services in India.

A related matter of concern is the indiscriminate use of the power of suspension of All India Service officers by State governments. A reference was made earlier to the apprehensions expressed in this regard by the Commission on Centre-State Relations. In recent years, these powers have been grossly misused, leading to demoralisation and resentment. A new and highly questionable record was set by Mayawati, former Chief Minister of Uttar Pradesh, by suspending a number of district magistrates, superintendents of police and deputy inspector general of police. The former Chief Minister of Maharashtra,

Sudhakarrao Naik, issued orders of suspension for the then Commissioner of Police, Nagpur at a meeting of the citizens convened in connection with the murder of an editor of a local newspaper although the officer had been commended for his work only a few months earlier. The same officer was later promoted to Director General of Police. Suspending senior officers on the spur of the moment to show one's authority can cause incalculable harm to the morale and image of the administration. It is not, therefore, surprising that demands are now being made to restrict the powers of the State governments pertaining to All India Service officers.

With increasingly rigorous selectivity for posts in the Centre, the States are left with a large pool of officers who fail to make the grade. They necessarily have to be provided for in the State. Claims for promotion are put forth by these officers on the ground that their batch mates at the Centre or in some other States have already been promoted; State governments have been finding it difficult to resist such pressures. As a result, a large number of posts have been created at senior levels in both the IAS and the IPS, often in utter disregard of the cadre rules on the subject. In most States, one now finds a number of posts carrying the same pay as the chief secretary and the director general of police. This has led to unexpected consequences. The politicians have often used this opportunity to select officers for the top posts who are politically convenient, pliable and therefore acceptable. Officers with backbone, integrity, honesty and calibre have been side-lined in equivalent posts so that they cannot complain of supercession. At times, incumbents of the highest posts in both the services have been shifted unceremoniously for resisting political pressures and unreasonable demands, and appointed to sinecures and inconsequential posts. Apart from the humiliation heaped on the officers concerned, this demoralises the entire service and effectively lays down the ground rules for a successful career causing a permanent damage to the fabric of the civil services.

It is time that a more effective method of weeding out officers who fail to make the grade at various levels is seriously examined and pursued; rather than carrying their burden till the normal age of retirement. It will, however, have to be ensured that the process of weeding out is carried out as judiciously, objectively and apolitically as possible. This responsibility could also be entrusted with the statutory Civil Service Boards proposed elsewhere in this paper.

Among the many debilitating factors afflicting the civil services is the recent trend to give extensions and re-employment to some officers. The myth of indispensability has to be dispelled with a firm hand. For a long time, there was a well-settled policy not to give extension or re-employment to officers beyond the age of retirement. This has now been breached with impunity, and a number of officers even at the level of cabinet secretary, secretaries and special secretaries in the Government of India are given extensions. None of these has ever been a tenure post. The State governments quickly followed suit. A number of officers in the States, particularly at the level of chief secretary and director general of police, have been given extensions up to six months by the state governments, first within their own powers and thereafter with the approval of the Government of India. Apart from creating two classes of persons in the same service, this leads to serious demoralisation in regards to the situation of career stagnation facing the officers. This has also resulted in seriously compromising the freedom and independence of the civil service. It is time a total stop is put to this highly pernicious practice.

A related question which deserves early and careful consideration pertains to the very concept of the All India Services. The original intention in setting up these services was to have a common pool of officers who could serve the States as well as the Central Government. The system of selecting officers to meet the needs of the Centre has undergone a change in so far as the IAS is concerned. The idea of a Central Pool of officers who would be selected early in their career and, thereafter, permanently seconded to the Centre was rightly given up and now officers are taken on deputation for a period of three to seven years at various levels ranging from under secretary to additional secretary.

There is an increasing tendency among officers to avoid going on deputation to the Government of India. By their training and background, the officers who are taken in the IAS from the State services and constitute 40 per cent of the total are generally reluctant to go to the Centre. The more disturbing trend is the disinclination among the direct recruits to go on deputation to the Centre. Also, direct recruits who do not belong to the State and are "outsiders" prefer to work in the Government of India. In most cases, the States also prefer to nominate such officers for deputation to the Government of India. As a result, the officers who work in a State largely belong to the same State and, in the process, one of the pre-eminent characteristics of the All India Services sets consciously and deliberately eroded. Yet another consequence of this development is that the officers who do not work in the Government of India at an early enough stage find it increasingly difficult to get a placement at the Centre at senior levels, which leads to considerable frustration and despondence.

Special mention must be made of the problems faced by the All India Services in Jammu and Kashmir and the north-east. There has been persistent reluctance on the part of these States to accept the All India Service officers so that they can promote a larger percentage of local officers to the IAS and the IPS. The Jammu and Kashmir government has been insisting on regularising State service officers working in various cadre posts. The number of direct recruits in the cadre is much lower than warranted according to the cadre rules. The Centre, irrespective of the political party in power, has been unable to make the State Government fall in line under the misplaced fear of offending local public opinion.

The creation of small, unviable, full-fledged States in the north-east has created serious problems in the governance of the area. The management of small cadres poses innumerable problems. But the States are opposed to the formation or continuance of joint cadres on the ground that it seriously erodes their autonomy and freedom to manage the cadres. The officers posted in these States, particularly "outsiders", are facing a number of problems. Some of them have even faced threats to their lives as well as to the lives of their families. There is overt discrimination against such officers in matters of promotion, postings and transfers. Often, these officers have been sidelined when top posts have become available. As a result, most of them prefer to spend long spells on deputation to the Government of India, and look for opportunities to change cadres. The State governments are only too willing to recommend such cases to the Centre.

A common complaint often heard from ministers and others in the States of the north-east is that most All India Service officers who do not belong to these areas keep their families in Delhi and elsewhere outside the State, and evince no interest in the well-being of the State. The officers, in turn, emphasise a number of overriding factors such as the need to supplement the income of the family (the wife is forced to take up employment), lack of facilities for the children's education, compulsions of looking after the elderly persons in the family, lack of adequate medical facilities in the remote areas, and so on.

With the existing legal provisions which prohibit "outsiders" from acquiring immovable property in the North-East and Jammu and Kashmir, these officers have a genuine grievance that they cannot own land or a house in the State they serve during their entire working life and, after retirement, they are treated as aliens in these States.

These genuine issues and concerns have never been addressed in depth or with political courage and far-sightedness by the Government of India. As such, the future of the All India Services in these sensitive States is in serious doubt. If any of these States is permitted to opt out of the All India Services scheme, many other States will also follow suit thereby eroding an important link in Centre-State relations.

In the past, the civil service was considered to be synonymous with the government. A civil servant could not have imagined being on the opposite side of the government in a court of law to get his personal grievances redressed. The situation has changed perceptibly during the last few years. With the dilution of standards of rectitude, honesty and integrity coupled with increasing political interference and the predominance of caste and other considerations in promotions, transfers and postings, litigation against the government has gone up by leaps and bounds. As many as 27,067 petitions were filed before the CAT in 1993 as compared to 18,602 in 1989. The answer to the malady cannot be found by mechanically increasing the number of benches of the tribunal. This malaise has to be looked into by carefully reviewing the factors which are giving rise to such large-scale discontent and frustration.

A related but equally important question which deserves further consideration is whether the mechanism of the administrative tribunals is adequate to deal with the rapidly deteriorating situation. Administrative tribunals were set up as alternatives to the high courts, and their jurisdiction restricted to the writ jurisdiction of the high courts. As a result, the administrative tribunals confine themselves to questions relevant to judicial review. They are helpless against the arbitrary actions of the government. The question of setting up Civil Service Tribunals which can go into the merits of the cases with CAT/SAT acting as appellate bodies needs to be seriously considered.

Soon after the installation of Rajiv Gandhi as Prime Minister, the creation of Civil Service Boards at the Centre and States was mooted as one of the major initiatives to address these issues. However, it remained only on paper. Considering the sharp deterioration in the situation since then, such boards can have some chance of success in addressing these problems only if they are put on a statutory basis. This is particularly important since the political executive has, in the past, shown scant respect for conventions, guidelines, precedents, and even rules and regulations, Moreover, a section of the bureaucracy itself has been found to be towing the line of the politicians to serve its own interests.

The situation could have also been retrieved to some extent if there was closer contact and interaction between senior and junior officers. Over the years, the seniors have stopped taking any interest in promoting fellow-feeling among the younger officers. They are not interested in knowing or understanding the problems faced by the service officers leave alone advising or supporting them. "Don't bring any problems to me; deal with them yourself" is the common refrain of the seniors. It is not surprising that this has led to disenchantment, disillusionment and demoralisation among the younger officers.

As is widely accepted, new situations call for a fresh look at the old practices and precepts. The various associations of All India Service officers had so far desisted from raising issues affecting their members except to file memoranda before the Pay Commissions set up from time to time. It was rightly felt that the members of the service which had such a large hand in running the government could not take a public position against the government and grievances, if any, could be raised directly with the government at the appropriate level.

With the surfeit of arbitrary actions pertaining to all aspects of the services referred to above, the administrative situation has changed completely. Several decisions are no longer based on the advice of senior civil servants. In some States, the cadres are divided on caste and other considerations. Functionaries such as secretary to chief minister or secretary (personnel) have often become alter egos of the political executive, thus sidelining the chief secretary. The chief ministers have repeatedly thrown to the wind rules, past practices and well-established conventions. These could not have damaged the system so quickly and irreparably if a section of the ambitious and politically well-connected officers had not subverted it from within to further their own prospects.

This gross abuse of power by the political executive has not been confined only to interfering in the administration of the cadres of All India Services. Some of the officers who have shown courage in resisting political pressures have been physically harmed. The most reprehensible instance of this kind was V.S. Chandralekha, an IAS officer of the Tamil Nadu cadre, who became a victim of an acid attack in 1992 after she exposed the underselling of government shares in a joint-sector company. A former health commissioner in Bihar was attacked in his office. A district magistrate in Bihar was wantonly killed. A number of officers in the north-east were threatened and even harmed. A former additional collector of Nagpur was slapped by a Congress (I) office-bearer and a legislator for rejecting a beer-bar licence.

In this period of turmoil and turbulence, the service associations have been found to be largely defunct, inactive and docile. This, in fact, has encouraged the political executive to take whatever action it wanted with utter disregard and contempt for the morale and image of the civil service. The fear complex is so widely prevalent that even the Central IAS Association did not raise its voice against matters which were causing incalculable damage to the services.

Fortunately, this position is now undergoing a change. For the first time, the service associations in the States are finally taking a public stand on these issues. Recently, the IAS Officers Association of Uttar Pradesh formally protested against the excesses of the State Government on transfers and suspension of officers and requested a review of the States' powers in this regard. The Association has also urged that disciplinary proceedings should not be initiated against officers without following the prescribed procedure. It suggested that various posts in the IAS cadre should be categorised according to seniority so that placement of officers is made accordingly. None of these are extraordinary demands. What was, however, extraordinary was the persistent demand by a section of officers that to deal with the widespread corruption in the service, the three most corrupt officers in the service be identified by a secret ballot. The move fell through. But the other grievances, more than anything else, underlined the complicity of a section of officers of the civil service with the political masters in bending the rules and subverting the system. This was also borne out by the resolution adopted by the IAS Association in Bihar which, *inter alia*, criticised the State Government for its "sustained efforts to subvert and denigrate the permanent civil services... through the gross abuse of executive and political power" and... "holding the rule of law to ransom".

But the Central IAS Association continues to be a silent spectator in these eventful and turbulent years in the life of the civil service. It cannot shirk responsibility to its own members any longer and will have to look beyond holding annual dinners, festival cricket matches and submitting memoranda to the pay commissions from time to time. It will have to provide leadership and take initiative in focussing attention on issues and concerns relevant to the image, morale, integrity and stature of the civil services. As a part of these efforts, it will have to lay down and rigorously enforce a code of conduct and ethics for its own members.

This brings us to the subject of public accountability of the civil service. There is a justifiable concern at the increasing ignorance and apathy of the civil service regarding the grievances and sufferings of the people. A Supreme Court judgement in November 1993 in the case of the Lucknow Development Authority against the National Consumer Disputes Redressal Commission (NCDRC) put the whole issue in a new perspective. The Court categorically held that public servants cannot shield themselves from personal responsibility to pay damages when the exercise of their discretionary powers is *mala fide* and the complainant has suffered mental agony and harassment. The judges observed that when the court directs payment of damages or compensation against the State, the common man is the ultimate sufferer. It is the tax payer who bears the brunt when officials fail to discharge their duty. Therefore, in cases where the NCDRC determines payment of compensation, the amount must eventually be recovered by the department concerned from one or more functionaries found guilty of dereliction of duty.

In the public mind, the civil service is now firmly associated with administrative and political excesses and even political corruption which is in sharp contrast to its historical image of integrity, probity and political neutrality. Earlier, there was a widespread belief that a civil servant could be relied upon to do justice irrespective of the political nuances of a case. This appreciation has undergone a drastic change in recent years.

The time has come to ask to whom is a civil servant finally responsible? In an orderly democratic society wedded to the rule of law, one would normally expect a government to be answerable to the people at large at periodical intervals. It is also expected that a government would conduct itself according to some well-established norms, conventions and moralities. The really difficult choices and questions arise when this does not happen and the civil service becomes a tool in the hands of unscrupulous politicians. What then are the responsibilities of the civil service to the public at large?

The answer lies in bringing about greater transparency and openness in the functioning of the government. There is a widespread feeling that too much power continues to be vested in the civil service at all levels and the system needs to be "opened up" by providing a larger role for the society. The insider-outsider culture must go. This would, *inter alia*, mean clearly laying down policies and parameters for making any decision, severely curtailing the discretionary powers both at the administrative and political levels, open and competitive bidding before accepting any offer or entering into any contract, and the utmost expedition in decision-making. This would also require willingness on the part of the government to place before the people and Parliament/legislatures, all relevant papers pertaining to any and every decision except those which affect the security and defence of the country.

This brings us to the provisions of the Official Secrets Act, 1923. The Act which is a vestige of colonial days deals with two aspects, espionage and disclosure of official information. The most obnoxious provision pertains to the widely worded Section 5 of the Act. The coverage of the persons having possession of official information who are liable under this Section is extremely wide. Further, not only is the person communicating the information guilty of an offence but also the person receiving it. The official information covered by the Section is also extremely wide. Nowhere have the words "secret" or "official secret" been defined in the Act. A literal reading of the Section indicates that disclosure of any kind of secret information will attract prosecution under the Act, whatever be the purpose or impact. There are no exceptions like communication of information for the public interest. The punishment extends up to three years' imprisonment or fine or both.

These provisions have been so useful and convenient to the Government that every effort to amend the Act has been cold-shouldered by the Congress (I) which has been ruling at the Centre for almost the entire period since Independence. During the short tenure of the V.P. Singh Government, an effort was made to review these provisions and enact a Right to Information Act. But this did not materialise before the change of government.

The Second Press Commission (1982) suggested repeal of Section 5 and its replacement by a provision that meets the ends "both of national security and other vital interests of the State as well as the right of the people to know the affairs of State affecting them". There is no doubt that the sweep of Section 5 needs to be circumscribed. A joint study by the Press Council of India and the Indian Law Institute recommended replacement of Section 5 by a suitable provision doing the following lines: Nothing shall be an offence under the Section if it predominantly and substantially subserves public interest, unless the communication or use of the "official secret" is made for the benefit of any foreign power or in any manner prejudicial to the safety of the State. A further safeguard against arbitrary action is suggested by prescribing that no one shall be prosecuted without the sanction of a committee consisting of the Attorney General, a nominee of the Chairman of the Press Council, and a nominee of the Chairman of the Bar Council of India, unless the accused is charged with communicating the "official secret" for the benefit of a foreign power, or in a manner prejudicial to the safety of the State.

An interesting off-shoot of the discussion in this regard was the suggestion in the September 1995 report of the Parliamentary Standing Committee on Defence that the report of the Committee on Defence Expenditure should be made public as early as possible. The Committee was of the view that a little more openness even in matters relating to defence would not militate against national interests. Thus, for example, defence purchases are currently treated with the same level of secrecy as defence strategy so that the price paid for equipment is seldom officially revealed. Since large sums of money are spent on such purchases, these ought to be treated on the same basis as public-funded civilian purchases. The public need not be told where and how the equipment is to be deployed, but the financial aspects of the transactions certainly need to be subjected to public scrutiny. This subject requires very early review keeping in view the serious abuse of political power and the use of the civil service to further the ends of political parties in power whether at the Centre or in the States.

It is often suggested that individual officers could be encouraged to come out publicly against the wrong-doings, corrupt practices and misuse of political and public office by any incumbent. The US Civil Service Reform Act, 1978, commonly known as the Whistle Blowers Act, protects a civil servant from any form of retaliation, legal action or demotion if he discloses to the Congress or the Press any evidence of violation of law, mismanagement, gross waste of funds, abuse of authority or any substantial danger to public health or safety. An organisation known as Public Concerns At Work in Britain has been making efforts since 1992 to give legal aid and assistance to public servants giving publicity to corrupt actions and practices.

To be successful, apart from giving legal protection as above, such an officer would have to be given vocal and unstinted support by various sections of society. He must have the confidence that he will be fully supported in his fight against vested interests in the government, industry, etc. Unfortunately, the present experience is exactly the opposite. The moment an officer is on the wrong side of the establishment and the powers-that-be, he is shunned by his colleagues and avoided even by his erstwhile well-wishers and friends. His career prospects are marred. Threats to his life and that of his family are not uncommon. Looking at these realities, it is unlikely that "whistle-blowers" will be prepared to come forward easily. But given the untenable situation in which Indian society find itself without any moral mooring, it would be worthwhile to take steps to put such a statute on the books. The system could also be "internalised" by making a provision to protect civil servants so as to encourage them to approach statutory agencies such as the Lok Pal, when established, and the Lok Ayukts.

Such efforts will, however, have to be differentiated from general activism by individual officers making pronouncements, while in service, on public platforms about the ills afflicting the society and denigrating the institutions of governance. Such officers are being increasingly associated in public mind with politicking. It is necessary to bear in mind that encouraging such actions by serving bureaucrats is a double-edged weapon. Apart from seriously undermining the discipline of the organised civil services, it will also encourage yet another breed of civil servants who would like to play politics while enjoying all the protection, perquisites and other advantages of office. Such efforts will not achieve anything beyond giving ephemeral publicity to the concerned officers.

The role of the civil service also needs to be seen in the perspective of the rapid social changes and convulsions in recent years. With the "Mandalisation" of the society, caste, creed and community have once again come to the fore. The SCs, STs, OBCs and minorities have started asserting themselves. Communalism has once again started raising its ugly head in several parts of the country. The dark shadows of terrorism are spreading in a number of States.

Added to these is the new phenomenon of political instability. A number of countries in the west have lived with it for a long time. For example, Italy has seen 58 governments since the Second World War. But this is a new reality in India both at the Centre and in the States after a long period of hegemony of a single political party. Uttar Pradesh has seen three governments in less than three years. Gujarat and Andhra Pradesh have seen a change of government in less than a year. There are political upheavals, rumblings and uncertainty in some other States as well. Coalition governments have become inevitable in States as well as at the Centre. In such a situation, as has been evident, the administration invariably has to pay a heavy price. There is no possibility of political stability returning soon.

The introduction of economic liberalisation has added a new dimension to the situation. Economic liberalisation, by definition, should mean less bureaucratic discretionary powers and, therefore, less scope for corruption. But the government, in public perception, continues to be as corrupt as ever, if not more. Several decisions of the government in major fields such as power, petroleum, banking, disinvestment of shares of public sector undertakings, telecommunications and foreign investment have lacked consistency or rationale. The economic administration has reached new levels of imperviousness and disdain for public accountability and transparency. It is pertinent to note that visiting trade and industry delegations from a number of countries have repeatedly and publicly urged that the framework of the new economic policies and the decision-making processes should be open and transparent.

The process of liberalisation, in the true sense of the term, cannot be carried too far without changing the mind-set of the civil services. The civil services' role will have to change from that of a regulator to a facilitator and co-ordinator. Dismantling the government can be a formidable, challenging and continuous task calling for innovation and breaking of new ground. Thatcherism and Reaganomics have caught the fancy of the world. The White House, for instance, has set healthy precedents by announcing a series of regulatory reforms aimed at ending or simplifying unnecessary and burdensome regulations. The new reforms eliminate some 16,000 pages of regulations and streamline another 31,000 pages. The reforms are stated to have already saved taxpayers $63 billion.

There is a genuine apprehension that the Indian bureaucracy is not yet mentally committed to implementing the economic reforms. In this context, a suggestion which is often heard is to permit civil servants to go on deputation to business and industry for a period of five to seven years. The underlying objectives are to give them exposure to industry and trade issues and enable them to get compensated for the low emoluments in the government. The latter objective is particularly nefarious and can seriously undercut the values on which the civil service is based. If this proposal is accepted, very soon one could see accredited representatives of various major industries and business houses within the government itself trying to further the interests of the concerned parties. Such solutions borrowed from abroad can do irreparable harm to the civil service.

But it has to be accepted that the new philosophy of economic liberalisation has not yet percolated at the various levels of the civil service. There is considerable lack of clarity on the issues. The Centre is largely responsible for this situation. It has never made any effort to involve the different players in evolving new policies. In fact, even at the Centre, there is a preponderant section of people who believe that the entire responsibility for the globalisation of the economy rests with the Finance Ministry. It is time these misconceptions are removed.

To be successful, the management of change will have to encompass the civil service from the stage of induction training. The civil servants will have to be enabled to improve their capacity to conceptualise the new role of governmental institutions. For example, the 73rd and the 74th amendments to the Constitution envisage substantial delegation of powers to institutions of local self-government at the municipal and panchayat levels. But these amendments were carried out in the early stages of economic reforms.

A fresh view will now be necessary to determine which responsibilities these institutions can delegate to the private sector and keeping only the powers of overall supervision and coordination. The role of the State government too will have to be redefined.

It is not correct to say that in the new regime of economic reforms and liberalisation, the administration will be less relevant to the common man. Nor would it be correct to assume that either economic liberalisation or democratic decentralisation will necessarily reduce corruption in the administration or the abuse of political power. With burgeoning population as well as widespread poverty, deprivation and destitution, the role of the civil service will continue to be critical for a long time to come. The civil service will have to accept the formidable challenges even though the political and social milieu will be difficult to understand and navigate.. The society has a large stake in ensuring that the civil service is equipped to overcome these obstacles with a new dedication and dynamism.

A number of points arise from the discussion in the foregoing paragraphs. Some of the more important ones may be summarised as follows:

1. The role of the higher civil service needs to be redefined as a vehicle of change in the context of the new thrust of economic liberalisation, globalisation and democratic decentralisation. The primary responsibility of the civil service to uphold the rule of law needs to be restated unambiguously. Political neutrality has to be accepted as a cornerstone of the edifice of the civil service.
2. Civil servants must be paid adequate emoluments to attract meritorious candidates, and to do away with the temptation for corruption.
3. A number of issues pertaining to the All India Services need to be examined afresh. These include the future in-take in the services, age of recruitment, number of chances to be permitted to a candidate to appear for the competitive examinations, weightage to be given to the preferences of candidates in making allotments to States within the quota of fifty per cent earmarked for the "outsiders", emphasising a value system and moral foundations in the training programmes, compulsory service in both the State of their allotment and the Centre, a review of procedures and laying down of clear criteria for selection of officers at every stage of

promotion, and the introduction of a system of weeding out officers through early retirement schemes.
4. Special problems of the cadres in small States such as Jammu and Kashmir, and those in the north-east need to be reviewed to ensure that the role of All India Services is not diluted in any way and their effectiveness is increased to cope with the serious problems of insurgency, alienation, corruption and slow pace of development.
5. The Centre and the States should lay down rules and regulations concerning the transfer of officers to ensure a reasonable term of three years in a post to any incumbent. The reasons for any departure from the prescribed rules must be recorded in writing and conveyed to the affected officer.
6. The powers of suspension which are being used indiscriminately by the State governments should be withdrawn so that the Centre and the UPSC would have a say in it.
7. No extension or re-employment should be allowed to any officer beyond the prescribed age of retirement.
8. The role of the civil service associations needs to be redefined. Apart from raising their voice against policies and actions which lead to demoralisation of the officers, the associations will have to set standards of conduct and safeguard the image, prestige and position of the service they represent.
9. Statutory Civil Service Boards should be established in the Centre and the States to oversee all matters pertaining to the services. Their recommendations must be binding on the concerned government. Any departure therefrom must be for reasons to be recorded in writing and open to review by the Civil Service Tribunals to be set up. The appeals over the decisions of these Tribunals will be presented before the CAT/SAT.
10. The right to information must be guaranteed to all citizens and a comprehensive Central legislation enacted for the purpose.
11. Simultaneously, the Official Secrets Act should be repealed and a new legislation enacted to confine its ambit only to safeguarding national security and defence concerns.
12. Steps should be initiated to bring in greater accountability and transparency in the functioning of the government.

Corruption, Political Interference and the Civil Service 87

13. A Legislation should be enacted to give protection to those officers who expose corruption, wrong-doing and mismanagement in government.
14. The Investigating agencies in the Centre and the States charged with the responsibility to investigate cases of corruption, excesses and misuse of power and position should be placed under statutorily created authorities with appropriate safeguards against political interference in their appointment and removal.

Notes and References
1. Quoted in B. Shiva Rao (Ed.) *The Framing of the Constitution of India*, N.M. Tripathi Pvt. Ltd., Bombay 1968, p. 715.
2. *Ibid*, pp. 721-22.
3. Government of India, *Report of the Commission on Centre-State Relations*, Part I, 1988, pp 229-30.

4
The Role of Audit in Tackling Corruption

Ramaswamy R. Iyer

By corruption, we commonly mean bribery, i.e., the payment of a sum of money to a government official, public sector official or politician for something which is in his or her power to do or refrain from doing, or for indirectly bringing about a desired result. Whether the payment is demanded or offered and whether it is meant for the private gain of an individual or goes to a political party or other organisation, are questions which make no difference, it is still corruption. The payment can, of course, be in kind rather than in cash; it could take the form of costly gifts, paid holidays, entertainment, alcoholic drinks, provision of services including sexual services, and so on.

There are many other kinds of improprieties or wrong-doings in our public systems, and the word 'corruption' itself is used in a wide range of senses such as degeneration, decay, putrefaction, moral deterioration, perversion of an institution or system, gross deviation from original purpose or rationale and so on. Indeed, in the widest sense of the word 'corruption', practically all the evils of our administrative and political systems and institutions, and of our society as a whole, can be brought under that rubric. However, such a wide coverage will not facilitate purposeful discussion or the prescription of specific remedies. In the present paper, the reference is to corruption in the narrower sense as defined in the previous paragraph. An attempt will be to examine whether or not constitutionally mandated audit machinery can be pressed into service as a useful and effective instrument to curb corruption in the public domain.

Thus, this paper will focus on a small part of a large canvas. Whatever is recommended in this paper will have to be read along with the recommendations of the other papers relating to the reform of the investigative agencies, the establishment of Ombudsmen and so on.

Audit: An Overview

CAG: Our SAI

The audit machinery referred to above is the Indian Audit Department (IAD) presided over by the Comptroller and Auditor General of India (CAG). The financial accountability of the Government, and the observance of 'regularity' (i.e., conformity to rules and procedures) and propriety in public financial transactions must be confined by the CAG. An important feature of Indian quasi-federalism is that there is a common CAG for both the Union and the States. The CAG is appointed by the President of India by the warrant under his hand and seal; he is given a term of office of six years and cannot be removed except in the same manner as a judge of the Supreme Court, i.e., by an impeachment process. His salary and other terms and conditions of service are fixed by statute and cannot be varied to his disadvantage after his appointment. The administrative expenses of the office of the CAG are 'charged' on the Consolidated Fund of India, i.e. they are not subjected to a vote of Parliament. After his term, the CAG cannot be appointed to further office under the Government either at the Centre or in any of the States. Thus, through a variety of provisions, some symbolic and some substantive, the CAG's status and independence are ensured. An important point to bear in mind is that the CAG, at the time of appointment, takes an oath similar to that taken by the judges of the Supreme Court, to "uphold the Constitution and the laws", whereas a minister has to swear an oath only to act "in accordance with the Constitution".

The CAG is our Supreme Audit Institution (SAI). There are SAIs in the form of CAGs, Comptrollers-General, Audit Commissions or Courts of Audit in different countries with diverse systems of governance. In the USA, the General Accounting Office (GAO), headed by the Comptroller General of the United States, has been declared to be a part of the legislative branch. In the UK, after the enactment of the National Audit Act of 1983, the CAG is an officer of the House of Commons. In contrast, the CAG of India is not formally an officer of Parliament, though he assists Parliament and the State Legislatures in ensuring the financial accountability of the executive government. However, his duties and powers are laid down by Parliament. Article 149 of the Constitution says that the CAG "shall perform such duties and exercise such powers in relation to the accounts of the Union and the States and of any other authority or body as may be prescribed by or under any law made by Parliament". In pursuance of this, Parliament has enacted The CAG's (Duties, Powers, and Conditions of Service) Act, 1971.

The organisations subject to the audit of the CAG are all government departments and offices, Central and State, including departmental commercial undertakings such as the Indian Railways and Posts and Telecommunications; government companies, Central and State (under special provisions relating to their audit in the Companies Act) and statutory corporations where the relevant statute provides for an audit by the CAG; a number of non-commercial autonomous bodies and authorities owned or controlled by the State and Central governments; and a large number of authorities and bodies substantially financed from Union or State revenues. The CAG also ensures uniformity in accounting: the accounts of the Union and the States are kept in the form prescribed by the President on the advice of the CAG. He continues to be responsible for the compilation of the accounts of many of the State Governments though this responsibility has been taken over by the Governments at the Centre and in some of the States.

CAG's Audit

The word 'audit' has not been defined either in the Constitution or in the CAG's Act, and has therefore to be understood in the light of common usage ("to make an official examination of accounts to ascertain their accuracy" — *The Oxford English Dictionary*), and the actual practices which have evolved over time. The CAG's audit has a wider scope than that of chartered accountants in the private sector. For instance, in the case of expenditures, the CAG's audit examines:
- the availability of funds for the expenditure which has been incurred (budget provision, a vote by the legislature, a valid re-appropriation order, whether the item constitutes a 'New Service' or 'New instrument of Service' requiring a fresh vote, etc.);
- the existence of proper authority for the expenditure (a valid sanction order by a competent authority); and
- procedural correctness and proper documentation and vouching ('regularity').

It goes one step beyond this when it scrutinises a sanction order itself for legality and constitutionality. It also examines whether an expenditure was avoidable, infructuous or clearly more than the object warranted. It goes even further when it examines the *prudence* or *propriety* of an expenditure or a financial decision.

The audit of receipts would include an examination whether the relevant law is being properly applied; whether there were reasoned grounds for all decisions; whether the interpretations of the law, if any, are based on existing case-law and rulings, or if new, are tenable; and, of course, whether the receipts have been correctly brought to account.

Accounts-related, Records-based

Most SAIs tend to interpret their audit functions expansively. In some cases, the extensions get written into the relevant statute. For instance, the National Audit Act, 1983 of the UK specifically enables the CAG to carry out examinations of economy, efficiency, and effectiveness (though in fact he had begun doing this earlier than 1983). The functions of the GAO of the USA have been expanded enormously over the years, and cover programme evaluations of the most diverse kind. In India, too, there has always been a tendency to stretch the audit function. Much of the 'stretching' (e.g., sanction audit, propriety audit, 'value-for-money' audit) remains within the bounds of what may be properly called 'audit', but in some cases (e.g., comprehensive 'appraisals' of public enterprises; reviews of governmental decisions or programmes which verge on 'policy audit'; reports on economic subjects such as public debt or the management of the balance of payments), there may be room for doubt whether or not the bounds of audit have been overstepped. If so, did the IAD have any special expertise in the areas in question or even a constitutional mandate for the activity? Without entering into that debate and confining ourselves to the essential concerns of this paper, we need to note two points:

(i) The first is that audit is essentially an activity relating to accounts and finance. Irregularities other than those relating to accounts or improprieties of a non-financial nature do not come within the purview of audit unless they also happen to have an accounting or financial aspect.

(ii) The second point is that the examination is with reference to vouchers, books of account, registers, ledgers, and other documents and related files. An audit can raise queries arising from that examination, ask for substantiation, draw attention to inconsistencies or evident improbabilities, seek clarification, explanations, further information, and so on; it can judge whether the replies and materials provided in response are adequate or warrant a comment. However, it does not, under the Indian System, undertake its own investigation of facts in the world outside those books, files and documents.

Keeping these two points in mind, we can examine how the audit processes can assist in controlling corruption.

Audit and Corruption

Corruption: Contexts and Forms

Corruption can occur in a wide range of contexts including but not limited to the following:
- ordinary governmental housekeeping (petty office purchases or minor works, passing of medical, travelling and other allowances and claims of government servants, allotment of government accommodation, etc.);
- administrative approvals (appointments, postings, transfers, etc.);
- major governmental or public sector contracts (large public works, purchases of commodities or equipment, project consultancy or construction, etc.);
- administration of tax laws (assessments, questions of classification, allowances and disallowances, applications for refunds, etc.);
- economic clearances/approvals, regulatory activities, etc.;
- provision of certain services to the people and related billing, etc.

Tell-tale Marks

In all such cases, any illegal gratification in cash or kind will necessarily be clandestine and is likely to take place outside the account books of the department or public enterprise concerned; it will therefore not come squarely within the purview of audit like the fraud or misappropriation of public funds might. However, the private occurrence of corruption might have some consequences in the public domain. Illegal gratification is aimed at securing a particular desired result and the effort on the part of officials or politicians to bring about that result, as a *quid pro quo* for favours received, could lead to deviations from the prescribed procedure, specious reasoning, special pleading in favour of a particular choice, course of action or manifestly erroneous, arbitrary or perverse decisions. There could be an exercise of undue patronage, the favouring of particular individuals or groups, failure to ensure adequate competition, excessively generous terms for a contractor, failure to safeguard the interests of the government or the public enterprise adequately and enforce penal clauses, poor choices in technology or equipment which subsequently give rise to problems, and so on. These are some of the tell-tale marks which could lead one to the possible presence of corruption.

Pointers to Corruption: Role of Audit

Procedural correctness and perfect documentation do not preclude the possibility of corruption. Procedural and documentational deficiencies do not necessarily warrant an inference of corruption. And a decision which has been influenced by corruption need not always be a bad one. All that can be said is that corruption is probably facilitated when there is procedural laxity and imperfection in documentation than when there is perfect conformity to all requirements, and insofar as corruption introduces an extraneous consideration into decision-making, there is a distinct possibility that the decision may be adversely affected. In drawing attention to procedural lapses or other ill-considered decision-making or mismanagement, Audit can provide pointers to the possibility of corruption.

Should Audit proceed beyond the kinds of query or comment indicated above and undertake further investigations of possible corruption on its own ? The answer has to be 'No'. Its constitutional mandate does not warrant this. Moreover, when we proceed from an examination of procedural lapses and internal inconsistencies in the world of accounts to an investigation of the possibility of corruption, the nature of the activity changes and demands a different kind of expertise and experience from what auditors possess. They could certainly acquire that expertise and experience, but they would then cease to be auditors; nor is there any need for them to do so, since specialized agencies which can investigate corruption are available. Corruption can be best controlled and investigated when Audit performs its own mandated and professional functions diligently and then leaving it to other specialised agencies to pursue further inquiries into possible corruption.

Selection of CAG

It is clear that if the audit machinery is to be used as an instrument (along with others) in the battle against corruption, it needs to be a strong and effective one. Unfortunately, it suffers from serious limitations, some external and some internal.

Absence of System

The first of these arises from the very system (if it can be so described) of selecting the CAG. Any institution, however exalted, is only as good as the incumbent. In singing a litany in praise of this high office we take it for granted that great care goes into the selection of the most suitable person for it. Unfortunately, the actual selection processes do not inspire confidence. They are entirely internal. No one outside the government has any knowledge of what criteria are applied, how names are short-listed, and how the final selection is made. Effectively, the choice is in the hands of the government of the day, i.e. the Prime Minister and the entrenched bureaucracy in the form of Cabinet Secretary and Principal Secretary to the Prime Minister, both officers of the Indian Administrative Service (IAS); it would appear that bureaucratic considerations play an important role in the selection process. This is hardly reassuring. We hypnotise ourselves with pious incantations of constitutional and statutory provisions and unctuous quotations from distinguished leaders of the past extolling the virtues of this high office, but the reality does not warrant such celebration. One may almost say that the CAG of the Constitution is a mythical creature, like the unicorn, which does not exist in reality, and that the current system of selection can only yield a pale simulacrum of that shining image. If, in fact, some CAGs have been not unworthy of their office, this is not because of but despite the system of selection.

The fact that the last three CAGs (and the newly appointed CAG) came from the IAS, has some functional implications which need to be noted. We are not concerned here with inter-service rivalries or resentments. No one can argue that the post of CAG should be treated as reserved for the Indian Audit and Accounts Service (IAAS); it is not even necessary that the CAG should be a former bureaucrat. However, by the year 2002, the Audit Department would have been under IAS officers continuously for 24 years; from the point of view of the IAAS, this looks like the systematic exclusion of that Service and the virtual absorption of the post of CAG in the IAS cadre. That view, right or wrong, has had a demoralising effect on the IAAS. The self-esteem of the Department, the firm belief in the virtues of an independent audit and the pride in performing constitutionally mandated functions, which used to be quite marked in the early years, are now much less in evidence. In its place, a spirit of cynicism seems to be growing. This is bound to affect the commitment and courage with which the audit function is performed. The answer to this morale problem is not to give any special vested rights to the IAAS over the post of CAG, but to ensure that the appointment processes are such as to leave no room at all for a sense of unfairness or suspicions of impropriety. Also, the selected person, drawn from whichever source, should be of such unquestionable suitability as to command respect both within and outside the Audit Department.

Need for a High Level Selection Committee

It is clearly necessary, then, to rescue this high constitutional and federal office from the hands of the ruling party and the entrenched bureaucracy by creating a wider field of choice and an objective selection process. In the UK, the CAG is appointed by the Crown on an address presented by the House of Commons, and the motion for such an address is made by the Prime Minister acting in agreement with the Chairman of the Public Accounts Committee. In the USA, the President appoints the Comptroller General subject to Senate confirmation, but under a new system introduced by the GAO Act of 1980, the President is expected, though not mandatorily required, to make a selection from a list prepared by a special congressional commission. In India, a pattern is available: The Protection of Human Rights Act 1993 provides for the appointment of the Chairperson and other members of the National Human Rights Commission to be based on the recommendations of a Committee consisting of the Prime Minister, the Home Minister, the Leaders of the Opposition in the two Houses of Parliament, the Speaker of the Lok Sabha and the Deputy Chairman of the Rajya Sabha. In the case of the CAG, considering the high constitutional position of the office and the nature of its functions, the Committee could include the Finance Minister instead of the Home Minister, and it may be appropriate to include the Chief Justice of India. The final selection and even the preliminary step of compiling a short list should be the responsibility of that Committee. The short list should include outstanding civil servants from the IAAS, IAS and some other Services as well as some distinguished names from sources outside the bureaucracy.

Need for Criteria

In this context, it is necessary to lay down in advance the criteria that should govern the selection of the CAG. Unfortunately, a writ petition to this effect, filed by H.D. Shourie, was not admitted by the Supreme Court. It is regrettable that the Supreme Court, which has lately been playing an 'activist' role and going into all kinds of issues — including industrial pollution, removal of city garbage, and so on — did not choose to interest itself in helping to determine the manner of selection of a high constitutional functionary. As such, the selection committee suggested above will have to lay down the job specifications and the selection criteria first before proceeding with the actual selection.

At the time of writing, a new CAG has just been appointed, and so there will be no new selection for another six years. Nevertheless, the reform proposed is an important one and needs to be debated by those who have public interest at heart.

Reorientation of IAD

Restoring Focus on Audit

The second limitation on the effectiveness of the audit function is one of orientation. From the very beginning, there has been a tendency in the IAD to regard the conventional audit activities such as the check of procedural correctness, proper documentation, and so on as *routine* or *formal* functions. There has been a constant search for higher functions. Perhaps the officers of the IAD derive greater satisfaction from writing reports on subjects such as *public debt*, undertaking *appraisals* of public enterprises, questioning decisions taken at high levels in Government, or venturing into policy audit rather than commenting on ordinary irregularities. Possibly, these activities were a defensive reaction to the usual criticisms of an audit as being 'wooden', 'unimaginative', 'pettifogging', etc. One wonders whether the Audit Department itself has become somewhat uncomfortable about its basic duties and tries to maintain its self-esteem by doing 'higher' things. Whatever the explanation, and however justified the extended and 'higher' functions, we have to recognise that it is an audit proper, and not the 'higher' activities, which could be of some assistance in curbing corruption. The basic audit function needs to be restored to a position of importance in the internal thinking and value system of the IAD. Other SAIs may take the prevalence of certain standards of integrity and probity in public administration and public life for granted, and concentrate on administrative audit, efficiency, value for money, and so on. Given the situation in this country, it seems reasonable to suggest that our SAI should pay special attention to the national problem of corruption, and give a special orientation to audit activity in order to remain on the watch for any incidence of corruption. As mentioned earlier, corruption may leave a trace or a smell and auditors need to develop a keen sense for this.

In operational terms, what does this mean? One is not advocating a presumption that the slightest procedural defect must be *mala fide,* the acceptance of a bid other than the lowest is necessarily indicative of corruption or every judgement or discretion has questionable motivations. That would paralyse the administration and place a premium on safe rather than sound decision-making. What is being suggested is that the possibility of corruption should be kept in view while carefully examining procedural lapses and deficiencies as well as exercises of judgement and discretion; there should always be a readiness to listen to explanations. A combination of rigorous scrutiny with an appreciation of the urgencies and compulsions of administrative and managerial decision-making is essential. That is no doubt a difficult combination to practice. It would be easy to slip either into undue suspiciousness and a wooden insistence on correctness or into an excessive readiness to accept plausible explanations for lapses and deviations. Both of these dangers have to be carefully avoided, but their presence does not invalidate the undertaking proposed or reduce its importance.

Rediscovering the Role of Detectives

Clearly, this will call for a major reorientation of attitudes in the IAD. An important element in such a reorientation would be to stress a forgotten aspect of the audit function, i.e. discovery or detection. An auditor is supposed to bring to light things which would otherwise have remained hidden. An audit notices errors, omissions, deficiencies, discrepancies and other oddities; it burrows deeper, asks for explanations. As a result, what looks innocent on the surface can turn out to be something more sinister: a fraud or misappropriation. Even a case of corruption could come to light. Yet, in recent years, it is difficult to recall instances of a major scandal having been ferreted out by the audit process. There was indeed one such case some years ago; the Kuo oil deal case which came to light as a result of audit queries. However, in recent years, most of the cases which have figured in public debates have come to light in other ways. Audit reports on the Bofors case, the securities scam, disinvestment in public enterprises, etc. were written long after the cases had been debated extensively in the media and Parliament. One almost wonders if the IAD picked up the cases from newspaper reports and discussions in Parliament. Perhaps that is not a fair comment, it is for the IAD itself to undertake an honest and objective self-examination on this matter. But it is not unfair to suggest that there is need for the Department to re-discover the role of auditors as financial and accounting detectives.

Strengthening the Hands of Audit

The effectiveness of the CAG's audit is greatly impaired by a number of factors and circumstances beyond its control. First, replies to audit objections and queries are often not received or only after long delays and several reminders. Most replies are grossly inadequate or evasive; sometimes, the replies are of an obfuscatory kind. Secondly, when Audit suspects that the reply is untrue or misleading, it is often handicapped in formulating a firm and sharp comment because of the aforementioned tradition that it does not undertake an external cross-check on its own. Thirdly, even when Audit clearly finds a particular expenditure or financial decision to be unacceptable or improper, it has no power to impose a sanction; it can only include a selective commentary in the ensuing Audit Report. Audit objections thus have no disagreeable consequences, in other words, audit lacks bite. Even, when an adverse comment is included in an Audit Report, it may be long after the event and therefore have little impact; furthermore, it may not get picked up for discussion by the Parliamentary Committee concerned. It is necessary to see whether these weaknesses can at least partially be remedied. Three possible measures suggest themselves.

The Role of Audit in Tackling Corruption 99

Power to Summon Officials

When the Accountant General (AG) — or by whatever title the head of the audit office is known — finds that he is not receiving a reply at all to his queries or that the reply is inadequate or misleading, it should be made possible for him to issue a notice to the departmental official concerned summoning him or her to appear in person and give evidence.

Limited External Checks

As mentioned earlier, Audit raises questions and objections to the contents of the accounts, vouchers, contracts, correspondence and files that come before it, and does not undertake its own investigation of the facts behind those documents externally. That is a sound principle, but it need not be allowed to become a crippling constraint on the effectiveness of audit. A limited and judicious recourse to external checks and the obtaining of information from sources other than the office being audited seem worth considering.

Ordering Recoveries

Where it is clear that an irregularity has occurred — e.g., an advance drawn has not been adjusted, the sanctioned amount has been exceeded, the unspent balance out of an advance has not been surrendered, a sanctioning authority has clearly exceeded its powers or has deliberately split a single work in order to bring it within its powers, pay and allowances have been overdrawn, there are elements in a claim which have to be disallowed as not being in accordance with the rules, and so on — it should be made possible for the AG to issue an order for the recovery of the appropriate amount from the official or officials concerned.

Power of SAIs in Other Countries

These are not novel suggestions. SAIs in certain other countries have powers of summoning witnesses and taking evidence; undertaking the physical verification of assets, stores, etc.; calling for information, material and witnesses from sources other than the offices under audit; ordering search and seizure; ordering recoveries or imposing financial penalties; demanding the institution of remedial or disciplinary measures; and so on. In some countries, failure or refusal to provide information and other material to the audit authorities, impeding or obstructing the audit process, etc., have been made offences punishable by fines or imprisonment. Diverse provisions of these kinds will be found in the statute books of France, Sri Lanka, Bangladesh, Kenya, Indonesia, the Republic of Korea, The Gambia and Zimbabwe. The laws and systems in those and other countries need to be studied and some of the features considered for adoption in this country through suitable amendments to the CAG's Act, other relevant statutes or even the Constitution. However, it may be possible to introduce some limited measures, e.g., asking departmental officials to appear in person to provide information or clarification, undertaking limited 'external' inquiries, etc., through decisions by the CAG even without statutory amendments.

Bihar Revelations

The Collapse in Bihar

At this stage, we should look at the appalling state of affairs in relation to finance and accounts in Bihar, because it highlights, among other things, serious weaknesses in the audit function.

Massive financial irregularities have been present in certain departments of the Bihar State government for some years now. What has become known as the Animal Husbandry Department scam or the fodder scam has often been in the news in recent months. The case appears to be one of misappropriation of government funds, but the possibility of corruption also being involved cannot perhaps be ruled out. In any case, the kinds of lapses, deficiencies and deviations from procedure which rendered the misappropriations possible could also have facilitated corruption. A study of the case could therefore be instructive in respect to the role of audit. However, we shall have to wait for the CBI's investigations to be completed to obtain a full picture of the scandal and the details of its *modus operandi*. The CBI will no doubt consult the IAD in regard to the budgetary, accounting and procedural aspects of the matter. Yet, even at this stage, three main features stand out.

Excesses Over Grants

First, year after year there were substantial excesses over the voted grants under various heads of expenditure, making a mockery of the basic system of the legislature's financial control over the executive. Excesses over voted grants do occur elsewhere too, but the magnitude of the excesses in Bihar is staggering. In theory, there is a procedure for regularising this; the excess has to be reported to the legislature and voted by it as an *ex post facto* grant. That would provide an opportunity for the legislature to take the executive to task, pass strictures, ask for responsibility to be fixed, and so on. However, the underlying assumption is that such cases would be exceptional and that the excess would be of a small order. If there are continuing and massive excesses which are in some cases as high as a multiple of the voted grant, what is the purpose of retrospective regularisation ?

Funds Drawn Freely from Treasuries

Secondly, it has been possible for various departmental authorities to draw funds freely from the treasuries without any limit and fail to account for sums drawn. Apart from the procedural slackness which facilitated this, it is clear that it would not have been possible without the collusion and active participation of large numbers of officials at all levels in numerous government departments and agencies; the network of collusion must have been vast.

Accounts not Rendered

The rendering of accounts by several treasuries to the Accountant General (AG) seems to have been in arrears for years not only making audit virtually impossible but also seriously affecting the accuracy and reliability of the State accounts as a whole. In the absence of treasury accounts, the AG can only make a simple observation ("accounts not received"), and cannot offer detailed comments on the accounts. That elementary failure can cover a multitude of sins as is evident in the case of Bihar.

Failures of Audit

The AG has no doubt been writing letters to the State Government at various levels regarding these matters, and they might also have been mentioned in the Audit Reports placed before the legislature. It may therefore be claimed that the Audit Department had in a technical sense discharged its responsibility, but the situation seems far from satisfactory. What then can be done in such a situation? The following is an attempt to explore some possible lines of action:

(i) The non-receipt of treasury accounts was evidence that the treasuries in question were not functioning properly. The AG could perhaps have undertaken in-depth and extensive inspections of treasuries and made special reports. Such inspections might have brought to light not only weaknesses in the treasury administration but also any dubious activities.

(ii) Excesses over budgetary allocations are possible in the Indian system because we do not have the kind of 'exchequer control' system that exists in the UK, wherein, immediately after the budget is passed every year by Parliament, the CAG authorizes the various Departments of the Government to draw funds from the Consolidated Fund up to the limit of the voted grants. In such a system, excesses over the vote would be impossible. During the debates in the Constituent Assembly, such a system was envisaged as a future possibility in this country, and the term 'Comptroller' was added to the designation of the Auditor General. Unfortunately, it has remained purely ornamental. The idea of exchequer control was given up fairly early because of certain perceived difficulties. Since then, there has been a separation of accounts from audit and the departmentalisation of the former at the Centre and in some States. Departmentalisation has been accompanied, at least at the Centre, by the further step of placing the departments in account with commercial banks. Thus, we have two payment systems: through cheques issued by departmental or centralised Pay and Accounts Offices or through old-style treasuries. In either case, the voted grant gets distributed over a large number of offices spread far and wide; that is the real difficulty in the introduction of exchequer control based on the UK model. However, it cannot be an insuperable one. In any case, it is absolutely necessary to obviate the possibility of an excess over the vote rather than allow excesses to occur and then go through regularisation procedures. Serious thought needs to be given to this problem which has assumed staggering proportions in Bihar. (Even under the present system, the AG is expected to conduct an 'appropriation audit' and issue warning memoranda if expenditure seems likely to exceed the appropriation. It is not clear whether that procedure was operating in Bihar or was rendered difficult by the non-receipt of treasury accounts).

(iii) In regards to the evil of funds being freely drawn from the treasuries, there are two possible explanations. First, fake vouchers and other documents might have been submitted, in which case the question arises whether or not this could have been detected in the treasuries or later in the AG's office. Secondly, funds could have been drawn on abstract contingent bills and not adjusted later through detailed bills. A simple remedy for this would be to insist that unless an earlier withdrawal has been adjusted no further funds can be drawn. If this is not considered feasible, an alternative check of some kind will have to be established. It is the responsibility of the CAG to ensure that this loophole is plugged.

(iv) This case is not a series of minor infractions but a massive complex of egregious failures of a fundamental nature. It would not be an exaggeration to describe this as a virtual breakdown of the machinery of the State: it is not merely the failure of the law-enforcement machinery that merits such a description. Considering that the CAG swears an oath to "uphold the Constitution and the laws", a possibility which suggests itself is that faced with such a collapse of the constitutionally ordained financial system the CAG could have gone beyond letters to the government bureaucracy or even the Chief Minister, and made special reports to the Governor of the State and perhaps the President of India for such action as they might have deemed appropriate. These reports could also have been simultaneously released to the Press. In the normal course, the CAG does not go to the Press with his findings. His reports become public only when they are placed before Parliament or the State legislature. However, that applies only to the regular Audit Reports. A report to the President or Governor that the constitutionally ordained financial system is not functioning is not an audit report in the ordinary sense. It is a special report detailing a breakdown. By making it public, the CAG would not be violating any provisions of the Constitution; on the contrary, he would be living up to his oath to uphold the Constitution.

Need for Independent Appraisal of IAD

The above suggestions, based on suppositions of what might have happened in Bihar, may have to be reviewed and perhaps modified when detailed examinations by the CBI and the IAD are complete.

However, what has already come to light is so shocking in terms of magnitude and implications that it could not be ignored in this paper. It seems fair to say that while there were massive failures on the part of the State Government departments and offices, the IAD cannot escape its share of blame for ignoring the grave irregularities which have occurred, particularly when we note that there is no separation of audit and accounts in Bihar and that the accounting function remains with the CAG.

The Bihar revelations go to corroborate two points made earlier in this paper: (i) the IAD has shifted its focus away from its main business, and (ii) the effectiveness of the IAD has been reduced by a number of weaknesses. We have already made some suggestions for improvement, such as a restoration of the importance of the basic audit function in the activities and internal value system of the IAD, and a strengthening of the hands of the department through the adoption of some of the features present in the SAI statutes of other countries. In addition, there is an urgent need to substantially reform the audit function in India based on a thorough, comprehensive and independent appraisal of its performance. The CAG himself should set up a high-level committee or commission for this purpose, and draw upon external consultants to provide it with expert assistance.

Pursuing Pointers to Corruption

Follow Up: Institutional Arrangements

We can now return to an earlier point regarding special institutional arrangements for a follow-up on the pointers indicating corruption, fraud, misappropriation, or the breakdown of a system emerging from an audit. Clearly, such pointers need to be taken note of quickly, examined further, investigated, and remedial and/or punitive measures promptly instituted. This would require (i) a system of reporting, (ii) co-operation in investigation (networking) and (iii) dissemination, i.e., making serious developments widely known.

Mechanisms for Early Identification

The first thing to do is to establish a mechanism for an early identification of matters which need prompt further investigation. There should be a unit for this purpose in each State Accountant

General's Office and the important Principal Audit Offices at the Central level. Perhaps a small special cell consisting of hand-picked experienced persons could review the results of the audit on a monthly basis and pick out all those cases which seem to warrant further investigation by the appropriate agencies. Once a month, the head of the audit office could write a letter to the government at the highest level (prime minister/chief minister) containing brief accounts of such cases. Simultaneously, a copy of the communication could also be sent to the Central Vigilance Commissioner or the corresponding functionary at the State level as well as the ombudsman if one has been established. It would then be for the ombudsman, CVC or another authority to have the cases investigated further. There may be nothing to report in certain months in which case the letter will say so, but a regular system of monthly reporting will provide an occasion to highlight matters that need attention before becoming serious problems. A question may be raised whether the CAG can report to anyone other than the President/Governor in terms of the constitutional provisions. The monthly letters suggested above would not be 'audit reports' but communications which would facilitate investigations. Further, so far as one knows, the constitutional provisions do not bar a working relationship between the government and the CAG.

Networking

The role of the Audit Department does not necessarily end with reporting. Its expert assistance may continue to be needed in the course of the investigations by the CVC, CBI or other agencies. If corruption, fraud and other grave irregularities are to be effectively dealt with, close collaboration among the various investigative agencies is essential. This kind of networking is perhaps best secured through a special committee for checking fraud and corruption, consisting of representatives from the CVC, CBI and other such agencies and committees at the State level. The CAG should have no hesitation in associating his representatives with such a committee. The governmental investigative agencies are entitled to expect the CAG's co-operation in such an important task and the CAG should not withhold that co-operation on the basis of a narrow interpretation of what his constitutional position entails. The committee should meet periodically, say, once a month, and review the progress of the investigations. In this context, it is interesting to note that in the UK there is an office known as the Serious Fraud Office, set up under the Criminal Justice Act, 1987, which is responsible for all the functions of detection, investigation and prosecution in relation to serious fraud cases. It is vested with special powers, including access to bank accounts, which would enable it to obtain information quickly and efficiently. It functions through multi-disciplinary teams including lawyers, accountants, police officers and support staff. In India, there may be need to establish a similar Fraud and Corruption Office either as a separate new institution or as a specialized part of the CBI. In either case, the CAG should both depute personnel to such an organisation and co-operate fully in its functions of detection, investigation and prosecution.

Dissemination

Apart from reporting and networking, the widest possible dissemination of the results of the audit is essential for the enforcement of accountability. The present arrangements leave much to be desired. The CAG reports only to the Government, and it is the Government which lays the reports before Parliament or the State Legislature; it is only then that the reports become public. Delays take place at every stage. By the time the reports are released, the events and transactions to which they relate would be at least a year old. Further delays can take place during the processes of consideration by the Parliamentary Committee concerned (the Public Accounts Committee and the Committee on Public Undertakings). The discussion, when it does take place, is very selective, and large numbers of paragraphs, and even entire reports, may not get discussed at all. There are even more delays in the finalisation of the reports by Committees, the Government's responses in the form of 'Action Taken Notes', their consideration by the Parliamentary Committees, and their further observations. Such a protracted and dilatory process greatly reduces the meaning of accountability. The irregularities and improprieties reported in the CAG's audit reports should be taken note of promptly, discussed in the House and appropriate remedial and disciplinary actions taken without delay, and the information and outcome made readily available to the general public. How can this be ensured?

Special or Concurrent Audit Reports

In the first place, audit reports themselves need to be expedited. There has been considerable improvement in this regard over the years, but there is scope for further improvement. This is linked with the completion of the accounts, which is a major subject in itself, but not our primary concern in this paper. However, we need not take the linkage with the accounting process as ineluctable. We have already suggested that there should be a monthly letter regarding cases which need investigation. What this implies is a delinking of audit findings from the accounting cycle and we can carry this further. There can be special audit reports throughout the year when important audits are completed. Some special audit reports are already being submitted, but the practice needs to be expanded. The more concurrent the audit process becomes, the more effective it will be. (By 'concurrent' we mean 'as soon as possible after the action or decision', and not 'during the course of executive action or decision-making'; audit must necessarily remain an *ex post facto* check). In respect to major purchases, works, projects or consultancy contracts, prompt completion of audit reports on the contracts themselves and periodical reports on their operation later may be among the most effective checks on corruption. This would also apply to the audit of other major decisions, such as the leasing of oilfields or mineral deposits for development and exploitation, the selection of bids for 'telecom' operations, raising of funds abroad, disinvestment of equity in public enterprises, and so on.

Such reports need not necessarily be 'thematic'; there could also be regular monthly or quarterly audit reports embodying the results of an audit of particular expenditures, receipts, sanctions, contracts or other decisions having financial implications as distinguished from the audit of accounts. In other words, there would be an annual audit report on the accounts containing the CAG's comments and a series of reports throughout the year on particular cases and special themes. When necessary, there could be special reports on serious accounting failures.

These monthly or quarterly or special audit reports will be presented to the President/Governor in the same way as conventional annual audit reports. However, all these will be taken note of by the Fraud and Corruption Office referred to earlier which will identify cases needing further investigation. Such cases will be included in the monthly letters suggested earlier, and will come within the purview of the investigative agencies and the committee to check fraud and corruption.

Making Reports Public

That still leaves the question of dissemination. Should the monthly letters, periodic audit reports, etc. suggested above, be released forthwith to the Press? There is much to be said for this. Everything should be in the public domain as much as possible. Transparency is the best safeguard against corruption, fraud and any other form of wrongdoing. In the USA, all GAO reports, unless classified for national security reasons, are available to the Press and the public immediately upon issue, or within a few weeks. We must move towards that position.

Audit on Request

Need for Positive Response

The special reports referred to above are those decided upon by the CAG. Should the CAG also undertake special checks at the request of others? It is possible that a department or ministry in the government may suspect the possibility of fraud or misappropriation or corruption and feel that a special audit is necessary. Similarly, Parliament or one of its Committees and another investigative agency may desire that certain matters should be looked at with the expertise available in the IAD. Thirdly, a member of the general public, voluntary organisation, or investigative journalist may propose a special examination by the CAG. In a sense, this would be similar to 'public interest litigation' in the legal domain. What should be the CAG's response to such requests?

Requests from Parliament will surely be on a special footing. The CAG may not be 'under' Parliament, but he is bound to give due weight to any suggestion emanating from that body. This would also apply to State Legislatures. Similarly, he is also bound to give due consideration to requests for special audits by the government. Requests or suggestions emanating from individuals, voluntary organisations or the media may not carry the same weight but these too should be given proper consideration. The CAG is no doubt a high constitutional functionary, but it does not follow that he should refrain from responding to suggestions or requests for special audits received from outside. It would certainly be for the CAG to consider the material submitted to him and decide whether the matter warrants further examination. If he decides in favour of a special audit, it could be undertaken as a regular departmental activity and not as a job taken up on behalf of another agency. It is understood that in the USA, in the context of the widespread concern arising from some emerging scandals in the late 70's, the GAO set up a nationwide toll-free 'hot line' through which federal employees or private citizens could communicate information regarding alleged instances of federal waste, fraud or abuse; a small special staff was established to follow up, investigate, and, where appropriate, initiate action on the basis of such calls.

Once the CAG has decided that a matter which has been brought to his notice needs to be examined, his report on the subject will be submitted in the usual manner to the government and not to those who had suggested the examination.

Expertise to be Made Available

There is another aspect to this. The IAD is not merely a constitutionally mandated watchdog agency; it is also a specialised professional organisation with certain skills and capabilities which might be of value to other bodies. When Parliament or its committees including Joint Parliamentary Committees set up for special purposes, or investigative agencies such as the CVC or the CBI undertake investigations into certain matters not necessarily arising from audit objections or reports, they may feel the need to enlist the expertise and experience available in the IAD for a thorough examination of the financial and accounting aspects. There should be a readiness on the part of the CAG to respond positively to such cases without compromising his right to comment on the matters in question later on in the discharge of his constitutional responsibilities. Similarly, if as a part of the effort to reform the electoral process, it is considered necessary to require political parties to get their accounts audited by the CAG, it seems desirable that the CAG to accept such a responsibility. Needless to say, in all these cases, the undertaking of an examination by the CAG would be on the basis of an agreement by him to do so, and not as, a responsibility cast on him by another agency.

Impact of Audit Reports

Speeding up Audit Reports

How can we ensure that Parliament and the State legislatures take note of the CAG's reports and insist on appropriate and prompt remedial or punitive action being taken by the government? It is difficult to suggest procedural remedies. It is really for Parliament and the State legislatures to enforce the accountability of the executive. If there is a lack of interest in this on their part, there are no answers left except perhaps public interest litigation by earnest persons or voluntary agencies who are deeply concerned about probity in public life. The only positive step that can be thought of is to ensure that the CAG's reports reach the public domain as early as possible. In this scenario Parliament may conceivably come under some degree of public pressure to take notice of the reports. As the reports become public only when they are placed before the Parliament or State legislature, it is necessary to see that they reach those bodies without delay. This can be achieved by laying down that all reports from the CAG should be placed before the Parliament or State legislature within three weeks from the date of their receipt by the President or Governor. This would apply only to proper audit reports whether monthly or quarterly or annual, and not to the monthly letters which we had suggested earlier in this paper, those would merely be communications for the purpose of facilitating an early start on investigations by the appropriate agencies, and it would be premature to give publicity to them at that stage.

Meanwhile, one possibility seems worth considering. There is now a vast accumulation of audit reports both at the Centre and in the States, and only a fraction of the reported matters have been discussed in Parliament, the State legislatures or the media. It may be useful if the CAG could have all those reports carefully reviewed by a special team of officers, and a small, compact volume (one for the Centre and one for each of the States) brought out which selectively brings to notice the significant deficiencies, irregularities and improprieties which deserve attention despite the passage of time. Such an effort could perhaps salvage at least a part of the valuable work done during the last several years and provide the basis for a useful debate in Parliament and elsewhere.

Summary of Recommendations

A number of suggestions and recommendations have been made in this paper. Some may require legislation or even constitutional amendments; some would need governmental decisions and orders. Others would call for decisions by the CAG and internal instructions within the IAD. A summary statement showing the necessary action needed, and by whom, is appended below:

Points Made	Addressed To	Nature of Action
1. Selection of CAG: High-level Committee (on the analogy of the NHRC law) to select CAG out of a wide field of choice, after laying down specific criteria for selection	Govt. of India/ Parliament	Constitutional Amendment (Article 148).
2. Re-orientation of IAD: Restore focus on basic audit function; re-discover role of auditors as financial/ accounting detectives.	CAG	Internal orders and guidelines in the IAD.
3. Strengthening the hands of Audit: Empowering the Audit Office to summon officials to appear in person; judicious recourse to external checks and to information from sources other than 'auditee' offices; empowering the Audit Office to order recoveries or impose penalties.	Partly CAG; partly GOI, Parliament	Instructions by CAG; amendments to the CAG's Act (based on study of SAI statutes in other countries).

(Contd...)

Points Made	Addressed To	Nature of Action
4. Bihar revelations:		
(a) Weaknesses in Audit Office and in State Govt. Dept. (control and check of treasuries, inadequacies of appropriation audit);	CAG/State Govt.	Enforce existing orders and procedures; tighten performance in IAD.
(b) Obviate excesses over voted grant through exchequer control or other measures;	CAG/GOI/Parliament	Work out a system; amend CAG's Act.
(c) Massive financial breakdown: special report by the CAG to Governor/President and release to press needed;	CAG	Decision by CAG
(d) Independent appraisal of IAD, with external consultancy.	CAG	CAG to establish a Committee; engage external consultants.
5. Pursuing pointers to corruption:		
(a) Establish special cell in audit office to identify cases needing investigation; monthly letter to PM/CM, with copy to CVC/ombudsman;	CAG	Internal decisions in IAD.
(b) Co-operation in investigations; a committee like the Serious Fraud Committee of the UK	GOI/State Govts/ CAG	Orders by CAG to Audit Offices; Government Resolution or Legislation establishing Committee.
(c) Delinking audit reports from accounting cycle; monthly/quarterly concurrent audit reports.	CAG	Internal decisions in IAD.

(Contd...)

Points Made	Addressed To	Nature of Action
6. Audit on request.		
(a) Need for positive response	CAG	Decisions by CAG (if necessary, amendments to CAG's Act).
(b) Expert assistance needed by CVC, CBI, JPC, etc.	CAG	
7. Impact of Audit Reports:		
(a) Speed up ARs	CAG	Internal action in IAD.
(b) ARs to reach Parliament/Legislature within 3 weeks after submission by CAG; make them public early.	Parliament/Legislatures; Govts — Central and State	Understanding between Govt and Parliament (parallel action in States); amendments to Constitution (Art. 151)
(c) Special review and compendium of past reports	CAG	Internal action in IAD.

Note: The author gratefully acknowledges the valuable comments received from the participants in a workshop organised by the Public Affairs Centre in Bangalore on 11-12 April 1996 at which an earlier version of this paper was presented and discussed, and also the help received from several active and retired officers of the IAAS with whom he held many informal consultations while writing this paper. Needless to say, none of them bears any responsibility for the views expressed or the errors in this paper.

5
The Right to Information

A.G. Noorani

"It has been established that more the effort at secrecy the greater the chances of abuse of authority by the functionaries".[1]

The Shah Commission had good cause to make this general observation, which its three reports bear out. Ironically, only a couple of years later, the Chairman of the Press Council of India, a former and highly respected judge of the Supreme Court, Mr. Justice A. N. Sen, described the situation at a Seminar organised by the Gujarat Daily Newspapers Association on December 20, 1987 at Ahmedabad in graphic detail. He said:

> "The major constraint on the freedom of the Press, as I see it, is the lack of a proper and necessary recognition of the right to information by the Press. The right of information which is ancillary and incidental to the fundamental right of freedom of Press...
>
> "Unfortunately, however, important information is at times sought to be withheld by the authority in power on the plea of the bar of the Official Secrets Act even in matters where the Act may not have any application at all, causing a great deal of harassment to the journalists and imposing improper curbs on the freedom of the Press. In various places, regional newspapers have complained to me of the very great harassment they have to suffer in the matters of collection of information from the authority concerned. In some States, only particular officers in districts and towns are authorised to brief the Press. The gentlemen so authorised in the districts are usually District Magistrates and the Superintendents of Police. Journalists come from far away places to get particular information and it so happens that on very many occasions these officers are not available and the journalists have to go back not only without getting the necessary information but also having incurred expenses and lost some very valuable time. Press Council of India had occasion to deal with complaints protesting

against such harassment as a result of the power to give information being placed only in some select hands. It may be expedient on the part of any State government to authorise only responsible persons for dissemination of information and news but the whole thing has to be so organised that information is not in any circumstances withheld and the journalists in the matter of furnishing legitimate information may amount to undue interference with the freedom of the Press. I feel that appropriate legislative measures should be adopted in our country not only for the right of the Press to information but also for proper implementation of this right."

Section 5 of the Official Secrets Act, 1923 is a replica of Section 2 of the British Official Secrets Act, 1911, a statute that was revised after two decades of agitation in Britain by the Secrets Act, 1989. But there is no sign of a serious effort to reform that law in India, let alone one to facilitate access to information. The Congress (I)'s Election Manifesto for the general Election in 1991 said: "Freedom of information is another precious right. The Congress will make a law in this behalf". The promised law was never so much as proposed. There were also no moves for a dialogue with the opposition parties on the subject. They are no less culpable.

The National Front's Government was none too active in this sphere during the brief months it was in power in 1990. Its manifesto for 1991 said: "The National Front reaffirms its pledge to inscribe the people's right to information as a fundamental right in the Constitution. From this solemn pledge shall follow the National Front's commitment to replace the present Official Secrets Act by such legislation as shall protect confidentially in matters of national security in conformity with the adherence to the principle of open government."

It is always open to the opposition in a parliamentary democracy — indeed, incumbent upon it — to urge Parliament to adopt its policies. No such bill was moved, however.

In his excellent essay, *Secrecy in Government in India*, Prof. Shriram Maheshwari recalled the moves towards "open government, which were made in the wake of the emergency".

The Janata Party made a special mention of promoting 'openness' in government in its manifesto of 1977. By way of fulfilling this commitment, the then Home Minister Charan Singh, constituted in 1977 a working group comprising of officials from the Cabinet

Secretariat, the Ministry of Home Affairs and the Ministries of Finance and Defence to find if the Official Secrets Act, framed in 1923, could be modified so as to enable greater dissemination of information to the public. The working group laboured for months to reiterate the soundness of retaining without change or abridgement the statute of 1923. It argued that there was nothing in the Official Secrets Act, 1923 which stood in the way of flow of necessary information to the public. The very composition of the working group ordained the kind of verdict which ultimately emanated from it. Secrecy is a well-known device which bureaucracy presses into service to strengthen its power position and to minimise criticism of its action. Bureaucracy revels in secrecy. The 'no change' recommendation made by the working group serves only to confirm that ancient truth. Indeed, any other kind of recommendation would have been a surprise."[2]

On August 30, 1978, Mr. Jyotirmoy Basu asked whether the Government "would bring an Act to guarantee access to all official documents other than the highly sensitive genuine ones dealing with national security."

The Government's answer was that, "The provisions of the Official Secrets Act 1923 are designed primarily to safeguard national security and not to prohibit legitimate access to official documents and, therefore, no legislation to guarantee access to official documents, other than those dealing with national security, is considered necessary."[3]

On June 4, 1979, it was announced by the Government of India that a working group which reviewed the Act had come to the conclusion that it needed no amendment as, in its view, it did not impose the flow of information to the people. The group comprised exclusively of officials from the Cabinet Secretariat and the ministries of Home, Defence and Finance. The States, predictably, endorsed their views. Thus ended the efforts of the Janata government.

On November 17, 1987, the Minister of State for Internal Security, Mr. P. Chidambaram, informed the Rajya Sabha that amendments to the Act were at an "advanced" stage of preparation and a bill incorporating them would be brought before Parliament "as soon as possible". The Congress Government did not propose any such legislation in the remaining two years of its tenure in office.

On December 20, 1989, President R. Venkataraman said in his address to the joint session of Parliament, that "a participating democracy required an enlightened and informed electorate. An open government functioning in full public view will minimise wrong doing. *The Official Secrets Act will be suitably amended* so that people have increased access to information. Legislative measures will be taken to have the *right to information enshrined in the* Constitution and to ensure free flow of information to the people " (Italics author's).

Two distinct though related pledges were made, *viz.* amendment of the Act in order to remove the impediments in the exercise of the right to know, and recognition of that right by constitutional amendment.

A 25-member Committee, headed by Mr. B.S. Lali, Joint Secretary in the Union Home Ministry, was set up. It was reported to have recommended appropriate amendments and a guarantee of the right. Askari H. Zaidi, a correspondent for the *Times of India*, noted:

"The Lali Committee has recommended, among other things, that barring a few sensitive areas like defence, intelligence and some financial matters, all other areas should be opened in public scrutiny which is the hallmark of democracy.

"The ministry is supposed to prepare a note based on the recommendations of the committee which will be presented for cabinet approval. Then the fate of the report would depend on the political will of the government. Both the National Front and the ruling Congress have promised right to information in their election manifestoes. The Congress manifesto says: 'Freedom of information is another precious right. The Congress will make a law in this behalf.'

"Unlike the present system, where even highly secret information having bearing on national security is leaked and most innocuous information is hidden from citizens, the Committee has recommended strengthening of the mechanism to protect leakage of information on the areas vital for the country's security and integrity.

"But it says that these areas should be limited in number so that all other spheres of government functioning could be made open to citizens. On payment of a nominal fee, ordinary people should be allowed access to government documents except those classified as vital, the report says.

"In case the government seeks to withhold certain information to a citizen on the pretext that it may cause injury to public interest, a pretext noticed too often under the system, the Lali Committee report makes it mandatory for the government to specify how a certain information would be injurious to public interest. The committee has also recommended setting up of a tribunal-type body".[4]

On the other hand, *The Hindu's* special correspondent reported that a Special Task Force had been set up "over one and a half years ago, on the subject, submitted its report" some time last week "and had recommended sweeping changes in the laws on five counts."[5] The correspondent proceeded to give details:

"These are an enactment of a statute on freedom of information, modification in the totality outdated Official Secrets Act, 1923: a close and comprehensive look at the issues relating to personal privacy, a more purposeful information dissemination system and appropriate changes in the related areas of record-keeping and archives.

"Sources said the Union Government has circulated copies of the two-volume report to the ministries of Home, Defence and Information and Broadcasting for their comments on the various issues raised by the Task Force. The ministries are expected to submit their response to the recommendations with specific reference to their bearing on the security and other related matters latest by December 19.

"On receipt of the comments from the various ministries, the Union Government is expected to process them and forward it to the Law Ministry for further consideration. 'The process might take a few months. The ultimate result might fall far short of expectations. But the commitment of the government on this issue can no longer be doubted,' said an official who is engaged in the exercise.

"Sources said there should not be any major hurdles in the acceptance of majority of the recommendations of the Task Force, as its report was the outcome of the inputs from 11 major ministries under the Union Government. The Task Force, though headed by a special Secretary in the Union Home Ministry, had members from all the important ministries of the Government.

"The first volume of the Task Force report primarily deals with the status report in India on freedom of information and records the experience of various advanced countries on the subject. Examples from the European Economic Community (EEC) member countries, United States of America, United Kingdom, Germany and Japan have been quoted.

"The second volume of the report deals with the recommendations of the Task Force which seeks to make freedom of information a reality in India within the security framework of the country. There is emphasis on the need for a comprehensive mechanism for dissemination of 'purposeful' information.

"Some of the issues discussed in the report give an idea of the changes desired to realise the goal of 'freedom of information'. For instance, there is reference to a legislation which would make it obligatory for the government to give information to any citizen on demand within a minimum period of one week to a maximum of one month.

"The report also makes reference to the legislation in the United States under which all government documents are deemed to be declassified or made open to public with a lapse of 12 years from the time of their coming into existence. Of course, there is an amendment to the legislation which provides for making certain categories of information or documents to be inaccessible in the national interest.

"The Task Force has dealt with issue of granting immunity to citizens from disclosing the source of information. Under the present legal frame-work, citizens in India have no immunity protection in the court of law. Such immunity, if granted, would be a boon to journalists,"

Four years have rolled by since without the legislation over which considerable public time and money had been spent. In the light of these reports by responsible corespondents, it is clear that the sole obstacle to reform is lack of political will. The civil servants are agreeable and, more so, the soldiers. Lt. Gen. Depinder Singh made a powerful plea for reform of the Act.[6] In his Foreword to the book, Field Marshall Sam Manekshaw urged greater facilities for Press coverage of "the theatre of operations"[7].

The Government's position was made plain in the Rajya Sabha on March 16, 1994 by the Union Home Minister, Mr. S. B. Chavan, in reply to an unstarred question. "Some suggestions/recommendations for amending the Official Secrets Act, 1923 have been received. At present, there is no proposal to amend the Act".[8]

A report entitled "Freedom of Information and Expression in India", published in October 1990 by Article 191, The International Centre on Censorship London noted: "Actual applications of the Official Secrets Act well demonstrate its potential for abuse". Faced by criticism of the Narmada dam, which required the relocation of tens of thousands of indigenous people, the Gujarat government simply declared the whole dam area to be off limits under Section 3 of the Official Secrets Act. It thus became impossible for journalists and activists to learn what was happening at the construction sites. When 8,000 people demonstrated in the area in January 1989, 5,000 were arrested, including journalists, and 18 were actually charged. Only after sustained and intense pressure from activist groups was the Act's application to the area lifted in March 1989.

"In 1986 several members of the Bhopal Information and Action Group were arrested under Section 5 of the Act for taking notes in an open and public meeting of scientists and doctors concerning the medical measures that should be taken for the rehabilitation of the Bhopal gas victims. The government has still declined to disclose information concerning the way in which the settlement of monetary damages for victims was reached."

On December 13, 1994, the Supreme Court ordered the Madhya Pradesh Government to publish the Jayant Patil Committee's Report on the Sardar Sarovar Project. Belatedly, on December 16, 1994, the Government of India agreed to deposit into Parliament's library the Gyan Prakash Report entitled "Preliminary administrative inquiry into the sugar shortage 1993-94" and that as "a precedent for the future" according to Mr. V. C. Shukla, the Minister for Parliamentary Affairs. The Report was not laid on the Parliament and thus not published for the nation.

Abuses in the States are common. A circular of October 30, 1995 issued by the Punjab Government to all senior civil servants stated: "The Chief Minister has desired that except with his prior approval, no administrative secretary or head of Department should issue any statement on Government policy. These instructions should be complied with immediately". As the corespondent Ms. Aunohita Mojumdar noted: "This, in effect, means that there is to be no interaction between the press and bureaucrats...."[9]. It took some time for the circular to become known to the press.

A similar edict was issued by the Government of Tamil Nadu in 1981 as the *Indian Express* reported (June 16, 1981). It said:

"Firstly, the government instructed the city police control room not to give any information to the Press. Since April 22 when the city police revolted and indulged in an orgy of violence, the control room has become silent.

"The police control room advises newsmen to talk to the public relations officer for any information. Secondly, instructions were given to all the police stations and senior police officers not to talk to reporters.

"Then the government opened a control room at the Circuit House Annexe manned by the personnel of the Information Department. It was from this control room that the government doles out information to the press about the daily law and order situation.

"Since the information given out to the press at these official briefings was found too inadequate, the reports used to get details about incidents of violence and arson from hospital and civic sources."

Vasant Sathe criticised the Tamil Nadu Government's order restraining its officials and employees from furnishing any information to the Press, AIR and Doordarshan. The Minister for Information and Broadcasting said that the Central Government believed that officials must share information fully with the Press to prevent misunderstanding on any issue.

Such orders are obviously unconstitutional. In *Pell* vs. *Procunier* 4174.s. 817 (1974), Justice William O. Douglas asked: "Could the government deny the Press access to all public institutions and prohibit interviews by all government employees ? Could it find constitutional footing by expanding the ban to deny access to everyone?" Justice William Douglas' questions were obviously rhetorical. He was emphatically denying the government's right to impose a ban on information by simply asking public servants not to give any information to their masters, the public, through their surrogates, the Press. He was aware of this possibility though he considered it most unlikely in the United States. But the potential remained: "A state might decide that criticism of its affairs could be reduced by prohibiting all its employees from discussing governmental operations in interviews with the media, leaving criticism of the state to those with the time, energy, ability and inclination to communicate through the mails."

The Supreme Court of India has ruled more than once in the last two decades that the citizen's right to know flows directly from this fundamental right to freedom of speech and expression guaranteed in Article 19(11)(a) of the Constitution. With this constitutional precedent, the provisions of the Official Secrets Act, 1923 would not survive. In *The State of U.P.* vs. *Raj Narain* A.I.R. 1975 S.C. 865, Mr. Justice K.K. Mathew said:

"The people of this country have a right to know every public act, everything that is done in a public way, by these public functionaries. They are entitled to know the particulars of every public transaction in all its hearings. The right to know, which is derived from the concept of speech, though not absolute, is a factor which should make one wary, when secrecy is claimed for transactions which can, at any rate, have no repercussions on public security".

In *Maneka Gandhi* vs. *Union of India*, AIR 1978 S.C. 597, Mr. Justice P. N. Bhagwati said that "freedom of speech and expression carries with it the right to gather information". In the famous High Court Judge's case, *S.P. Gupta* vs. *Union of India* AIR 1981 S.C. 149, the Court struck a powerful blow for open government. It interpreted Sections 123 and 162 of the Evidence Act to restrict severely the area of privileged secrecy and asserted the power of judicial review in deciding between competing claims of privileges against disclosure and the public interest in the disclosure. The governing test was whether the public interest would be harmed by the disclosure. Mr. Justice Bhagwati said: "The concept of an open government is the direct manation from the right to know which seems to be implicit in the right of free speech and expression guaranteed under Article 19(1)(a)".

More recently, the right to know was affirmed in *Secretary, Ministry of Information & Broadcasting* vs. *Cricket Association of Bengal & Others*. (1995) 2 SCC 161.

It is not widely known, although it should be, that a Freedom of Information Act exists already in an embryonic form in a colonial statute which is a masterpiece of its kind. This is the Indian Evidence Act, 1872. Section 74 defines public documents as (1) documents forming the act or records of the acts (i) of the sovereign authority, (ii) of public officers, legislative, judicial and executive, of any part of India or of the Commonwealth, or of a foreign country, and (2) public records kept in any state of private documents.

Section 75 says that "all other documents are private".

Next comes the important Section 76. It reads: "Every public officer having the custody of a public document, *which any person has a right to inspect*, shall give that person on demand a copy of it on payment of the legal fees therefore, together with a certificate written at the foot of such copy that it is a true copy of such document and such copies so certified copies."

The italicised words are crucial — "which any person has a right to inspect". Who decides whether the person concerned has a right or not? The custodian of the document, the government or the bureaucrat? The person aggrieved by a refusal can, of course, take the government to court. It will be for the court to decide whether he has "a right to inspect" or not. A simple writ of mandamus is all that is required. A civil suit also lies.

The court will be able to construe Section 76. So far, there are few decided cases on it. Judicial creativity has a fine opportunity to express itself here.

But, of course, this statute risks being curtailed by a later one, the Act of 1923. Therefore a reform of the Secrets Act is imperative. It is important to bear in mind its background in order to appreciate its provisions. Structures on its British model not only have direct relevance but added force. In India, the politician in power decides on whether or not to prosecute; in Britain, the Attorney General alone makes the decision. As Lord Shawcross pointed out in a letter to *The Times* (November 19, 1970), "Although the Attorney General is a political appointee, his actions as Attorney-General and the way in which he exercises his discretion are entirely non-political. I know of no instance (since the Campbell case) in which the Cabinet has been called upon to decide whether or not a prosecution should take any such decision on political grounds." In India, the executive controls the launching and, as recent experience shows, even the withdrawal of prosecutions.

The background to the Official Secrets Act, 1923 shows that replication of British law on the subject was a practice faithfully followed over the years. An analysis of its provisions confirms this. It is necessary intrinsically for two reasons. First, to know what the law is and, next, to consider its effect on freedom of the Press and its validity in the light of the provisions of the Constitution. Debates in Britain on comparable provisions in the law are relevant in so far as they throw light on the scope of the provisions in our statute.

The Background

No sooner had Britain passed its first Official Secrets Act in 1889, than the Indian Official Secrets Act was passed by the Imperial Legislative Assembly, the same year. Section 5 of the British statute provided that if "the Legislatures of any British possession" made provisions which appeared to the Crown "to be of the like effect of those contained in this Act" the Crown could by Order in Council suspend the operation of the British statute in that colony.

Already, by then, the Indian Press had asserted its right to reveal information of public interest even if it was classified as secret. In October 1889, the *Amrit Bazar Patrika* published the full text of a memorandum by the Foreign Secretary Sir H.M. Durand, dated May 6, 1888, opposing the British Resident in Kashmir Mr. Plowden's proposal to annex Gilgit. The paper teasingly wrote that the Viceroy Lord Lansdowne would find the original of the document in the Foreign office.[10]

The publication was used as a pretext for a secrets law. Four years later, the Viceroy, Lord Curzon, set about improving the Act. The result was the Indian Official Secrets (Amendment) Act, 1904. It was trenchantly criticised in the Imperial Legislative Assembly by Gopal Krishna Gokhale, Asutosh Mukherjee and others whose comments have a strong contemporary relevance.

Gokhale's reaction was: "The proper and only remedy worthy of the British Government is not to gag newspapers as proposed in this Bill but to discourage the issue of confidential circulars... The criticism of the Indian Press is the only outward check operating continuously upon the conduct of a bureaucracy possessing absolute and uncontrolled power".

Asutosh Mukherjee remarked: "A journalist may obtain, most innocently, important information relating to civil affairs; before he can publish it, he must satisfy himself that it will not be treated as an official secret under this Act; *in other words, that it will not be regarded as of such a confidential nature that the public interest would suffer by its disclosure.* So far as I know, he has no means of ascertaining this with any degree of certainty, and he must either face the risk of a prosecution — be the prosecution ultimately successful — or, unsuccessful what is more within the range of probabilities, he will think it safer to leave the subject alone".

Meanwhile, in 1911, the British Parliament passed the Official Secrets Act, 1911 which held sway till 1989. Like its predecessor of 1889, Section 11 of this Act gave the colonies the option either to legislate to "like effect" or be governed by the British Act. It was amended in 1920 in light of experience gained in Word War I.

The Indian Official Secrets Act, 1923, as it was originally called, was a replica of the British Acts of 1911 and 1923. Like them, it is directed against two distinct acts: espionage (Section 3) and unauthorised communication of information to outsiders (Section 5).

A great jurist, Sir Hari Singh Gour, attacked its provisions in the Central Legislative Assembly: "Your provisions are so wide that you will have no difficulty whatever in running in anybody who peeps into an office for the purpose of making some, it may be entirely innocent, enquiry as to when there is going to be the next meeting of the Assembly or whether a certain report on the census of India has come out and what is the population of India recorded in that period".[11] The Act of 1923 is still in force, however, as amended by Act 24 of 1967.

Analysis of the Official Secrets Act, 1923

The Act deals with espionage as well as the unauthorised disclosure of official information to outsiders. Only the latter part is discussed in this paper since its aim is to consider primarily the impact of this statute on the right to information.

In this context, the most important provision is Section 5 of the Act which is virtually a replica of the infamous Section 2 of the British Act of 1911 as amended by the Act of 1920. The texts of the two provisions are set out herein below to facilitate comparison:

Section 2 of the British Act of 1911 (as amended):

"(1) If any person having in his possession or control any secret official code word, or password, or any sketch, plan, model, article, note, document or information which relates to or is used in a prohibited place of anything in such a place or which has been made or obtained in contravention of this Act, or which has been entrusted in confidence to him by any person holding office under Her Majesty or which he has obtained or to which he has had access owing to his position as a person who holds or has held office under Her Majesty, or as a person who holds or has held a contract made on behalf of Her Majesty or as a person who is or has been employed under a person who holds or has held such an office or contract —

"(a) communicates the code word, password, sketch, plan, model, note, document, or information to any person, other than a person to whom he is authorised to communicate it, or a person to whom it is in the interest of the State his duty communicate it; or "(aa) uses the information in his possession for the benefit of any foreign Power or in any other manner prejudicial to the safety or interests of the state.

"(b) retains the sketch, plan, model, article, note, or document in his possession or control when he has no right to retain or when it is contrary to his duty to retain it, or fails to comply with all directions issued by lawful authority with regard to the return or disposal thereof; or

"(c) fails to take reasonable care of, or so conducts himself as to endanger the safety of the sketch, plan, model article, note, document, secret official code or password or information;

that person shall be guilty of a misdemeanour.

"(1A) If any person having in his possession or control any sketch, plan, model, article, note, document, or information which relates to munitions of war, communicates it directly or indirectly to any foreign power, or in any other manner prejudicial to the safety or interests of the State, that person shall be guilty of a misdemeanour.

"(2) If any person receives any secret official code word, or password, or sketch, plan, model, article, note, document, or information, knowing or having reasonable ground to believe, at the time when he receives it, that the code word, password, sketch, plan, model article, note, document, or information is communicated to him in contravention of this Act, he shall be guilty of a misdemeanour, unless he proves that the communication to him of the code word, password, sketch, plan, model, article, note, document or information was contrary to his desire."

Its Indian replica, Section 5 reads thus:

"(1) If any person having in his possession or control any secret official code or password or any sketch, plan, model, article, note, document or information which relates to anything in such a place, or which is likely to assist, directly or indirectly, an enemy or which relates to a matter the disclosure of which is likely to affect the sovereignty and integrity of India, the security of this Act; or which has been entrusted in confidence to him by any person holding office under Government, or which he has obtained or to which he has had access owing to his position as a person who holds or has held a contract made on behalf of Government, or as a person who is or has been employed under a person who holds or has held such an office or contract —

"(a) wilfully communicates the code or password, sketch, plan, model, article, note, document or information to any person other than a person to whom he authorised to communicate it, or a Court of Justice or a person to whom it is, in the interests of the State, his duty to communicate it; or

"(b) uses the information in his possession for the benefit of any foreign power or in any other manner prejudicial to the safety of the State; or

"(c) retains the sketch, plan, model, article, note or document in his possession or control when it is contrary when he has no right to retain it, or when it is contrary to his duty to retain it, or wilfully fails to comply with all directions issued by lawful authority with all directions issued by lawful authority with regard to the return or disposal thereof; or

"(d) fails to take reasonable care of, or so conducts himself as to endanger the safety of, the sketch, plan, model, article, note, document, secret official code or password or information; he shall be guilty of an offence under this section.

"(2) If any person voluntarily receives any secret official code or passwords or any sketch, plan, model, article, note, document or information knowing or having reasonable ground to believe, at the time when he receives it, that the code, password, sketch, plan, model, article, note, document or information is communication in contravention of this Act, he shall be guilty of an offence under this section.

"(3) If any person having in his possession or control any sketch, plan, model, article, note, document or information, which relates to munitions of war, communicates it, directly or indirectly, to the safety or interests of the State, he shall be guilty of an offence under this section.

"(4) A person guilty of an offence under this Section shall be punishable with imprisonment for a term which may extend to three years, or with fine, or with both."

A comparison of Section 5 of the Indian Act with Section 2 of the British Act shows the following points of departure:

(1) The words in Section 5 (1) referring to "information," etc. and "or which is likely to assist, directly or indirectly, an enemy or which is likely to affect the sovereignty and integrity of India, the security of the State or friendly relations with foreign States" were inserted by the Amending Act 24 of 1967. The expression "friendly relation with foreign States" is particularly liable to be abused to prevent disclosure

which expose mistakes in the conduct of foreign policy by the regime of the day.

(2) Use of the word "wilfully" in clause (a) of Section 5(1) to qualify communication of information *is one of the few welcome departures from the British Act* as is the exception "or a court of justice" in the same clause. However, the clause was drafted in light of Sections 123 and 124 of the Evidence Act, 1873 on privilege as to evidence relating to the affairs of State and official communications. In recent years, the Supreme Court has narrowed the scope of the privilege.

(3) Clause (b) refers only to "the *safety* of the State" whereas Clause (aa) of Section 2 of the British Act refers also to "the *interests* of the State".

(4) *Clause (d) of Section 5 (1) is not found in the British Act.* It is vaguely worded. A person who has in his "possession or control" any "information" or document of the kind mentioned in the provision and "fails to take reasonable care of it" or "so conducts himself as to endanger the safety" thereof will be guilty of an offence.

(5) Section 5(3) is an exact replica of Section 2(1A) of the British Act. The definition of "munitions of War" in Section 2(5) of our Act is identical to that in Section 12 of the British Act. It is wide enough to include any ship or aircraft "intended or adopted for use in War". To take a concrete case: if a person who has any "information" about the Bofors gun communicates it, "directly or indirectly" in a manner prejudicial to the "interests of the state", he will be guilty of an offence.

(6) The remaining parts of Section 5 and Section 2 are identical. The former retains all the latter's features which have been authoritatively criticised in Britain in recent decades — its "catch all quality", its self-serving nature for the men in power, and the like. It is relevant in this context to note that under Section 8 of the British Act of 1911, a prosecution for an offence under the Act can be instituted only by, or with the consent of the Attorney General who it is well settled, acts with his own discretion in such cases. Under Section 13(3) of the Indian statute, prosecution can be launched only with the sanction of "the appropriate Government" or some officer authorised by it. In relation to any offence under Section 5 "not connected with a prohibited place or with a foreign power", it is "the State Government" which is "the appropriate Government."

Section 14 empowers the court to order trial in camera on an application by the prosecution "but the passing of sentence shall in any case take place in public".

Section 15 refers to offences by companies. It makes "every person" in "charge of, and was responsible to, the company for the conduct" of its business liable unless he proves absence of knowledge or exercise of "due diligence to prevent the commission of such offence". Since most dailies and periodicals are owned by limited companies, Section 15 would apply to the staff, editorial and managerial, of the company which is concerned with the actual publication of the impugned matter.

On the crucial and fundamentally important question of the scope of judicial review, Section 5 is identical to Section 2. Is it open to one charged with the offence to contend that he communicated the information or document ' to a person to whom it is, in the interests of the State, his duty to communicate it' construing the expression "the interests of the State" to mean the interests of the nation, as distinct from those of the men in power ?

It is pertinent to recall the views expressed by the two Press Commissions, the Press Council of India, and some judicial precedents.

In 1948, the Press Laws Enquiry Committee said: "We are unable to accept the contention that the application of this Act should be confined to a national emergency or war emergency, and that the scope of the definition of document, information, etc. in Section 5 should be narrowed down to the documents or information likely to imperil public safety in times of emergency..... We have no doubt that the Government must be the sole judge in this matter; and we trust that popular democratic government in India would utilise the provisions of this Act only in case of genuine necessity and in the larger interests of the State and the public".

Two members, Mr. S. A. Brelvi and Mr. Kasturi Srinivasan, dissented and opined that "the application of the Act must be confined, as the recent Geneva Conference on freedom of information has recommended, only to matters which must remain secret in the interests of national safety".

The AINEC initially took a bold stand but retreated from it later. It argued in its memorandum to this Committee that "while the Press cannot claim any right to publish information likely to be useful to the enemy in times of war and confidential Government information likely to imperil public safety in times of emergency, it cannot accept the claim that every circular or note or instructions becomes a prohibited secret because it is marked 'secret and confidential'. The Press claims the right to publish Confidential Government information when publication is in the interest of the public and the two limitations mentioned above do not apply. Indeed it would be a matter of professional honour and distinction for a newspaper to expose secret moves when public interests justify such exposure".

Only a few years later, the AINEC changed its position when the First Press Commission was appointed in 1952. "In view of the international tensions and consequent need for ensuring that secret policies are not divulged, they did not recommend modification of the provisions of the Act". (Para 1046 of the Press Commission's Report. It noted that the AINEC had "modified" its opinion).

The Commission reported in 1954 that "in view of the eminently reasonable manner in which the Act is being administered, we refrain from making any recommendation for an amendment of the Act".

Eighteen years later, in 1982, the Second Press Commission opined that "one of the chief obstacles to the free flow of legitimate information to the people is the existence of certain provisions in the official Secrets Act, 1923" (para 47). It mentioned in particular Section 5 which, in its view, "has a chilling effect on the freedom of the press". It added that: "there can be no doubt that the Section 5 as it stands can prevent any information about any affair of Government being disclosed to the public and there is widespread public opinion in the country that the Section has to be modified or replaced and substituted by a more liberal one" (Para 50). However, it is important to note that in its view *"mens rea* (the guilty mind) is a necessary ingredient of an offence under the Act" (Para 49).

The Commission urged the repeal of Section 5, instead of its amendment, and its substitute by provisions which would meet both the needs of "national security and other vital interests of the State as well as the right of the people to know the affairs of the State affecting them" (Para 52).

The Press Council of India commissioned a study by the late Dr. S. N. Jain jointly with the Indian Law Institute of which he was Director, and adopted a draft of Section 5 to replace the existing provision. The draft embodies this very essential defence: "Nothing shall be an offence under the Section if it predominantly and substantially subserves public interest unless the communication or use of the 'official secret' is made for the benefit of any foreign power or in any manner prejudicial to the safety of the state".[12]

In Britain, it came to be universally recognised by the early '70s that Section 2 of the Act of 1911 was wholly inappropriate in a democracy. In 1971, the *Sunday Telegraph*, its editor and two others along the chain of communication were prosecuted when the paper published a confidential assessment of the situation in Nigeria written by the Advisor to the Britain High Commission in Lagos. They were all acquitted in February 1971. In the course of his summing up, Mr. Justice Caulfield made the memorable remark that Section 2 should be "pensioned off". Soon, there were demands for its repeal. The British Government adopted the classic remedy of appointing a Committee that year. It was headed by Lord Franks and comprised distinguished civil servants, diplomats, MPs and a leading QC Brian Neill [Departmental Committee on Section 2 of the Committee (Cmnd. 5104; HMSO London)].

The Franks Report, submitted in August 1972, condemned Section 2 in unequivocal terms: "The main offence which Section 2 creates is the unauthorised Communication of official information (including documents) by a Crown servant. *The leading characteristic of this offence is its catch-all quality.* It catches all official documents and information. It makes no distinction of kind, and no distinctions of degree. All information which a Crown servant learns in the course of his duty is 'official' for the purposes of Section 2, whatever its nature, whatever its importance, whatever its original source. A blanket is thrown over everything, nothing escapes. The Section catches all Crown servants as well as all official information".

Correspondingly, anyone, whether a newsman or a lay person, who receives such information is liable to punishment once it is proved that he either actually knew or had reasonable ground to believe that the information was communicated to breach of the Act. Both the giver and the receiver of the information are liable to imprisonment for a term which may extend to three years.

There is an additional issue to which the Franks Committee drew pointed attention: "*Ministers are, in effect, self-authorising.* They decide for themselves what to reveal. Senior civil servants exercise a considerable degree of personal judgement in deciding what disclosures of official information they may properly make and to whom".

Such communication is regarded as "authorised" communication. The result is that while official leaks, a fertile source of disinformation, are protected, their exposure by unravelling the whole truth is forbidden. Lord Devlin's censure of Section 2 is very apt: "It installs as the judges of what ought to be revealed men whose interests it is to conceal".

Two English decisions bear directly on the issue of judicial review. One decided by the House of Lords, is *Chandler* vs. *Director of Public Prosecutions (1964) A.C. 763*. Six members of the Committee of 100, part of the Campaign for Nuclear Disarmament, were convicted under the Act for organising a sit-in at an airfield. Bertrand Russell led the defence witnesses to explain the purpose of the campaign, to make known the horrors of nuclear warfare. The evidence was excluded as being irrelevant. The defence that aircraft armed with nuclear bombs were not "in the interests of the State" was rejected. But the expression divided the Lords.

Lord Reid warned about "what can happen if you personify and almost deify the State". He said the State "does not mean the government or the executive" and it cannot have "the last word" about what is or is not in the public interest. Lord Devlin took a similar view. "The fact to be proved is the existence of a purpose prejudicial to the State — not a purpose which 'appears to the Crown' to be prejudicial to the state". Lords Radcliffe and Pearce differed while Lord Hodson avoided the issue.

Prof. Harry Street and other jurists criticised the Lords for "the dangerous doctrine that whatever is Crown policy is necessarily in the interests of the State". Though Lords Reid and Devlin had clearly rejected the doctrine they upheld the conviction because they rejected the defence on the grounds immobilising an airfield for hours cannot be in public interest.

However, official deception can make disclosure of an official document an act "in the interests of the State", albeit not in those of the Government. A high authority on constitutional law, Prof. H.W.R. Wade, testified at the Ponting trial that if a civil servant was convinced of deception by the ministers it "might be in the public interest for him to give his information direct to Parliament" as is done by accounting officers. "For, the Government of the country could not be run as it does now if Parliament was consistently fed with information".

In the case of Mr. Clive Ponting, a senior official of the Ministry of Defence, the trial judge, Mr. Justice McCowan, in his summing up to the jury interpreted the words "in the interest of the State" to mean "the policies laid down by those recognised organs of Government and authority".[13] The jury rejected the interpretation and brought a verdict of "not guilty". In the House of Lords, Lord Denning welcomed the verdict and criticised the Judge's interpretation. In his view, the words mean "the interests of the country or realm".[14]

In the changed climate of opinion, the views expressed by Lords Reid and Devlin are likely to prevail should the issue be decided today. The following extracts from their rulings delivered a quarter century ago are, therefore, relevant. Lord Reid said:

"Next comes the question of what is meant by the safety or interests of the State. 'State' is not an easy word. It does not mean the Government or the Executive. *L'Etat c'est moi'* was a shrewd remark, but can hardly have been intended as a definition even in the France of the time. And I do not think it means islands. Again, we have seen only too clearly in some other countries what can happen if you personify and almost deify the State. Perhaps the country or the realm are as good synonyms as one can find and I would be prepared to accept organised community as coming as near to a definition as one can get.

"Who, then, is to determine what is and what is not prejudicial to the safety and interests of the State? The question more frequently arises as to what is or is not in the public interest. I do not subscribe to the view that the Government or a Minister must always or even as a general rule have the last word. But here we are dealing with a very special matter interfering with a prohibited place which Wethersfield was".

That tilted the decision against the accused. Lord Devlin said:

"The fact to be proved is the existence of a purpose prejudicial to the State — not a purpose which 'appears to the Crown' to be prejudicial to the State. Words of that sort could have been written into the statute. In emergency legislation they frequently are. In exceptional cases they can be implied: *Liversidge* vs *Anderson*. But there has been no suggestion that they are to be implied into this statute. Their place cannot be filed by common law. There is no rule of common law that whenever questions of national security are considered by any court for any purpose, it is what the Crown thinks to be necessary or expedient in fact. If there were, the reasoning in *Liversidge* v *Anderson* would, in effect, be part of the common law instead of the exigencies of an emergency regulation.

"Consequently, the Crown's opinion as to what is or not prejudicial in this case is just as inadmissible as the appellant's. The Crown's evidence about what its interests are is an entirely different matter. They can be proved by an officer of the Crown wherever it may be necessary to do so. In a case like the present, it may be presumed that it is contrary to the interests of the Crown to have one of its airfields immobilised just as it may be presumed that it is contrary to the interests of an industrialist to have his factory immobilised. The thing speaks for itself, as the Attorney General submitted. But the presumption is not irrebuttable. Men can exaggerate the extent of their interests and so can the Crown. The servants of the Crown, like other men animated by the highest motives, are capable of formulating a policy *ad hoc* so as to prevent the citizen from doing something that the Crown does not want him to do. It is the duty of the courts to be as alert now as they always been to prevent abuse of the prerogative. But in the present case there is nothing at all to suggest that the Crown's interest in the proper operation of its airfields is not what it may naturally be presumed to be or that it was exaggerating the perils of interference with their effectiveness."

In July 1978, the British Government published a White Paper on "Reform of Section 2 the Official Secrets Act 1911" (Cmnd. 7285) followed by another, in June 1988 with the same title (Cm. 408). It divided offences relating to the disclosure of secrets into two categories. One was the absolute category where disclosure itself is an offence; for instance, information supplied in confidence by another government. The defence of "serious injury" to the nation, recommended by the Franks Report, was rejected; so was one of revealing wrong doing. In the other category, proof of harm was necessary, but proof of public interest was not relevant. The upshot was that the Official Secrets Act, 1989, which is an advance on the previous law, falls short of what is desired in a modern democracy. It studiously omits the defence of "public interest" in the disclosure. The White Paper of 1988 had said that motives are relevant only in sentencing. The offence itself turns "on the nature and degree of the harm which their acts may cause." The new element of "damage", thus introduced, is applied in different ways.

Even in the clime of 1972, the Franks Report had recommended that "the citizen should have the defence that he did not know, and had no reason to believe that disclosure of the document might cause serious injury to the interest of the nation, "as distinct from damage simpliciter. A devastating critique of the White Paper was made by Richard Shepherd in an article in *The Times* (London) of July 18, 1988 entitled, *Secrets: freedom at risk.* He pointed out that "revealing iniquity would be no defence" and "the possible benefit to the public interest could not be argued."

The criticism was ignored and the Official Secrets Act, 1989, became law. It covers disclosure of information concerning security or intelligence, defence (which, however, is precisely defined in Section 2); international relations (including relations with international organisations); and crime investigation (also precisely defined). Section 5(2) makes it an offence for a person into whose possession has come such information or document to disclose it without lawful authority "knowing or having reason to believe that it is protected against disclosure by the Act." Note that mere unauthorised receipt of an official secret is no offence unless the receiver, in turn, discloses it. The prosecution must prove that the disclosure was "damaging" and was made in the knowledge or with "reasonable cause to believe" that it would have that effect. The offence by the original communicator of the official secret is open to the same defence.

As Geoffrey Robertson, Q.C., pointed out, the defence that "the benefit of revelation outweighed any damage which might be caused by it" is denied by the law. For example, under it *The Hindu* would have been liable to prosecution for publishing the Bofors documents. Mark his words: "disclosure of a public scandal — such as corruption in naval procurement... will be a criminal offence if it is 'damaging' as defined by the Act... the virtue of the disclosure and the social value of its consequences will be irrelevant."[15] Publication of the same information abroad was no defence, either.

Revelations about any aspect of intelligence work by persons engaged or formerly engaged in it are absolute offences. Information obtained by telephone tapping or burglaries authorised by the Home Secretary's warrant is protected absolutely. "It will not only be an offence to blow the whistle, but even in some cases to hear it."

After this Act became law in the UK, the Press Council of India (PCI), now headed by Justice R. S. Sarkaria, did the incredible. It backtracked on its own draft of 1982 and propounded, a new one in 1990 based on its own draft of 1989. It said that "fresh thinking was initiated *in the matter in 1989 with official support*"[16]. Its recommendations were communicated to the Government of India in August 1990. It urged the repeal of the Act of 1923 and the enactment of a Freedom of Information Act making "privacy" a ground of exemption. It said that "a constitutional amendment incorporating the right to information is not absolutely necessary at this stage, as this been upheld by the Supreme Court to be implicit in Article 19 (1) (a). However, such an amendment can be made at a later stage to make explicit in Article".

The PCI proposed new draft amendments as Sections 5, 5A, and 5B of the Act of 1923 which were far worse than the PCI's own draft of 1982. The defence of the public interest, ironically, is denied to a person who reveals an official secret in respect of three matters of the greatest public interest: "the sovereignty and integrity of India" (itself an expression perilously vague as compared to "defence"), "the security of the state" (which acquires, by juxtaposition with the first formulation, a vaguer connotation); and "international relations".

In effect, the Press Council discarded its liberal draft of 1982 and enthusiastically endorsed the Thatcher Government's conservative law of 1989. In one vital respect, the Press Council rendered its draft worse than the British law. Under the latter, the prosecution needs to prove that unauthorised disclosure of relations was in fact "likely" to endanger or obstruct the promotion of the interests of the United Kingdom abroad or the safety of its citizens.

But the Press Council, in its zeal, went one step further by introducing a legal fiction, a deeming clause, to shut out the defence thus: "Any matter which another State or with an international organisation, shall be deemed to be 'likely to damage international relations.' The Thatcher law penalised the offender only if there was a real probability, a *likelihood*, of damage. The Press Council forcibly identifies mere *possibility*, or *capability* with probability and would have a man sent to prison on the mere possibility of a disclosure on foreign affairs causing damage. Any officer from the Ministry of External Affairs can step into the witness box and testify that the disclosure had such a *capability*. Deprived of the defence of public interest, the accused would be convicted even if he exposed a gross betrayal of national interest in foreign affairs by the regime of the day.

The other interests which the Press Council's draft protects are public order and preservation of the confidentiality of information held in confidence. Only on these two is the defence of public interest allowed, albeit in a qualified form.

Again, unlike the 1989 British law, the Council's draft would punish a person who consciously received an official secret in breach of the law even if he keeps that secret to himself.

It is pathetic to see a body entrusted by statute with the duties "to preserve the freedom of the press" and to keep a vigil on "any development likely to restrict the supply and dissemination of news of public interest and importance" suggesting a law which will effectively curb that freedom, especially in the vital realm of international relations, and impede the dissemination of news of public importance.[17]

On June 30, 1993, the PCI formulated *Guidelines for Investigative Journalism* in a case decided on a complaint by Mr. R. C. Bhargava, Chairman of Maruti Udyog, against *The Statesmen*. One wonders what guidance a guideline such as this can provide the Press: "There being a conflict between the factors which require openness and those which necessitate secrecy, the investigative journalist should strike and maintain in his report a proper balance between openness on the one hand and secrecy on the other, placing the public good above every thing. There are a number of laws, such as Section 5, Official Secrets Act; Sections 123,124, Evidence Act, 'which stare the journalist coldly in print.' As far as possible, the investigative reporter should avoid a head-on collision with the consequences, for the sake of overriding public interest and benefit, without prejudicing the chances of fair trial to the subject (i.e. public figure) whose conduct he investigates."[18]

On July 15, 1993 the British government published a White Paper on *Open Government* (Cm. 2290). It left the law alone but promised relaxation of *executive* control in many fields, e.g. public records.

In light of the censures of the law by judges and committees in Britain and by the Press Commission and PCI in India, the question arises whether Section 5 of the Act of 1923 is at all constitutionally valid.

In his Endowment Lecture 1984 at the Advocate's Association, Bangalore, Mr. Justice E.S. Venkataramaiah, later a Chief Justice of India, commented on the constitutional validity of Section 5. He said:

"There is the question of constitutionality of the catch-all provision of the Official Secrets Act under Article 19 (1) (a) (2). Without passing any judgement on the same, let me mention the American Supreme Court decision in the *Landmark Communications, Inc.* Vs. *Commonwealth of Virginia.* In this case, a newspaper owner was tried and convicted in the Circuit Court of the city of Norfolk, Virginia, for violation of a Virginia statute making it a crime for any person to divulge information regarding proceedings of the Virginia Judicial Inquiry and Review Commission — an organisation authorised to hear complaints concerning the disability or misconduct of judges — which proceedings are declared to be confidential by the Constitution and statutes of Virginia. The basis for the newspaper's conviction was the rejection of its contention that the Virginia criminal statute violated the First Amendment. On appeal, the United States Supreme Court reversed the judgement of the Supreme Court of Virginia and remanded the case. In the judgement of Chief Justice Warren E. Burger, joined by Justices White, Marshall, Blackmun, Renquist and Stevens, it was held that the First Amendment which guaranteed freedom of speech and press did not permit the criminal punishment of third persons, including the news media, who were non-participants in the Commission's investigative proceedings for divulging or publishing truthful information regarding the Commission's confidential proceedings, such encroachment on the First Amendment not being justified either on the ground that the absence of criminal sanctions would undermine the objectives of the State's statutory scheme for confidentially or on the ground of Virginia's interests in protecting the reputation of its judges and in maintaining the institutional integrity of its courts. Justice Stewart wrote a concurring judgement."

An analysis of Section 5 in light of the authoritative comments on it in India and on Section 2 in Britain establishes that:

(1) Section 5 is incontestably unreasonable as a restriction on the fundamental right to freedom of speech and expression. In *R.S. Nayak* vs. *A.R. Antulay* (1984) 2 SCC 1983 (decided on February 16, 1984), the Supreme Court ruled that "reports of the committee which preceded the enactment of a legislation, reports of joint parliamentary committee information leading to the enactment are permissible

external aids to construction". These observations are even the more relevant when it is the Constitution, and not a mere statute, which is being construed. No court will ignore the reports of the Press Commission, the Franks Committee, recommendations of the Press Council or the two White Papers published by the British Government on *Reform of Section 2 of the Official Secrets Act 1911* in July 1978 and June 1988.

(2) For the same reasons, Section 5 is violative also of Article 21 of the Constitution. The definition of the offence is impermissibly vague.

(3) Constitutionality apart, like any provision creating an offence, Section 5 must be construed strictly. The Second Press Commission observed in Para 49 of Chapter IV of its report that "the only redeeming feature is that *mens rea* is a necessary ingredient of the offence under the Act". It must be proved that the person giving, or the person voluntarily receiving, the information knew or had reasonable grounds to believe that such information was being given in contravention of the Act. All the elements of the breach will have to be proved beyond reasonable doubt.

(4) The defence of "public interest" should be available to the accused. Correspondingly, the prosecution will have to establish that the disclosure is "likely to affect.... the security of the State", etc., or was made or obtained "in contravention of the Act" and was communicated "wilfully" to a person other than one to whom he is authorised to communicate it. The likelihood of harm to the public interest or "the interests of the State" is an essential ingredient of the offence. Here, the observations of Lord Reid and Lord Devlin are relevant.

(5) Judicial review is always available in respect of each ingredient of the offence. A provision which bars judicial review will, *per se*, be unconstitutional. The fact that the fundamental rights alleviate the vigour is no reason for not repealing the Act.

The Second Press Commission commended Part II of the British Freedom of Information Bill "as a model in framing the new provisions" after the repeal of Section 5. Its text is reproduced in Vol. II of the Report (p. 113). Part II was to be a replacement of the Act of 1989. Part I of the Bill provided for "Access to Official Documents". The Press Commission said that Part I "can be studied with the profit and our legislation modelled on that part with appropriate changes".

A major effort was made in the Right to Know Bill, moved by Mr. Mark Fisher, a Labour MP. It was supported by MPs from all parties, had its second reading in the House of Commons on February 19, 1993 and was referred to a Committee for detailed examination. On March 24, 1993, however, Mr. Robert Jackson, Parliamentary Secretary for the office of Public Service and Science, told the Committee that the Government would not support the bill.

The U.S. Freedom of Information Act, 1966, an amendment to the Administrative Procedures Act, was improved by the Act of 1974 and is one of the most successful of its kind. The specific document need not be mentioned. It is enough for the request to "reasonably describe such records." It is also sufficient to request all the documents on a specified matter. The documents can be had for inspection. A search fee of $ 7.50 is payable although this is waived by some agencies if the request is for disclosure in the public interest rather than for personal reasons. Photocopies can be had for a fee.

There are nine categories of matters which are exempted from the duty of disclosure. They are, first, matters which are specified by the President, "to be kept secret in the interest of national defence or foreign policy." The court can, however, examine the records for itself, *in camera* if need be, to ensure that the refusal does not exceed the terms of the Presidential Order. On this point, the court can also require considerable preliminary disclosure to the lawyer for the applicant.

The eight other exempted categories relate to matters concerning internal personnel rules, inter agency memoranda, personal and medical files, trade secrets, certain records compiled for law enforcement purposes, records of agencies responsible for supervision of financial institutions, geological and geophysical data concerning wells, and matters specifically exempted from disclosure by other statutes.

The Act confers jurisdiction on the Federal District Court to hear compliments against refusals of disclosure. "In such a case, the court shall determine the matter *de novo*, and may examine the contents of such agency records *in camera* to determine whether such records or any of the exemptions set forth in the Act." However, "the burden is on the agency to sustain its action."

In India, an effort in this direction was made in the Karnataka Freedom of Press Bill, 1988 (L. A. Bill No. 12 of 1988). Clause 2 conferred on journalists "immunity from disclosure of source of information." Clause 3 provided a detailed procedure for the exercise of "right to access to a public document".

The PCI, headed by Justice A.N. Sen, made detailed comments on the Bill recommending changes in order to improve the procedure. It opined: "In the Council's view it would be eminently desirable if the Parliament chooses to pass such a Bill which will have effect throughout the country. The fact that the Parliament has not chosen to pass any such Bill may not constitute any bar on any State Legislature to the passing of the Bill." [19]

One last category of publishers of information deserves special mention — "the whistle blower". The U.S. Civil Service Reform Act, 1978, known as "the Whistle Blowers Act", protects civil servants from any form of retaliation, legal action or demotion if they disclose to Congress or to the Press any evidence of violation of the law, mismanagement, gross waste of funds, abuse of authority or any substantial danger to public health or safety.

In Britain, on July 4, 1988, a few days after the publication of the White Paper, the 35th Report from the Committee of Public Accounts was published. It was on the "Ministry of Defence, Procurement Irregularities." It recognised the role of the "whistle-blower". Is a member of the intelligence services who blows the whistle on a gigantic fraud in defence purchases to be punished, then ?

However, the civil servants right to "blow the whistle" is more appropriately dealt with in the service rules as it has been in the U.S. Act of 1978. What is needed in India is drastic reform of the Official Secrets Act plus a Freedom of Information Act.

Conclusions

(1) The Official Secrets Act should be reformed; not on the lines of the draft proposed by the Press Council of India in 1990 but on the basis of its recommendations in 1982; specifically, Clause (2) of draft Section 5 which made "public interest" a good defence. This might well protect the "whistle blower" in the public services from prosecution; disciplinary action apart.

The draft listed only six categories of official information for protection. Information relating to defence or security, foreign relations, monetary policy, foreign exchange policy, etc. But only "where premature disclosure may harm the national interest or provide interests"; information likely to facilitate commission of crime, affect prison security, impede crime detection or apprehension of offenders; private information given to the State in confidence and trade secrets.

(2) A Freedom of Information Act, as well as Part I of the U.K. Bill commended by the Second Press Commission, the U.S. Act of 1966 can be drawn upon, the basic structure is more or less the same. The right of access to official documents is explicitly guaranteed, subject to the provisions of the law. Procedure for the access is laid down by application to a prescribed authority and on payment of a reasonable fee. The rule of the matter lies in the categories of documents exempt from disclosure. The Schedule to the UK Bill delineates six categories to be exempt from disclosure — matters relating to defence, foreign affairs; crime detection, etc.; matters otherwise privileged in law; matters affecting the privacy of any individual and Cabinet Papers.

The Karnataka Bill followed the same pattern. The documents exempt from disclosure were ones relating to defence; foreign relations, those privileged under Section 123 and 124 of the Evidence Act; Union-State or inter-State correspondence; trade secrets; private information given to government in confidence; and "monetary policy" (using the formulation in the Press Council's draft).

The Bill laid down the procedure for access — "application to the competent authority in the department concerned" in a prescribed form; a decision thereon within 20 days of its receipt; failure to notify the same to be treated as refusal; expeditious access in the event of its acceptance. Refusal would, of course, be subject to court jurisdiction.

It is, however, imperative that the decision to decline access should be notified to the applicant and the reasons for the same set out clearly enough. An appeal could also be provided for.

Notes & References

1. *Report of the Shah Commission of Inquiry* (Third and Final Report), Controller of Publications, Government of India, 1978. p. 231.
2. T.N. Chaturvedi (Ed.), *Secrecy in Government*, Indian Institute of Public Administration, 1978. p.126.
3. T. N. Chaturvedi, no. 2 above. P. 127.
4. *The Times of India*, August 15, 1991.
5. *The Hindu*, December 13, 1991.

6. Lt. Gen. Depinder Singh, *The IPKF in Sri Lanka*, Trishul Publications, New Delhi.
7. See A.G. Noorani, 'In Defence of Openness: The Armed Forces and the Media', *Frontline*, February 25, 1994.
8. See *The Hindu*, April 19, 1994, for an informed resume of the background.
9. *The Statesman*, January 11, 1996.
10. William Digby, *Condemned Unheard: The Government of India and H.H The Maharaja of Kashmir*, London: 1890, pp. 99 - 112
11. T. N. Chaturvedi, no. 2 above, p. 123.
12. See N. M. Tripathi P. Ltd., *Official Secrecy and the Press*, 1982; p.p. 43-44 for the text of the Press Council's recommendation in the form of a draft of a new Section 5.
13. *The Times*, February 2, 1985
14. *The Guardian*, March 21, 1985
15. Geoffrey Robertson, *Freedom, the Individual and the Law*, Penguin Book, 1989, pp. 139- 144.
16. See Press Council of India, *12th Annual Report, April 1, 1990-March 31, 1991.*
17. A.G. Noorani,' Shelter in Secrecy', *Frontline*, December 6, 1991.
18. Press Council of India, *15th Annual Report 1993-94*. p. 139.
19. Press Council of India, *10th Annual Report (Chapter V- Press Bills)*, p. 288.

6
Corruption in Public Service Delivery

Samuel Paul and Manubhai Shah

While political and corporate corruption at high levels tends to evoke considerable criticism among citizens and the media, corruption in the public agencies that regulate or deliver services to the people is seldom monitored or widely debated in most developing societies. "Grand" corruption involving large sums of money or favours understandably attracts greater public attention. But "retail" corruption (in relative terms) of the kind that is associated with public services also needs to be taken seriously because it impacts the lives of large numbers of people and can have highly adverse allocational and distributive consequences. Furthermore, in many countries, there are strong links between grand corruption and retail corruption. Corrupt political regimes tend to create a favourable environment for the practice of retail corruption. Politicians who have to raise funds for their elections may try to recover their investments by auctioning off jobs in public utilities and other agencies under their control. This is not to deny that retail corruption could exist independently of what happens at high political or corporate levels. For instance, past practices tend to continue and low levels of compensation may encourage petty corruption.

All acts of corruption arise out of the abuse of the principal-agent relationship. In a government elected by the people, all public officials are expected to act as agents for the citizens. An agent who has the power to allocate resources may sell his decisions or services for personal gain thus sacrificing the interests of citizens in the process although the latter are his or her principals. The salaried managers in a private corporation who are agents for the shareholders may also behave the same way. Corruption in any form thus entails a conflict of interest[1]. Conflicts of interest can arise in a government's purchase and sale of goods and services, its regulation of economic or other activities and the supervision and control of its assets and organisations. Correspondingly, the potential for corrupt practices exist in all these areas. The growing size and complexity of governments and the impersonal relationships between bureaucrats and citizens have steadily expanded the scope for corruption. Nevertheless, it is significant that the spread of "retail" corruption has substantially declined in most developed countries. The phenomenon of "grand" corruption continues to persist in these countries, but the vast majority of the population is spared the harassment and costs of retail corruption. This is no small achievement.

In this paper, our focus will be on corruption in the services that the government provides its citizens through its various departments, agencies and enterprises. As noted above, these services are the interface through which the vast majority of citizens come to know their government. They include public utility services such as water and power, a wide range of civic services and regulatory activities such as taxation and law enforcement. We shall first examine the major factors that contribute to corruption in public services. Then, the extent and manifestations of this problem in India will be assessed although the paucity of quantitative data is a serious constraint to this exercise. Finally, we present a set of recommendations to reduce the scope for corruption in public services in the Indian context while recognising that eradicating this problem will be a most difficult task. Specifically, our proposals are meant to reduce the incentives and opportunities for corruption in public services.

1. Contributory Factors

The public debate on corruption has identified two sets of contributing factors. The first set, which we shall label *popular hypotheses about corruption,* are factors that may sound plausible, but cannot stand the test of careful scrutiny. The second set consists of factors that, in our view, are more defensible in both theoretical and empirical terms. Let us start with the popular hypotheses.

Hypothesis 1: Corruption is an Efficient Lubricant in the Economic Development Process

This is a proposition that economists tend to support on the plea that in a highly-regulated and slow-moving economic environment, corruption enables economic actors to cross barriers and move forward. If speed money is not paid, decisions are delayed and services are denied. Corruption is the price to be paid to cut through these problems. What is ignored here is the adverse impact corruption may have on the efficient and equitable allocation and distribution of resources. Licences, permits and tax benefits may not go to the efficient, but to those most willing to bribe or use the power of connections. When politicians take money for the appointment and transfer of officials, the resultant allocation of personnel may be far from efficient or equitable. When credit and other services for the poor are allocated based on the influence of corruption, neither efficiency nor equity will be served.

Hypothesis 2: Corruption is the Result of Shortages in the Economy

It is true that the potential for corrupt practices increases with the severity of shortages. The temptation to jump the queue or invoke connections is high where shortages abound. What is often overlooked, however, is the fact that corruption prevails even when no physical shortage is present. Many regulatory services (e.g., driver's licence, registration of land sale, etc.) do not involve any shortages in the supply sense. Regulatory controls are used to simulate shortages or create delays, but this is a far cry from shortages that are beyond the control of the authorities concerned. Furthermore, when genuine supply shortages are present, pricing can be used to retain demand. This may be inappropriate or difficult in some cases, but it can be used as a remedy in a wide variety of situations without violating the concern for equity and justice.

Hypothesis 3: Corruption is a Rational Response to Low Public Salaries

There is a germ of truth in this myth as in others. Low government salaries may encourage corruption and a tendency to sell favours. Implied here is the hypothesis that corruption would disappear once government compensation policies are reformed. This is difficult to accept for the simple reason that grand corruption is associated with those with high incomes and assets. It would seem as though the appetite for more goes up with one's income level. The level of compensation does not therefore explain the ubiquity of the corruption phenomenon. It has, no doubt, an influence on corruption, but it is by no means the dominant factor.

Hypothesis 4: Rampant Corruption is Unique to Some Societies and Cultures

It is true that corruption in the public services which concern the average citizen is minimal in most developed countries. It is also pointed out that corruption was rampant in the same countries in an earlier era. There is a tendency, therefore, to conclude that corruption is a manifestation of the socio-economic backwardness of a country. Here again, the socio-economic transformation of a society will no doubt have a bearing on the behaviour of its public officials and citizens. But to assume that this is such a long-term process that no perceptible change can be expected in the medium-term is perhaps too pessimistic. In our own life-time, Singapore, which was known for its corruption, has substantially eradicated the problem. Chile, though surrounded by several countries known for widespread corruption, is known for its relatively non-corrupt public services and institutions. This shows that leadership, economic reforms and proper incentive structures to reduce corruption need not wait for socio-economic backwardness to disappear in order to make an impact.

It is reasonable to conclude that while the foregoing hypotheses highlight a few plausible factors underlying corruption, they do not offer a satisfactory explanation of why corruption persists in poor countries, especially in the area of public services. Admittedly, it is unrealistic to expect that corruption can be explained in terms of a mix of factors that apply across countries. The hypotheses discussed above, for example, are too general to adequately shed light on the complexity and spread of corruption in India. We, therefore, present below a more concrete set of contributory factors that can both explain the prevalence of corruption and point to policy guidelines applicable to India's public services.

The first significant factor that contributes to corruption in public services is a *monopoly* in the supply of public goods and services[2]. Absence of competition tends to create opportunities for corruption either by restricting supply deliberately or through inefficiency. This can occur in both public and private sectors. When customers have no other option, they are more vulnerable to the pressures of monopolistic service providers. Monopoly is natural in some sectors for reasons such as economies of scale (e.g., water supply). Regulatory activities have to be managed by authorities designated for the purpose and cannot be left to competitive forces (e.g., licences for buildings, vehicles, etc.). The point to note is that the inherent monopolistic nature of some of these services create a fertile environment for arbitrary decisions and corrupt practices which an individual citizen cannot easily monitor or fight.

A second contributory factor is the *discretion* that monopolistic public agencies enjoy in their decision-making and allocative roles. If, for example, the rules and criteria are simple and unambiguous, the validity of their decisions and actions could easily be checked by citizens. When multiple criteria are involved and all cases are not alike, the use of judgement becomes necessary. But this situation also creates opportunities and incentives for those involved to engage in corrupt practices. Often the decision makers, their supervisors and clients collude and take advantage of the discretionary facility. Here again, the remedy may not lie in the elimination of discretion, but rather in clarifying and demystifying the decision-making process, disseminating information on rules, specification of criteria, and providing for greater transparency and the right to appeal decision.

A third factor is the relative *lack of accountability* of the service providers except in the nominal sense of presenting annual audited accounts to Parliament or other superior authorities. Part of the problem here stems from the collusive tendencies referred to above. When those who are expected to supervise the agents are themselves party to collusion with the latter, the enforcement of accountability becomes extremely difficult. The problem is exacerbated by the difficulties in measuring the performance of the agents and the outcome of their decisions. The lack of proper reporting systems and supervisory controls add to the severity of the problem. Last, but not the least, accountability is viewed as hierarchical, with little attention paid to the need to be accountable to the clients (citizens).

In addition to these three factors, which Klitgaard also highlights in his work, we need to add a fourth, the role of *information barriers* in contributing to corruption. Corruption involves both givers and takers. In public services, the givers are mostly citizens or other users of services who have limited information about the rules of the game and the standards of service they can expect from public providers. Service providers may behave opportunistically because they have access to information that citizens do not have. Existing legislation in India contributes to this situation as public agencies are not required to divulge information concerning specific decisions or actions to the public. Citizens, having been brought up in this tradition are not used to demanding information. They are often unaware of their rights *vis-a-vis* service providers and of the remedies available if justice is denied to them. That the right to information is a fundamental right of citizens and consumers, whether it be in relation to the attributes of the goods they buy or to the benefit schemes provided by the State, is not a notion fully accepted by Indian leaders and representatives. Under these conditions, information barriers tend to create a setting in which incentives and opportunities for corruption gain strength.

Finally, the exposure of the average citizen to corruption in public services tends to be *episodic*. If a person does not encounter the problem frequently, it is unlikely that he will invest his time and resources in a systemic reform. This is a major reason why it is difficult to organise effective collective action against corruption in public services.

These *five factors* taken together explain a substantial part of the phenomenon of "retail" corruption in India. This is not to deny that broader underlying factors such as low public compensation levels or socio-cultural traditions have no bearing on corruption. But monopoly, wide discretion in decision-making, poor accountability systems and information barriers are more proximate causes and may offer valuable insights into the kind of reforms that could make a difference. For example, it is well known that most public services are delivered by mostly State-owned monopolies. That they are often insensitive to customers and withhold information to the detriment of the latter is also widely observed. We also know that their decision-making processes, rules and practices are seldom transparent and probably lead to the abuse of the discretionary powers vested in them. Information such as this points to the directions of change required to improve public services and reduce the scope for corruption.

2. Magnitude of the Problem

The institutional framework for dealing with the problem of corruption in public services is not uniform within the Indian government apparatus. A number of State governments have established the office of Lok Ayukt, comparable to an ombudsman, while the Central Government has yet to appoint a Lok Pal, the counterpart of the Lok

Ayukt. Citizens can take their complaints to the Lok Ayukt, but the number of such cases varies significantly between States. Ministries and departments of both Central and State governments have vigilance officers who are expected to monitor and deal with corruption complaints. Many of the larger public utilities also have their own vigilance officers while others deal with corruption cases as and when they arise through their established management structures. In serious cases, these agencies may set up their own inquiry commissions or ask the Lok Ayukt in their State to investigate specific cases. These diverse institutional arrangements and practices mean that there is no uniform approach to the treating, reporting or monitoring corruption cases. Nor is there any attempt within or without the government to analyse the data on corruption on a regular basis. Consequently, systematic information on this subject, including assessments of the magnitude and trends in corruption, are not easy to come by.

For these and other related reasons, it is not easy to quantitatively assess the extent and severity of corruption in the public services of India. One has to turn to other sources to fill this gap. Transparency International, a non-profit group that monitors corruption across countries, has stated that India, along with Indonesia and China, is among the most corrupt countries in the world[3]. The study was based on a survey of those who do business in various countries. It is reasonable to conclude that the phenomenon assessed is a mix of "grand" corruption and "retail" corruption. Nonetheless, it is difficult to generalise on the severity or extent of the corruption in public services alone based only on the country rankings given by Transparency International.

There are very few studies that have attempted to quantify corruption in India. A recent study analysed the complaints on corruption received by the Anti-Corruption Bureau, Vigilance Commissioner and Lok Ayukt in Karnataka and compared them with similar data in some other States[4]. The findings of this study confirm that retail corruption arising from the transactions of public service providers with citizens is the most pervasive form of corruption. For Karnataka, the study concluded that the departments of revenue, police, education, health and public works accounted for nearly three-fourths of all corruption complaints in recent years. The study further noted that corruption in local bodies was increasing and that in departments like commercial taxes, excise, road transport, weights and measures, etc. corruption had remained steady. Of the different types of complaints, corruption in the issuance of certificates, licences and permits occupied the first position (15% of the total), followed by bribes for the use of certain facilities and allied services like admission to public hospitals, appointments and transfers, and the release of grants and passing of bills in the education department (11%). There are fixed rates for certain services and favours, and the study gave examples of how the bribes are shared within the public hierarchy.

The authors also compared the volume of complaints in Karnataka with similar complaints from other States. An interesting finding was that complaints in Karnataka were much higher compared to those in Andhra Pradesh, Madhya Pradesh, Uttar Pradesh, Maharashtra and Bihar. This may, however, merely mean that people are more indifferent and are unable to access the anti-corruption bodies in their respective States than the possibility that corruption is much less in these other States. The study also found that over two-thirds of all complaints received were from urban areas. In addition, many aggrieved persons avoid lodging complaints, and are afraid of retaliation from officials and of the high costs of pursuing their cases.

The findings of the Public Affairs Centre's recent studies provide more relevant evidence on the extent of "retail" corruption in India. This again offers only partial evidence as the studies were confined to urban areas. The cities of Ahmedabad, Bangalore, Madras, Pune and Calcutta were surveyed on a variety of public service related issues including corruption. Feedback through personal interviews with citizens was obtained from slum dwellers as well as the general population (non-poor).

Table 1 presents a comparative picture of the extent of retail corruption in these cities. It shows, for example, that in Madras, every fourth person in the general population ends up paying a bribe when dealing with agencies such as the urban development authority, electricity board, municipal corporation and telephones[5]. In Bangalore, it is one in eight persons, in Pune, it is only one in seventeen that pays a bribe. With respect to slum dwellers, Madras and Bangalore lead other cities in the matter of retail corruption. The average amount paid as bribe per case was also estimated. Bangalore led in this regard (Rs. 850), followed by Ahmedabad (Rs. 500), and Pune (Rs. 350).

Table 1

The Speed Money Phenomenon

	(% of persons who paid)	
City	Among the urban poor	Among general households
Ahmedabad	20	10
Bangalore	33	14
Calcutta	12	2.4
Madras	26	22
Pune	6	4

Even the poor living in slums is not spared. In Bangalore, every third slum dweller claims to have paid a bribe for getting a service or solving a problem with a public agency. In Madras, every fourth person pays a bribe. Pune, again, reported the lowest incidence of this problem. Although the five cities are a small sample and represent only our large and industrialised urban areas, it is reasonable to conclude from this evidence that corruption is a pervasive phenomenon in India's public services. Others might add that this statement applies equally to rural areas even if systematic surveys have not been conducted there.

Though the practice of corruption is widespread, the proportion of people who consider it abhorrent ranges from two-thirds to four-fifths. Over half the respondents in these cities claim that bribes are demanded of them by officials. Personal views of this kind should always be taken with a pinch of salt. Some officials are likely to argue that citizens who wish to violate laws tempt them to accept money or use influence to bend the rules. But the fact remains that officials have better information and control the systems they operate. The feedback given by the respondents in the five cities confirm that they face a moral dilemma when faced with corrupt demands and that they would rather avoid having to pay bribes and would prefer to pay a little more officially provided they get efficient service from public agencies.

Even when higher prices for services are charged, public officials have found ingenious ways to practise corruption. The Telephone Department has a *Tatkal Scheme* to enable customers to get new connections within a short period on a payment of Rs. 30,000. The only qualification is that the staff have to first ascertain the feasibility of installing a telephone in the location requested. There are cases where the staff would inform the customer that feasibility can be checked out only after the full deposit is made. The customer is naturally concerned that his money will be blocked if the finding is negative. Agents are available to see that the feasibility test results in a positive finding. This, of course, calls for an extra payment! This is a case where, although a higher price has been used to provide a speedy service, the purpose has been defeated by adding conditions that are vague or difficult for the customer to verify.

3. Remedies: Proposals for Action

Before proposing recommendations for action, it is proper that we review what the government has done so far to tackle the problem of corruption in public services. Here we need to scan public actions taken on a wide front as corruption can often be addressed along with other problems. A good example is the Consumer Protection Act of 1986 and the establishment of district consumer courts. Though these mechanisms are meant to protect consumers from arbitrariness and abuses of various kinds, they have helped to deal with corruption too by bringing under the Act's purview at least those public services for which fees or user charges are paid by citizens. Similarly, the Lok Ayukt Act provides for cases of corruption in public services to be dealt with along with wider forms of corruption.

In this section, we propose to present a set of actionable ideas to reduce the incentives and opportunities for public officials and citizens alike to engage in corrupt practices. The scope of our proposals is limited to the area of public services which, as noted above, concern the vast majority of our population. The initiative for acting on these proposals must be taken by the government for obvious reasons. Nevertheless, the media, public interest groups and other non-governmental organisations can play a proactive and facilitating role by putting these ideas on the agenda for public debate and encouraging citizen groups to understand the issues involved and cooperate with the government when corrective measures are taken.

The proposals discussed below can be divided into two categories, preventive and curative. Preventive actions are steps that can be taken in advance so as to minimise the emergence of opportunities for corruption in public services. These measures therefore endeavour to deal with the underlying causes to the extent feasible. Preventive measures may not always fully succeed in eliminating "retail" corruption. Hence, there is the need to track and respond to corruption cases once they surface. This is comparable to curative or corrective measures since the mechanisms are activated only after the problem has been detected. A combination of both preventive and corrective actions will doubtless be more effective in curbing retail corruption than either approach alone. Needless to say, most of the measures presented below will impact not only on corruption, but also on other important problems. Thus, the elimination of excessive controls or the specification of service standards tends to improve the efficiency of public sector performance. Improved information sharing strengthens the working of democratic processes in the society. An Ombudsman may deal with corruption cases as well as other grievances. In this paper, however, we shall not examine the multiple benefits of the proposed measures. Our sole concern here will be to see what they can do to control corruption in public services.

Preventive Measures

1. Reduce Opportunities for Retail Corruption through Deregulation and Elimination of Unnecessary Controls

The process of deregulation initiated by the Government of India has focussed largely on industry and trade. It has had a positive impact on the corruption front despite the irritants that remain. These reforms, however, have not yet been extended to the State and local levels where the maximum interaction between public officials and citizens take place. Legislation on public utilities has created public monopolies, but they are exempt from responsibility for services or outputs. There is statutory control over what ought to be administrative decisions. Overlapping statutes abound in many areas of activity. These are major problems that often create opportunities for corrupt practices. A systematic review of the laws and regulations governing public utilities and municipalities with a view to simplifying them and improving their transparency deserves early attention.

As noted earlier, the existence of monopolistic conditions tends to create favourable conditions for the practice of corruption. Where there is competition, people have the option to choose more efficient and less corrupt service providers. The presence of competition can thus dampen the spread and severity of corruption. Even in service sectors that were considered natural monopolies, there is now evidence that competitive options can be made available to citizens. The long distance segment of telecommunications, electricity and transport are services where multiple service providers are able to operate in many countries. A systematic attempt to encourage multiple providers to enter the public utility arena in India, wherever it is feasible, may not only generate efficiency gains, but also discourage the practice of "retail" corruption.

2. Decentralise Services and Involve Citizens in Monitoring Them so that the Scope for Corruption is Reduced

This applies in particular to municipal and other local services for which people pay taxes or user charges. The creation of ward offices in large cities can make officials more accessible to the residents. Local residents or NGOs being on ward committees plus plans, budgets and problems being discussed in such forums tend to make the internal working of civic bodies more transparent and their officials more responsive to public needs. Monitoring and questioning by citizens will make the collusion and hiding of information more difficult. The provisions of the 74th Amendment hopefully will make the creation of ward committees a reality. What remains to be seen is how the committees will be constituted and what role they will play in performing the tasks mentioned above. Decentralisation cannot possibly be expected to eliminate all forms of corruption. But at least in respect of many day-to-day service related problems that people face, the scope for and severity of corruption may get reduced. A recent example comes from Pune where decentralised ward-level services are said to have improved citizen access and participation and increased the transparency of operations. In Bangalore, experimentation with ward offices and committees is under way. Still, decentralisation of services has yet to be seriously attempted in India.

It is often argued that decentralisation tends to strengthen the hands of the local elites who may use their proximity to decentralised power centres to engage in corrupt practices even more effectively. While there is some validity to this argument, centralised control is also vulnerable. The real question is whether the easier access due to proximity to decision-making, reduced transaction costs and increased transparency enjoyed by non-elites will empower them to resist corruption more than before, if not immediately, in the medium or long term. Evidence on decentralisation from other countries provides modest grounds for optimism in this regard.

3. Modify the Official Secrets Act so as to Improve Citizens' Access to Public Information

There are legitimate reasons why governments withhold information in the national interest. But the Official Secrets Act has been used to hide abuses of power, and according to knowledgeable observers, it is a convenient spawning ground for corruption. In the area of public services, it has enabled officials to withhold information from the public even when no security or concern for national interest is involved. Perhaps the most damaging consequence of this legislation is the generally secretive behaviour ("discretionary secrecy") it has instilled in the Indian bureaucracy. India inherited this tradition from the UK which has been behind other developed countries with respect to access to information[6]. But UK has of late moved forward in its stance on access to information while we, in India, have yet to recognise the need for reform in this area.

The Consumer Education and Research Centre, Ahmedabad (CERC) recently prepared an Access to Information Bill, comparable to Right to Information Acts in other countries, which CERC hopes will be introduced in Parliament in the near future. Initiatives of this nature deserve to be widely debated and supported. A more open government, while it cannot guarantee the end of corruption, will at least create an environment that is more hostile to corruption.

Another example of an initiative to deal with the lack of information and administrative accountability is the Administrative Procedure Bill, 1991 that was introduced in the Karnataka Legislature but not passed. This Bill sought to simplify and streamline administrative procedures and promote open and participatory governance. In specific terms, it required public authorities to display in their offices information on the procedures being used, including those for filing petitions or grievances. It also mandated that notice be given to the public on proposed rules and interested persons be given opportunities to participate in the rule making process through the submission of written proposals and views. Legislation to streamline rules and procedures along these lines and make them known to the public is essential especially when a decentralised administration is being put in place throughout the country.

4. Service Providers should be Permitted to Charge Higher Fees or User Charges to Customers who Wish to have Speedy or Special Services.

The role that the pricing of services can play in reducing the scope for corruption is not well understood by most people, including administrators. The provision of free services in the name of equity or other laudable goals has often had the perverse effect of creating excess demand for such services and attracting corrupt middlemen and other well-connected persons who divert these benefits to less deserving people. This is not an argument for abolishing all free or subsidised public services. The conditions under which free services are provided must be more tightly stipulated so that incentives to divert these benefits are eliminated. Whether free or highly subsidised services are what the poor need also deserves to be assessed. It is well known by now that subsidised credit often does not get to the intended persons and costs them much more than was anticipated. On the other hand, several urban and rural credit groups have now demonstrated in India that the poor are able to use timely credit at close to market rates of interest productively and regularly repay the loans. Through the imaginative use of pricing, these credit agencies have effectively cut down the scope for corruption and diversion of benefits in this socially important activity.

An important reason for the presence of corruption in some of the public services is the failure of service providers to match services to the differing needs of users and their ability and willingness to pay for such services. When services are rigidly standardised, those with special needs tend to exert undue pressure or bribe officials to get what they want. Thus, unofficial multiple tracks of services are created resulting in corruption or the abuse of power in the process. Alternately, public officials may use their contacts and network to claim priority and special treatment from service providers. Business houses appoint agents who are adept at getting services on priority simply through the use of connections and money. In both cases, the State-run public utilities do not benefit as they can charge only for their standard services. They are unable to generate more resources and improve the volume and quality of their services. The pressure on their services increases and the scope for corruption is further enlarged in the process.

This is a complex problem that does not lend itself to any simple remedy. Whether governments need to pre-empt most services and facilities through liberal quotas is itself a moot point. Even if the case for some pre-emption is accepted, the question still remains whether or not providing services to meet the varying needs of customers in terms of urgency or special features is justified, both in terms of meeting the objectives of efficiency and resource generation as well as reducing the scope for corruption. It is typically argued that dual or multiple tracks of services will lead to the neglect of services for the ordinary citizen. A case in point is the alleged adverse impact of speed post on ordinary mail service. The problem here is that some people view the quantum of work that the Postal Department can do as fixed. If it gets into speed post operations, its staff cannot attend to the ordinary mail service. But this may well be a problem of internal planning and supervision. If the volume of business expands, or its nature changes, dynamic organisations will plan ahead to recruit and train more people, introduce new organisational reforms and monitor their diverse operations systematically. In the absence of such approaches, organisations will get overloaded and perform poorly. But there is nothing in diversification that dictates that one service can be delivered only at the expense of another. Needless to say, multiple services and prices may not be relevant to all public utilities and services. The challenge is to think creatively about the relevance of this option in as many services as possible so that the incentives and opportunities for corruption are reduced. The basic point to note is that when services are poorly matched to customer needs or are given free or at subsidised prices, there will be a strong tendency for public officials and middlemen to collect "rents", a euphemism for corruption.

Dual or multiple track pricing of services is one way to reduce the load on service providers while meeting customer needs more effectively. The underlying assumption here is that those who need services with special characteristics or urgency are more vulnerable to the use of influence and speed money. All the citizen feedback studies done by the Public Affairs Centre so far have reaffirmed the willingness of customers to pay higher official fees than bribes provided services are more efficiently delivered[7]. In a way, this is not surprising as any payment is a cost to the customer irrespective of its form or destination. Public transport often provides services using the dual track approach thus meeting the special needs of a segment of the population who might otherwise have competed with the rest of the population. In the process, the service provider also generates additional resources that could be used to cross subsidise deserving segments of the population. Many countries have adopted this approach with respect to public services for which fees or user charges are levied. This is especially relevant to business enterprises that need to obtain documents, permits and authorisations on an urgent basis. Singapore, for example, is well known for innovative applications of this approach. Specified time frames such as 24 or 48 hours are announced for getting certain services. The conditions for getting the services are also clearly specified so that there is no ambiguity or uncertainty about their meaning or the actions required. In India too, dual pricing has been tried out in some services such as telephones and cooking gas. But, as noted above, the terms and conditions of the dual track's working needs to be carefully designed so that they are not exploited by interested parties to extract bribes on top of the increased fees. In the *Tatkal Telephone* case, there should be no ambiguity about the technical feasibility condition when customers are asked to pay a substantially higher amount. There should be a periodical announcement as to the locations where feasibility is not a problem so that people know that when the payment is made, a telephone connection is assured within a specified period.

The dual track pricing approach merits attention because of its potential to reduce the pressure on citizens to pay speed money. It encourages the flow of speed money or at least a good part of it into public coffers. The additional resources thus collected could be used to improve the service facilities and infrastructure not only to serve customers better, but also to improve the working environment and morale of the staff of public agencies. A moot question is whether those who opt for the slow or normal track will be neglected by service providers. Here again, conscious steps will need to be taken to avoid this tendency. For example, standards of service will have to be laid down for the normal track of service as explained below. Careful monitoring of how these customers are treated will have to be institutionalised. In brief, dual track pricing should be viewed as a means to provide wider choices to customers and reduce the incentives and opportunities for corruption. It should not become a subtle tool for serving one set of customers at the cost of another.

5. Every Service Provider or Regulatory Agency should Widely Disseminate Information on its Standards of Service

Some public agencies do have well-defined standards and norms for their services. More often than not, they are not made known to the public. Moreover, when changes in norms and standards occur, no updating is done, and no effort is made to keep the public informed of such changes. It is a common attitude of our public agencies that they do not feel any obligation to inform and educate citizens on how to transact business with them efficiently. The time required for service delivery, the conditions and sequential steps to be met and remedies available in the event of unsatisfactory agency response are usually unavailable. Even well-intentioned public leaders seem to be unaware that informed citizens who know what their entitlements are can help curb corruption in public services. Consequently, the movement to define service standards has hardly touched India. In contrast, standards for over 1,500 specific services offered by government agencies in the United States have been widely disseminated.

In the UK, Citizen Charters have defined standards for most service oriented departments of the government. For example, the British Rail's 'Passenger's Charter' was launched in March 1992. The Charter has set targets for the reliability and punctuality of each line, contains a clear commitment to improving the quality of service, outlines provisions for compensation for customer inconveniences, and requires the wearing of name badges as well as detailing performance related pay. The British Government's Competition and Service Utilities Act of 1992 provides new statutory powers for regulators to set and monitor standards for specified public services, help make customers aware of standards, provide for compensation when guaranteed standards are not met, improve the complaints procedure, and facilitate greater competition in the provision of water and sewerage services. This approach has helped demystify service delivery and empowered citizens by informing them about their rights and what they should expect from their service providers. In the process, it encourages citizens to demand greater accountability from public officials.

A serious problem in India is that the legislation governing most public utilities does not require the authorities to lay down measurable standards of service and ensure the proper dissemination of this information to the public. It is left to those in charge of these organisations to specify standards, review and update them periodically and disseminate information as they deem fit. As a result, there is considerable unevenness in the actions taken on this front by the responsible authorities. It will be a major step forward if service providers are required by law to specify their standards of service and to make this information easily accessible to the public. Ready access to this information will strengthen the hands of the users of services to resist extortionary tendencies of public officials.

We recommend that every public service provider be required to take the following steps:
- Survey its customers to understand what problems they face in their transactions with the agency and identify the kinds of information that can minimise these problems.
- Define the standards which the agency will maintain in the provision of its services and the conditions customers should fulfil in order to qualify for the services.
- Specify who can provide additional information or clarification if customers require such assistance.
- Announce the remedies and appeal procedures available if customers are dissatisfied.
- Display the above information and guidelines clearly in agency offices and disseminate the same widely and periodically to the public through the media and other forums.

Corrective Measures

1. Major Public Utilities should Appoint Independent Ombudsmen whom Citizens can Approach to Redress Their Grievances, Including Corruption. Smaller Agencies may Share an Ombudsman in the Same Location

Corruption cases are today reported to the agencies themselves or to other bodies, such as the Lok Ayukt, which are part of the executive arm of the government. A recent development is the appointment of ombudsmen by the Reserve Bank of India with a mandate to investigate complaints about banking services in different geographical areas. If the banks fail to comply with the decisions of the ombudsmen, there is provision for the RBI to use its regulatory authority to direct banks to implement them. The same model should apply to all other public utilities. To begin with, an ombudsman may be appointed for all the public utilities in a State if the total load is modest. Depending on the nature and extent of the complaints received and after periodical reviews, a State may decide to appoint additional ombudsmen.

2. In addition to the above, there is a need to create a High Level, Constitutionally Protected Authority to entertain Complaints about Corruption from Citizens and to award Compensation to the Aggrieved for Loss or Injury as a result of their Refusal to submit to the Corrupt Demands of Public Officials including Politicians.

Some States have appointed Lok Ayukts and Lok Pals for this purpose. Experience has shown that this institutional mechanism has not been very effective. This mechanism will work only when it can act as a quasi-judicial authority, with citizens having the right to lodge complaints, lead evidence followed by public hearings and speaking orders, and directions to provide not only for the punishment of corrupt officials, but also award compensation for loss or injury suffered by the aggrieved.

This quasi-judicial authority will be comparable to the Election Commission in terms of its independence. There should be one such authority in each State, and its performance reviewed every two years. Depending upon the findings of the review, steps could be taken to strengthen this institutional mechanism in respect to compensation, *modus operandi*, overload in terms of cases, etc. The single most important prerequisite for its success must be the independence and political neutrality of its members. To minimise the politicisation of appointments, we recommend a panel nominated by the Chief Justice, Chairman of the State Consumer Protection Council and similar high level persons least vulnerable to political influence. This panel should identify suitable candidates to be appointed to the proposed commission. While the structure proposed here has an exclusive focus on helping citizens to seek relief in terms of compensation for loss or injury suffered by them, the underlying approach is equally applicable to investigating larger scandals and related policy and reform issues.

Notes

1. M. Naim, 'Corruption Eruption', *The Brown Journal of World Affairs*, Summer 1995.
2. R. Klitgaard, *Controlling Corruption*, University of California Press, Berkeley, 1988.
3. Transparency International, *National Integrity Systems: The TI Source Book*, Berlin, 1996.
4. S.N. Sangita, 'Institutional Arrangement for Controlling Corruption in Public Life: Karnataka Experience', *Indian Journal of Public Administration*, Vol. XLI, No. 1, January-March 1995, pp. 45-67.
5. S. Paul, *A Report Card on Three Indian Cities: A View from Below*, Public Affairs Centre, Bangalore, 1995.
   S. Paul, *Public Services for the Urban Poor*, Public Affairs Centre, Bangalore, 1995.
   S. Shekhar, *Public Services and the Urban Poor: A Comparative Assessment Based on Citizen Feedback from Five Indian Cities*, Public Affairs Centre, Bangalore, 1996.
6. R. Chapman & M. Hunt (eds.), *Open Government*, Croomhell, London, 1987.
7. S. Paul, 1995 (see No. 5 above).

7
Corruption and Administrative Discretion

S. P. Sathe

Corruption: Meaning and Concept

Corruption means taking gratification for the exercise of a public function. The range of such gratification varies between a bribe which a petty civil servant takes for rendering a service or exercising power in favour of or against someone to granting a largess or conferring a privilege on a minister or highly-placed civil servant. Gratification may take diverse forms, such as money, property, a woman, wine, a job, educational facilities for the son, daughter or near relative or a foreign trip for the official or his near ones.

Types of Corruption

(1) When services or actions in favour of or against another person are required urgently, gratification, otherwise known as speed money, is given for expediting it. (2) When an authority has power which he or she chooses to exercise in favour of or against a person in return for some money or such other consideration, it is a bribe; examples of this would be giving employment or admission to professional education or ministers taking bribes for making appointments to public offices. (3) When an authority has discretion to do or not to do a thing or to choose one person out of those who seek a privilege and exercises such discretion for an illegal consideration, it is an abuse of power; granting of licences, permits, exemptions or monopolies, dealerships, etc., in favour of a person on consideration other than merit falls into this category. All cases of abuse of power and *mala fide* exercise of power are cases of corruption.

Corruption — Penal Remedies

A person who accepts illegal gratification is punishable for offence under the Indian Penal Code as well as the Prevention of Corruption Act, 1988 (which replaces the Prevention of Corruption Act, 1947). These penal sanctions operate only after the corruption actually occurs. Since there are penal sanctions, the guilt of the person must be established beyond reasonable doubt. This is often difficult and so there are few convictions; moreover, where high officials are involved in corruption, criminal proceedings seldom succeed. People do not come forward to give evidence. There is the possibility of the matter being hushed up. A good deal of evidence gets lost due to delay. Moreover, corruption can be successfully punished only if its incidence is minimised through preventive measures. Further, more benign methods of giving justice than those used in the criminal justice system would be preferable for introducing accountability on the part of those who exercise power. We have to turn towards administrative law for this purpose.

Administrative Law: Types of Administrative Action

Administrative law has been described as the law relating to the control of governmental powers[1]. It deals with the following questions: (1) What are the powers of the administration?; (2) What are the limits of such powers?; (3) What are the ways in which the administration is kept within those limits?; (4) What procedures does the administration have to follow in the exercise of its powers? and (5) What remedies are available to the individual against the illegal acts of the administration?[2]

Administrative law offers parameters for the exercise of administrative power. An administrative action may be of three types: (a) quasi-legislative, (b) quasi-judicial and (c) administrative. Where the administration announces a policy in accordance with which it would exercise its discretion through a government resolution, circular or notification, it performs a legislative function. This is in addition to the power of subordinate legislation which the government has by virtue of the power delegated by the statute. Through the exercise of quasi-legislative power, the administration is continuously circumscribing its discretionary power. Where an administrative action is likely to result in deprivation of a right or has an adverse effect on an interest, the action is required to be preceded by a fair inquiry in accordance with a procedure governed by the rules of natural justice. The observance of such a procedure involves a notice of the proposed action, the opportunity of being heard by the person concerned as to why such an action should not be taken and a decision based on reasons. It also requires that the person who decides is not biased or prejudiced in favour of or against the person in whose respect the decision is to be taken. This kind of decision-making is known in administrative law as a quasi-judicial decision. Both quasi-legislative as well as quasi-judicial actions involve the exercise of discretionary power but the exercise of discretion is made objective by the legislative or judicial processes through which it is required to be exercised. Both can, however, be ritualised, meaning that the procedures can be followed without complying with the spirit underlying them. We often hear that in many quasi-judicial or quasi-legislative actions, public hearings are held for namesake only. For example, a notice of such a hearing is given inconspicuously and very little time is allocated for people to give their reactions.

Discretion and Rule of Law

The possibility of the abuse of discretion is, however, much greater when it is part of a non-quasi-legislative or non-quasi-judicial administrative action. Discretion means freedom to act or not to act and freedom to choose one or a few among many who are applicants for a privilege, licence or other such largess. A writ of *mandamus* is not issued where an authority has the discretion to compel it to act in one way rather than another. A writ may be issued to compel it to act where such an authority is bound to act. Where the discretion is not merely regarding how to act but also regarding whether to act, no compulsion can be made by a court to the authority to act. Discretion is often conferred by statutes through phrases such as "if he is satisfied" or "is of the opinion of" or "has reasonable grounds to believe" which give it the freedom to act as well not to act.

Prof. A.V. Dicey, in his monumental treatise on Constitutional Law, described discretion as being inconsistent with the rule of law[3].

Many years later, Prof. Wade said that if the existence of discretion negated the rule of law, there could not be rule of law in any civilised democratic country.[4] The emergence of the welfare State increased the functions of the State and with it the powers and particularly the discretionary powers of the administrative authorities. Today, although we concede to Prof. Wade's point and admit that discretionary power cannot altogether be eliminated, we also share Prof. Dicey's apprehensions about the inconsistency between administrative discretion and the rule of law. Therefore, the courts have been most reluctant to concede absolute discretion to an administrative authority. The courts of England as well as India have acted vigilantly while reviewing the exercise of discretion.

Canalisation of Discretion through Judicial Review

The courts in England took a passive attitude towards discretion before the end of the Second World War. *Liversidge* vs *Anderson* was the highest watermark of judicial restraint. Under the Defence of the Realm Act, regulation 14 B provided that if the Home Secretary had "reasonable grounds to believe" that a person was of hostile origin (i.e. German), he could be held in preventive detention. The House of Lords was invited to interpret that provision. There were two possible interpretations: one was that the Home Secretary must have reasonable grounds to believe thereby implying that the reasonableness of the grounds was justifiable, and another that if the Home Secretary believed that there were reasonable grounds, the court would not examine whether the grounds were reasonable. The majority of the Lords adopted the latter interpretation thereby giving the Home Secretary the last word on whether the grounds were reasonable. Lord Atkin, in his memorable dissent, admonished his brethren for being more executive-minded than the executive and spoke the following words: "In this country, amidst the clash of arms, the laws are not silent. They may be changed, but they speak the same language in war as they speak in peace." The courts in England, however, have not adopted such a positivistic interpretation of regulation 14B in subsequent cases. Judicial restraint shown during or before the Second World War was slowly abandoned by the English courts during the post-Second World War years; lately, they have become much more jealous of the Executive's discretionary powers. Possibly, the honeymoon with the Welfare State ended, and the courts became more critical of discretionary powers and their exercise.[5] Absolute discretion has been held to be a constitutional monstrosity, and the courts have insisted that the exercise of such discretionary power must be subjected to the strictest judicial scrutiny.

In India, the written Constitution with a declaration of fundamental rights gives the courts much greater power of judicial review than what the courts in England possess. A court in England cannot strike down a law as being unconstitutional due to the doctrine of parliamentary sovereignty. The Supreme Court of India and the High Courts can declare any law or administrative action void if it is inconsistent with, takes away or abridges any of the fundamental rights guaranteed by Part III of the Constitution. The courts have used this power to control not only the exercise of discretionary power but also the grant of discretionary power.[6]

The Supreme Court of India has held that if a law vests unguided or absolute discretion in the Executive, such a law would be held to be violative of the right to equality guaranteed by Article 14 and an unreasonable restriction on the rights guaranteed by Article 19 of the Constitution. The fact that the executive is required to exercise such discretion in a quasi-judicial manner may be one of the mitigating factors which may save the grant of absolute discretion from being held unconstitutional.

Although the Court has laid down a sound policy with regard to the grant of discretionary power to the Executive, the courts have generally leaned heavily in favour of the legislature, and upheld the grant of discretion when there was a broad statement of policy. The courts usually avoid striking down legislation and prefer to entertain a complaint regarding the improper exercise of discretion. The courts have insisted that the discretion must be exercised strictly in accordance with the parameters laid down in the Act concerned. An administrative action may be struck down if the power is not exercised for the purpose for which it has been given or if it is exercised *mala fide*. When the exercise of discretion is contingent upon the satisfaction or opinion of the administrative authority, the courts want to find out whether such satisfaction is based on relevant considerations [*Barium Chemicals Ltd.* vs. *Company Law Board*]. All the cases regarding the grant of petrol pumps to the relatives of the ministers, the transfer of a customs official who insisted a minister pay customs duty for the contraband articles imported from abroad or the waiving of arrears on rent payable by retired ministers or government officials, which recently came up before the courts, were cases of alleged abuse of discretionary power.

One important bottleneck to penetrating judicial review is the inaccessibility of the materials on the basis of which the administrative decisions were made. For a long time, the government frustrated such judicial probes by pleading its privilege not to disclose certain documents is given to the Government by Sections 122 and 123 of the Indian Evidence Act. The Supreme Court has now held that any claim of privilege to withhold disclosure of documents is reviewable by courts to make sure that it is not unnecessary [*S. P. Gupta* vs. *India*]. Another difficulty is that rarely are such decisions made through reasoned orders. In a recent decision [*Mohd Zafer* vs. *India*], Justice P. B. Sawant castigated the government for merely writing the reasons in its file but not communicating them to the person concerned. This was a case under the Unlawful Activities (Prevention) Act where an association had been declared unlawful. The law required the government to state the reasons. Justice Sawant wondered what would be the use of the government merely stating the reasons in its file but not communicating them to the organisation concerned. The government order was, therefore, held unconstitutional. Also, the reasons recorded in the file were not always intelligible.

The grant of discretion is so omnibus, and the methods of abuse of discretion are so subtle and sophisticated, that judicial review is bound to play a marginal role in tracking down the abuse of discretion. There are two reasons for this: (i) by its very nature, judicial review exercised by the High Courts under Articles 226 and 227 of the Constitution and the Supreme Court under Articles 32 and 136 of the Constitution tends to be sporadic and peripheral; (ii) the information required for proving the allegations of corruption or abuse of power is not easily available because it is locked up in government files.

Peripheral Nature of Judicial Review

Judicial review tends to be sporadic and peripheral because it does not envisage determination of questions on merit by the courts.[7] It is supposed to merely stop the administrative authorities from acting beyond their powers and in violation of certain minimal procedural norms. The basic rule of judicial review is that the courts should not substitute their decision or view for that of the administrative authority whom the legislature has thought to be fit and proper to decide that matter. In administrative law, there is a celebrated quote which says that administrative authorities can decide rightly as well as wrongly as long as they are acting within their powers. Over the years, the courts have expanded the scope of judicial review by intervening when they find that administrative authority is perverse or when such an authority commits error of law apparent on the face of the record.

The courts of England and India have shown a tendency to convert any error of law into an error apparent on the face of the record [*Anisminic Ltd.* vs. *Foreign Compensation Commission*]. Thus, they have increased the scope of judicial review and have subjected administrative actions to critical scrutiny. Judicial activism of this type is a feature of almost all countries of the Anglo-Saxon system. However, in spite of such activism, the courts cannot transcend the limitations of judicial review except marginally. The fact remains that there is no review by an independent agency as regard the merits of the exercise of discretion. Judicial review also tends to be formal, time-consuming and expensive. We have a few cases in which administrative actions were held invalid because of *mala fide* exercise of power or abuse of discretion. Further, barring the solitary instance of A.R. Antulay, no minister was ever prosecuted for corruption.[8] It was only because of the public interest litigation undertaken by some public-spirited citizens that cases of corruption against ministers and high officials have come up before the courts.

The second difficulty in bringing the matter to court is that the aggrieved person rarely has the necessary information on which he can build up a case. Since he does not know who the other applicants were and why they were preferred, he cannot adequately allege that he has been discriminated against. The authorities do not co-operate with him, and he normally cannot mobilise resources for this purpose, and it was only because of the emergence of the public interest litigation that some such cases involving adverse effects on the environment or corruption or abuse of power in respect to matters relating to development could come up in the courts. Organised social action groups have conducted PIL in a professional manner, and that is why we see that the tip of the iceberg of corruption has become visible. Readers will recall how persistent enquiries had to be made by courts in matters involving allotment of petrol pump, LPG and kerosene agencies, the transfer of a customs official, Ms. Shakuntala, who had demanded customs duty from a minister for articles imported from abroad, or out-of-turn allotments of government houses by ministers. This research could not have been achieved through the effort of an ordinary citizen. Moreover, given the costs of judicial processes and technicalities of the adversary procedures, the chances of abuse of discretion being successfully prosecuted are rare. Power can be abused without much likelihood of being legally caught.

Instances of Abuse of Discretion

It is not possible to catalogue all the instances of abuse of discretion in this paper. However, what we are trying to do is to pinpoint a few statutes under which the abuse of discretion can and has taken place. There are potential sources of corruption by politicians and civil servants. One of the most significant and fertile areas of corruption is that of urban property. Corruption takes place when agricultural land is converted into non-agricultural land. Agricultural land cannot be used for building houses but the scarcity of housing in cities makes the demand for housing shoot up. Consequently, builders search for land on the out-skirts to utilise for housing. These lands are agricultural. Under the Maharashtra Land Revenue Code, 1966, it has been provided that no land used for agriculture shall be used for any non-agricultural purpose "except with the permission of the Collector."[9]

An application for conversion of agricultural land into non-agricultural land is required. The Collector may, after due enquiry, either grant permission on such terms and conditions as he may specify subject to any rules made in this behalf by the State Government, he can refuse the permission applied for if it is necessary to do so to secure public health, safety and convenience, or if such use is contrary to any scheme for the planned development of a village, town or city in force under any law for the time-being in force. When an application is rejected, the Collector shall state the reasons in writing of such rejection. Obviously, the extent of discretion given to the Collector is considerable. If he gives reasons, does any one verify whether those are valid ? Are such reasons given to the applicant ?

When the stakes are so high and the discretion so absolute, such discretion is susceptible to abuse. With real property in urban places being so expensive, it is no wonder this power has become a source of corruption. Although power is vested in the Collector, he is often made to use it according to the wishes of the higher-ups. In fact, in districts where land prices are very high, only those persons are chosen to be Collectors who would agree to quietly use their power according to the wishes of higher-ups. Such corruption would be difficult to prove in a court of law, much less in a review court.

Town Planning: Law and Discretion

Town planning is necessary to regulate the growth of cities while conserving and promoting ecological balance and providing for various needs such as schools, parking places, gardens and markets. Town Planning Acts usually provide for elaborate procedures for the publication of the schemes of town planning and hearing of objections from people; the aim of such activity is to facilitate people's participation in decision-making. In practice, such hearings become mere rituals which are performed for satisfying the procedural requirement of the law. The plans show reservation for schools, parks, playgrounds, etc. and in many cases, these schemes cannot come into being because of the paucity of funds held by the municipal authorities.[10] If a land is not acquired within ten years, the landlord can serve a notice to the concerned Corporation and, if nothing is done thereafter within six months, the reservation lapses.[11] The Supreme Court observed that since development and planning were primarily for the benefit of the public, the Corporation was under obligation to perform its duty in accordance with the law [*Municipal Corporation of Greater Bombay* vs *Advance Builders (India) Pvt. Ltd.*]. Under the Maharashtra Regional Town Planning Act, 1966, the Planning Authority can ask the State Government to acquire land, and the compensation payable under that Act is lower than that under the Land Acquisition Act. Why are lands not acquired? According to one writer, only 4% of the area of land reserved for public purposes in the Development Plan for Pune (1966-76) could be acquired.[12] In Bombay, only 10% of the proposed works, which took 38% of the expenditure, could be implemented during the Plan period. Are reservations purposely allowed to lapse?

Under Section 50 of the MRTP Act, the appropriate government, if satisfied that the land is not required for the public purpose for which it was designated, reserved or allocated in the interim or draft development plan, may request the planning authority to sanction the deletion of such designation or reservation from the plan. In recent years, the power of de-reservation has been used by the State governments rather too often and some such de-reservations have become controversial. In spite of fulfilling the norms laid down by the Supreme Court for the conferment of discretion, the discretion given by the law is so wide and extensive that its abuse is inevitable. It is difficult to prove *mala fide* exercise of power on the part of the Government. But the fact remains that the powers which have been given for social justice are often used for promoting the interests of the builders and other wealthy sections of society which cannot happen without *quid pro quo*.[13]

The Urban Land Ceiling and Regulation Act, 1976

This Act was passed to provide for the imposition of a ceiling on vacant land in urban agglomerations, acquisition of such excess land and to regulate construction of buildings on such lands with a view to preventing concentration of urban land in the hands of a few persons, speculation and profiteering therein and with a view to bringing about equitable distribution of land in urban agglomerations to subserve the common good. The Act has laid down the maximum land that a person can hold and the excess land which can be acquired on payment of compensation which shall not exceed Rs. 2 lakh.[14] This provision was upheld by the Supreme Court in *Bhimsinghji* vs *India* thus confirming the high stakes involved in obtaining exemption under the Act.

Section 20 of the Act gives the State Government the power to grant exemption. The exemption is to be granted if the State Government is satisfied that "having regard to the location of such land, the purpose for which such land is being or is proposed to be used and such other relevant factors as the circumstances of the case may require, it is necessary or expedient in the public interest so to do". Further, the State Government may also exempt any person holding excess land from the provisions of the Act if it is satisfied that the application of the provisions "would cause undue hardship to such person". Section 21 says that excess vacant land is not to be treated as excess in certain cases. The landowner has to apply to the Government submitting that he intends to utilise such land for the construction of dwelling units (each such unit having a plinth area not exceeding 80 sq. m.) for the accommodation of the weaker sections of the society, in accordance with any scheme approved by any authority as the State Government may, by notification in the official gazette, specify. The State Government has issued detailed administrative instructions for the exercise of these powers.[15]

Section 21 has been used by Government officials to provide housing to their relations and friends. In *Shantistar Builders* vs. *Narayana Khimalal Totame*, the Supreme Court laid down the following guidelines: (a) allotment should be on the basis of one family-one flat basis-family consisting of husband, wife and dependant children; (b) the government nominees must belong to weaker sections and their number should not exceed five percent of the total accommodation available; and (c) builders must maintain a register of applications, give receipt of application to the applicant and send a copy of the application to the committee. The Court also asked the Government to formulate a test for identifying those who belonged to the weaker sections of the society. It suggested that a means test could be used for this purpose and the income of the family should not exceed Rs. 18,000 per annum.

The implementation of the ULCA has not been satisfactory. It has bred corruption which has acted against the interests of the weaker sections of the society and to the benefit of the builders and property owners. It has sky-rocketed the prices of the real property.

Government Contracts

Next after urban property is the area of government contracts which has the greatest propensity for corruption. The modern welfare State is required to enter into contract for the supply of goods as well as services. Sometimes, these contracts are with multinational corporations. The Supreme Court has laid down the law regarding judicial review of such contract-making to ensure that (a) the terms and conditions of such contracts are not detrimental to public interest; and (b) contracts are granted after giving equal opportunities to all potential competitors to bid. The principles of government contract were laid down by the Supreme Court in *R.D. Shetty* vs. *International Airport Authority*. Since then, in a number of cases, the Court has insisted upon transparency in government contracts. Such contracts often contain secret clauses and commissions are paid by traders to clinch a deal. Here again, the limitations of judicial review become quite obvious. A review court does not go into the merits of the terms and conditions of a contract but merely satisfies itself as to whether tenders and quotations were invited from all eligible competitors and whether they were accepted or rejected by giving reasons. Even if such requisites are satisfied, there can be an invisible exchange of favours.

How Exercise of Discretion can be Made Accountable

The administrative law developed by the courts highlights how discretion should not be exercised. If an authority acts *mala fide*, decides without applying his mind, takes irrelevant considerations or does not take relevant considerations while deciding a matter, the decision is held to be vitiated and is, therefore, void. But not enough has been said about how discretion should be exercised. In this section, we propose to examine what reforms need be made in order to make the exercise of discretion more predictable and objective.

Administrative Instructions

One way to minimise the abuse of discretion is to minimise the unpredictability of the exercise of this power. This could be done by laying down, through administrative instructions, the policy in accordance with which such discretion is to be exercised. A book containing a statement of policy is often issued in respect to discretion under the Import and Export Control Act. Administrative instructions have the advantage of greater flexibility than any legislative instrument. The Government may change its policy and, therefore, replace one set of instructions with another. Though such instructions do not have the force of law in the sense that they cannot be invoked for obtaining a writ of *mandamus* for their enforcement,[16] they doubtless provide parameters for judging whether the discretion has been properly exercised.

Sometimes, administrative instructions contain guidelines as to how Government largess is to be distributed. An administrative instruction provided that a person whose spouse, father, mother, brother, sister, son, daughter, son-in-law or daughter-in-law already possessed a dealership, would not be eligible to apply for one, was held to be valid by the Supreme Court in *Mahinder Kumar Gupta* vs. *India*. It had been contended that the above restriction on eligibility to apply violated the fundamental right of a citizen to carry on any trade or business guaranteed by Article 19(1)(g). Such a restriction may be necessary for preventing concentration of such largess in a few hands but it is sufficient to prevent the allocation of scarce resources on considerations other than merit ? In fact, it could legitimately be asked why a person could be disqualified because some other relation has a dealership. If getting a largess because of a family relationship is bad, is not denial of an opportunity to compete because of family connections also bad?

The crux of the whole issue of corruption is that such largess should be distributed equitably as well as impartially. The administrative instructions could lay down who would be preferred and why, and the decision-making should rest with an independent and impartial body. Being a relation of a minister would not be objected to if the decision is taken not by the minister but by an independent body on considerations of the candidate's suitability for the largess. The criteria of such suitability ought to be clearly laid down through administrative instructions. All decisions regarding the distribution of largess should be in writing with reasons, and be accessible to anyone who desires to verify its proper allocation.

Principles of Natural Justice

Administrative actions which entail adverse actions against others resulting in a loss of privilege, right or adversely affect some interest are required to be exercised after complying with the principles of natural justice. This means that the person against whom such an action is likely to be taken must be informed of the grounds on which the action is proposed to be taken; also, he must be given an opportunity to say why it should not be taken against him. As much as possible, the authority taking a decision must give reasons. The rules of natural justice tend to make administrative decisions transparent and objective. These rules are, however, not relevant where the decision does not result in the infringement of a right or does not have adverse effect on an interest. For example, it was held that before giving sanction for the prosecution of a public servant for an offence under the Prevention of Corruption Act, 1988, the concerned public servant need not be given an opportunity of being heard [*Superintendent of Police (CBI)* vs *Deepak Chowdhury*]. The requirement of sanction has been provided with a view to protecting the honest civil servant from vexatious proceedings which ultimately subserves the cause of good administration. The requirement of sanction to prosecute is a matter of public policy and not the right of a public servant. If the sanction to prosecute is refused, such refusal could be challenged on the ground that the power was exercised *mala fide*. In another case [*India* vs *W. N. Chadha*], it was held that the accused could not claim a right of hearing before a court issued a letter rogatory to a foreign court (letter rogatory means a request by an Indian court to a court abroad to take the testimony of a person residing within its jurisdiction and transmit the same to it). An accused does not have a right to say what evidence should be collected against him during investigation of crime. He, of course, would get an opportunity to rebut any evidence produced against him by the prosecution.

Reasoned Decisions

Although the rules of natural justice, which include the two principles, (i) that no one who has interest in the disposal of a matter should hear that matter; and (ii) no one should be condemned unheard, are applicable only when the action is quasi-judicial. It is desirable that the first of the two rules become applicable even in respect of the discharge of the discretionary functions. In fact, in administrative law, greater flexibility in the application of such principles is being injected through decisional law. Although the selection of persons for jobs or higher posts is not a quasi-judicial function, the Supreme Court held that a person who was himself a candidate for such promotion could not sit on the selection committee for recommending persons for such promotion [*A. K. Kraipak* vs *India*]. A person is disqualified to be an examiner in the university examinations if any of his near-relations are appearing for such examination. This is because a mere likelihood of bias would disqualify a person from being a judge of someone's suitability for an entitlement. This principle, in our submission, should now apply to all decisions involving the exercise of discretionary powers. Further, all such decisions must be reasoned decisions. Reasoned decisions are necessary for satisfying the respondent's right to information and making the administration transparent.

Right to Information

Although the Supreme Court has held that the right to information is included within the right to freedom of speech and expression, this writer has submitted elsewhere that the right to information emanates from a number of constitutional provisions other than the right to freedom of speech and expression.[17] For example, Article 22 (1) of the Constitution says that no person who is arrested shall be detained in custody without being informed, as soon as may be, of the ground for such arrest. Right to information is to be found in a number of constitutional provisions such as Article 311(2) which says that no government servant shall be dismissed or removed or reduced in rank without being informed of the charges against him and having been given an opportunity to contradict those charges. Even the principles of natural justice, by implication, recognise the right to information. But the citizen's right to information about how decisions are taken by ministers, how largess is allocated, on what basis are contracts made for the supply of commodities or services, how regulatory agencies such as the Pollution Control Boards or the Securities Exchange Board of India [SEBI] Act need to be specifically guaranteed and enforced. Such a right will make the administration transparent. The right to information about these matters emanates directly from the citizen's right to a good and honest government which is implicit in his right to vote. A comprehensive legislation providing for such a right, specifying limitations thereupon, is urgently required. The right to information is subject to the right to privacy, and the scope of the right to privacy also needs to be delineated. The Supreme Court has held that the right to life and personal liberty guaranteed by Article 21 of the Constitution includes the right to privacy as an aspect of personal liberty [*Kharak Singh* vs. *U.P.*]. The Supreme Court has recently drawn limits of the right to privacy that could be claimed by public functionaries. We shall consider these cases briefly.

In *R. Rajagopal* vs. *Tamil Nadu*, the petitioner was the editor, printer and publisher of a Tamil weekly. He had agreed to serialise an autobiography of one Shankar who had been convicted of murder and sentenced to death. The autobiography was to reveal the close association of some police officers in the crimes committed by him. The police authorities issued a warning to the petitioner against publishing this book because (1) he had no authority to do so since Shankar could not give him the power of attorney since such attorney could be given only through the prison authorities and that had not been done; (2) his action of publishing the said autobiography would amount to attempt to blackmail and would be liable to action.

The petitioner, therefore, urged the Court to restrain the police from interfering with publication of the book which was his fundamental right to publish. In their counter affidavit, the respondents said that the publication of the above book would compromise the right to privacy of various police officers who were likely to be referred to by the author in his book.

The relevant question for the Court's determination was whether the police officers could invoke their right to privacy for stopping the magazine from serialising the autobiography. The Court was, therefore, required to go into the scope of the right to privacy available to persons performing public functions in respect of matters which fell within the domain of their public duties.

Justice B. P. Jeevan Reddy, in his judgement, traced the decisional laws in the United States and India on the right to privacy as being part of the right to personal liberty. The learned Judge held that the petitioner had a right to publish, what he alleged to be the life story/autobiography of Shankar insofar as it appeared from public records even without his consent or authorisation. If he went beyond such records, he might be violating the right to privacy of the person concerned i.e., Shankar. If such a person voluntarily gave information about himself, he would have forfeited his right to privacy to that extent. However, others who were affected by the disclosures contained in such an autobiography might sue the author as well as the publisher for defamation or infringement of privacy. Such persons, whether government officials or the Government on their behalf, could not impose any prior restraint against the publication of such an autobiography. They could, however, sue them for defamation. Such a remedy, however, could be availed of by the public officials/public figures only after publication and would be governed by ordinary law. The judge, however, further circumscribed the scope of the remedy in respect to public officials or the public figures as follows:

"In the case of public officials, it is obvious, right to privacy, or for that matter, the remedy for action for damages, is simply not available with respect to their acts and conduct relevant to the discharge of their official duties. This is so even where the publication is based upon facts and statements which are not true, unless the official establishes that the publication was made (by the defendant) with reckless disregard for truth. In such a case, it would be enough for the defendant (member of the press or media) to prove that he acted after a reasonable verification of the facts; it is not necessary for him to prove that what he has written is true."

This changes the law of privacy insofar as public figures or officials are concerned. The press or the media would not have to establish truth in their defence if they have written about the public acts of the public figures. It will be enough if they prove that they took reasonable care to verify that what was written was authentic. The Court made it clear that it had not gone into the impact of Article 19(1) (a) on the law of defamation contained in Sections 499 and 500 of the IPC. That might have to await a proper case. The above observations, however, mean a significant empowerment of the media against the public officials/figures in respect of their public acts. The Court, after perusing the decisions of the United States Supreme Court in which it had been held that the constitutional guarantee contained in the First Amendment prohibited a public official from recovering damages for a defamatory falsehood relating to his official conduct unless he proved that the statement was made with actual malice, observed that the citizen had a legitimate and substantial interest in the conduct of such public officials and that the freedom of the Press extended to engaging in an uninhibited debate about the involvement of public figures in public issues and events.

Another significant case on freedom of speech and expression was *Gadakh Yashwantrao Kanakrao* vs. *Balasaheb Vikhe Patil*. The election of Gadakh had been held invalid on the ground that he had committed corrupt practice as defined in Section 123(4) of the Representation of the People Act, 1951. Sharad Pawar, Chief Minister of Maharashtra, was also named for being guilty of such a corrupt practice and served with notice as per the requirement of the RPA. Section 123(4) declares that publication by a candidate or his agent, or by any other person with the consent of the candidate or his agent, of any statement which is false, and which he either believes to be false or does not believe to be true, in relation to the personal character or conduct of any candidate, or in relation to the candidature or withdrawal of any candidate, being a statement reasonably calculated to prejudice the prospects of that candidate's election, as a corrupt practice. Both Gadakh as well as Pawar had accused Vikhe Patil of giving money to the voters and Pawar went to the extent of saying that even if the rival candidate offered money, the voters should accept it but vote for Gadakh. Ashok Desai, who argued on behalf of one of the appellants, said that in view of the fall in the ethical standards of political people in general, such allegations were not likely to prejudice the electoral prospects of a candidate. Ram Jethmalani went further and said that such allegations were desirable because they educated the electorate about the malpractices which were not uncommon in elections. Justice Verma, speaking on behalf of N.P. Singh, N. Venkatachala JJ and himself, observed that "the growth of this unhealthy trend (of malpractices mentioned above) is a cause for serious concern" for the proper functioning of democracy. His Lordship, however, described the lament of Gadakh and Pawar about the financial might of Vikhe Patil as being "farcical and comical in view of their own considerable resources." The Judge also deplored the speeches but held that they did not constitute corrupt practice.

The Judge said:

"It is clear that every statement of fact in relation to the personal character of any candidate does not amount to a corrupt practice under Section 123(4) unless all the requirements of the provision are satisfied, notwithstanding the fact that such a statement may be defamatory in character. The additional requirements to constitute a corrupt practice are obviously to maintain the delicate balance between the freedom of speech of an individual and the public interest of giving full information to the electorate of the candidates."

It is submitted that the balance is to be maintained not between freedom of speech and the right of information of the electorate, because both are aspects of the same freedom and not poised against each other. The balance is to be maintained between freedom of speech and decency in elections. Section 123(4) imposes a reasonable restriction in the interest of decency on freedom of speech and expression guaranteed by Article 19(1)(a) if all the requisites mentioned therein are satisfied. The primary requirement of Section 123(4) is that the statement should be of a fact which is false and which the maker either believes to be false or does not believe to be true; that it should relate to the personal character or conduct, etc. of any candidate and that it should be reasonably calculated to prejudice the prospects of that candidate's election. Unless all these requirements were satisfied, the statement did not become a corrupt practice under Section 123(4) of the RPA. Unlike in the law of defamation, the falsity of the statement is not presumed but is required to be proved by the candidate against whom it is made.

Both the cases discussed above expose public persons to greater public criticism and scrutiny and deny them certain presumptions of law which are available to an ordinary person. The public persons cannot now invoke the right to privacy against acts which they do as public functionaries and cannot allege a corrupt practice on the part of their rival in an election if he uses false stories against them, unless they show that they were false, were believed to be false by the maker and they were likely to prejudice their chances in the election. We hope the Court will in the near future explain the scope of the law of defamation in relation to political or public persons so as to make it consistent with the freedom of the Press which includes the people's right to know.

Independent Administrative Agencies

All decisions regarding economic benefits or social benefits should, as far as possible, be taken by autonomous administrative agencies which will be directly accountable to Parliament. While their policies will be subject to the government's approval, the Government shall not interfere in the day-to-day administration. The chairman and members of such regulatory bodies shall be experts in the respective subjects and they shall be appointed by the government subject to approval of the Upper House of Parliament. We are not in favour of having such appointments made on the recommendations of a selection committee consisting of the Prime Minister's nominee, a nominee of the Leader of the Opposition, the Speaker and the Chief Justice of India, which is usually considered as a panacea against improper appointments. Some statutes like the Protection of Human Rights Act, 1993, contain such a provision for the appointment of the chairperson and members of the commission. We have come to believe that such a provision could become a mere ritual and might not prevent undesirable appointments. Therefore, the only way to reinforce peer group control is to make such appointments more transparent and subject to legislative control. Such legislative control should not only be restricted to the appointments of the personnel but should also extend to the work and recommendations of the concerned administrative agency. For example, the recommendations of the MRTP Commission regarding the monopolistic character of a business organisation are at present submitted to the Central Government, and the Government is not bound to abide by it. The reports of such a Commission should be laid on the table of each of the Houses of Parliament and the Government must give an adequate and convincing explanation as to why it disagrees with the Commission's recommendation. All important regulatory authorities such as SEBI, Reserve Bank of India and Environmental Control Authority should have autonomy; and their reports annually submitted must be published and made available for a modest price. We wish to make it clear that all such administrative agencies should have autonomy, not independence, from the Government. They will have to be accountable to the Government which, in turn, must be accountable to Parliament or legislature. We say so because often the words "independent" and "autonomous" are used interchangeably but the two concepts are distinct.

The need for an independent and autonomous regulatory authority to regulate the use of airwaves was stressed by the Supreme Court in *Secretary, Ministry of Information and Broadcasting* vs. *Cricket Association of Bengal*. The Court observed that the broadcasting medium is subject to the freedom of speech and expression guaranteed to the citizen of India. Hence, monopoly of the medium whether by Government or an individual body or organisation is unacceptable. The citizen must have the benefit of plurality of opinions on all public issues. Unlike trade or business which can be monopolised by the State [Article 19 (6)(ii)] broadcasting or telecasting which is subject to freedom of speech and expression cannot be monopolised by the State. However, the electronic media needs to be regulated so that the airwaves which are a public property are used for the maximum public good. The electronic media should be under the control of a public as distinguished from a governmental authority. The Court observed:

"The broadcasting media should be under the control of the public as distinct from Government. This is the command implicit in Article 19 (1)(a). It should be operated by a public statutory corporation or corporations, as the case may be, whose constitution and composition must be such as to ensure its/their impartiality in political, economic and social matters and on all other public issues."

What is true of the broadcasting or electronic medium regulatory authorities could also apply to the other regulatory authorities which have to apply standards of efficiency in public interest to other trades like insurance and banking, which are also now open to private enterprise.

Such bodies have to be autonomous but can they be independent of the Government? They cannot be independent in the sense that the judiciary is independent. The judiciary has to do justice in accordance with the law and the Constitution. It is independent in the discharge of that function. However, the judges are liable to be removed by Parliament [Article 124(4), Article 217(1) Proviso (b)] and appointments of the judges are made by the President. [Article 124(2), Article 217(1)]. No authority which is performing a legislative or administrative function can be totally independent of the Government and Parliament. Such independence would be contrary to the system of parliamentary democracy. We do not know what the Court means when it says that the media regulatory authority should be subject to public control but not governmental control. Public control, after all, is exercised through the Government which is elected by the people. It is respectfully submitted that in our enthusiasm to weed out corruption, we should not think of setting up bodies or authorities which would be accountable to no one.

Punishment of Corrupt Officials

Civil servants and political persons accused of corruption must be fairly tried before an independent judicial authority. The standard of proof required for the conviction of a person in a criminal case is far higher than that required for holding him guilty in a disciplinary enquiry. In a criminal case, the accused officer must be held guilty beyond reasonable doubt. In departmental actions, the probability of his being guilty may suffice. Criminal law punishes a person whereas the administrative law merely relieves the administrative powers of an officer whose integrity is suspect. The civil servants are protected under the Constitution from arbitrary actions resulting in their dismissal, removal or reduction in rank by a provision which assures that a government servant would not be so punished unless he is informed of the charges against him and given a reasonable opportunity of being heard in respect of those charges [Article 311(2)]. Although in exceptional cases, an enquiry before dismissal can be dispensed with [Second Proviso to Article 311(2)] an elaborate procedure for such enquiry has been prescribed. In spite of this, arbitrary actions might take place. While there should be adequate protection against arbitrary action, there should be enough deterrence against those who indulge in corruption.

At present, a civil servant can approach an administrative tribunal set up under the Administrative Tribunals Act, 1985 against a decision of the departmental authorities. The Administrative Tribunal was set up as an alternative to the High Court and its jurisdiction restricted to the writ jurisdiction of the High Court [*S. P. Sampath Kumar* vs. *India*]. An appeal against the decision of this Tribunal lies only with Supreme Court. This works to the great disadvantage of the civil servant because going to the Supreme Court is extremely expensive for him. Since the Administrative Tribunal does not decide matters on merit but confines itself to the threshold questions relevant to judicial review[18], he is helpless against the arbitrary actions of his department. The appellate jurisdiction of the Supreme Court is also not broad enough to include an examination of the allegedly wrong administrative actions on merits. It is necessary to develop an internal appellate procedure, may be in the form of a service tribunal, which will consider his case on its merits. Such a tribunal may consist of an experienced civil servant with a good background in law. The procedures to be followed by such a service tribunal will not be adversary as are followed by courts but may be inquisitorial like the administrative courts in France.

Ombudsmanning the Administration

The ombudsman is a Scandinavian institution through which administrative actions are overseen by an independent authority with a view to ridding them of maladministration and abuse of discretion. Such an authority had been recommended by the Administrative Reforms Commission in 1966 and a Bill was accordingly passed by the Fourth Lok Sabha. The Bill lapsed on the dissolution of the Lok Sabha in 1970. Since then it has reappeared several times but in a variety of forms. The original concept of ombudsman seems to have been replaced by a permanent Inquiry Commission against high placed public persons[19]. The ombudsman essentially advises the administration to avoid taking wrong decisions and only when the administration is not amenable to its recommendations does it report to Parliament. This is how the institution functions in England under the name Parliamentary Commissioner. In India, if we were to replicate the English model, the Lok Pal would make recommendations to Parliament. The cases involving allegations of *mala fide* exercise of power, such as those involving preference of a party for a government contract on ulterior considerations or with unfair terms, or the transfer of an official of CBI with a view to frustrating investigation of a crime involving high dignitaries, or preference to the kith and kin of ministers in the allotment of largess are cases which require in depth probes which might not be possible through the adversary judicial processes. What the Supreme Court of India is doing at present is really the function of an ombudsman. The setting up of the office of the Lok Pal may relieve the Supreme Court of dealing with cases of that type. The office of the Lok Pal will, however, become meaningful only if Parliamentary control over the Executive becomes more active and vigilant. A person held guilty by the Lok Pal may not be sent to jail that can happen only when a competent criminal court convicts him of an offence but such a person should lose his political legitimacy.

India may have to transplant the continental system of administrative justice to its soil without disrupting the common law system of judicial process. A combination of tribunals following inquisitorial processes and ombudsmen may be the right solution for preventing and minimising corruption.

Conclusion

(1) Discretion given in broad terms must be narrowed by administrative instructions stating the policy in accordance with which such discretion is to be exercised.

(2) Decisions involving exercise of discretion must become transparent and accompanied with reasons.

(3) Authorities taking decisions regarding the allotment of largess should be independent and should not be disqualified on the ground of bias as understood in administrative law.

(4) An Act specifying various aspects of the right to information should be enacted. The limits of the right to privacy must be clearly stated. This will have to be done consistently with the law laid down by the Supreme Court in respect of the right to privacy that could be claimed by persons holding public office.

(5) An administrative appellate tribunal should be set up for hearing appeals against the decisions of the administrative authorities, including ministers in respect of the grant of exemptions, privileges or largess. These tribunals should follow inquisitorial procedures. No appeal shall lie from the decision of the tribunal to any court. The decision of the tribunal shall, however, be subject to judicial review under Articles 226 and 227 of the Constitution.

(6) Service tribunals manned by senior civil servants should be set up to hear appeals against the departmental actions against civil servants resulting in transfer, demotion, reduction in rank, removal and dismissal on merit. These tribunals should follow inquisitorial procedures. An appeal shall lie from the decision of the tribunal to the administrative tribunal set up under the Administrative Tribunals Act, 1985.

(7) The present Administrative Tribunals Act should be amended to confer administrative tribunals appellate jurisdiction over the decisions of the service tribunals in the above matters. These tribunals should in addition continue to possess the powers of a High Court under Article 226 of the Constitution.

(8) Ombudsmen should be set up at various levels and the office of the Lok Pal may be set up at the apex of such a network of ombudsmen. The Lok Pal and other ombudsmen should deal with cases of maladministration, abuse of discretion, delays or callousness which are not within the purview of the courts. The Lok Pal should not

merely be a recommendatory authority as in other countries but ought to be given specific jurisdiction in matters which do not fall within the purview of the courts.

Notes & References

1. Wade and Phillips, *Constitutional and Administrative Law* (Edited by A. N. Bradley) 9th ed. 1978. p.4.
2. Sathe, S. P., *Administrative Law* (5th ed. 1991), N. M. Tripathi, Bombay. p.6.
3. Dicey, *Introduction to the Study of the Law of the Constitution*, 9th Ed. (Macmillan, 1952).
4. Wade and Phillips, No. 1 above.
5. De Smith, S. A., *Judicial Review of Administrative Action*, Stevens & Sons 1980, pp. 31-35.
6. Sathe, No. 2 above, p.7.
7. De Smith, No. 5 above, p.3.
8. Baxi, Upendra, *Liberty and Corruption: The Antulay Case and Beyond*, Eastern Book Company, 1989.
9. S. 42, *The Maharashtra Land Revenue Code*, 1966.
10. Bapat, Meera, 'The Myth of Housing for All', *Janata* 25 (Independence Day) 1988.
11. S. 127, *The Maharashtra Regional and Town Planning Act*, 1966.
12. Bapat, No. 10 above.
13. Sathe, S. P., 'Right to Shelter: Review of Housing Law and Policy in Maharashtra', *Journal of the Indian Law Institute*, 35. p.1332.
14. S. 10, 11(6), *The Urban Land Ceiling and Regulation Act*, 1976.
15. Administrative Instructions [U.L.C.R. Act, 1976] G.S.R. 85 (E) dated Feb. 17, 1976 published in Gazette of India, Extraordinary, pt. II, sec. 3 (I); GSR No. 765 (E) dated December 1977 Gazette of India, extraordinary, pt. II, sec. 3; GSR. 271 (E) dated 26 April 1979, Gazette of India, extraordinary, pt. II, sec. 3(i) and G.S. R. 7 (E) dated 29 December 1981, Gazette of India, extraordinary Pt. II, sec. 3 (I) dated 8th January 1982.
16. Sathe, No. 2 above.
17. Sathe, S. P., *The Right to Know*, N. M. Tripathi, Bombay, 1991.
18. Sathe, S. P., *Tribunal System of India* (in Press), N.M. Tripathi, Bombay, 1996.
19. Dhavan, Rajeev, 'Engrafting the Ombudsman Idea on a Parliamentary Democracy — A Comment on the Lok Pal Bill, 1977', *Journal of the Indian Law Institute*, Vol. 19, p. 257, 1977.

8
Lok Pal and Lok Ayukt

A.G. Noorani

> "Law has reached its finest moments when it has freed men from the unlimited discretion of some ruler, some civil or military official, some bureaucrat. Where discretion is absolute, man has always suffered. At times, it has been his property that has been invaded; at times, his privacy; at times, his liberty of movement; at times, his freedom of thought; at times, his life. Absolute discretion is a ruthless master. It is more destructive of freedom than any of man's other inventions"[1].

Time has demonstrated that this ideal cannot be attained by the classic institutions provided by democratic forms of government; legislatures elected by the people in free elections held periodically with executive heads responsible to them, or themselves elected directly by the people. An independent judiciary and a free Press are only the barest minimum essentials for the functioning of a democratic polity.

These institutions themselves are sorely in need of reform, especially in India. However, even at their best, they ensure neither the government's accountability to the people nor an effective mechanism for the redress of grievances. An *"elective despotism"* is how the British system has been commonly described in recent years.

What Michael Meacher, Labour Party's social security spokesman, said of that system on May 26, 1992, applies to the Indian system with far greater force. The Prime Minister, he said, now had more untrammeled power than the King before the Revolution of 1688. Meacher said "the corrupt proliferation of patronage, the opium of the elite; the rise of unelected confidants in the No. 10 office who can be more powerful and less accountable than elected Ministers; the all-pervading blanket of secrecy around most sensitive decisions, which excludes even Cabinet members — all these should be reduced or ended[2]."

In June 1969, a UN Seminar held in Stockholm on *Ways of Safeguarding the Rights of Individuals against the Abuse of Administrative Power* discussed five principal means of ensuring such protection:
- Parliamentary Commissions of Inquiry;
- Procuracy of the Soviet Type;
- Judicial Remedies of the English Legal System;
- The French Conseil d'Etat; and
- The Ombudsman of Scandinavia.

By then, the ombudsman had already acquired a reputation in India. Addressing the All India Congress Committee at Jaipur, on November 3, 1963, Prime Minister Jawaharlal Nehru said he was fascinated by the idea of an ombudsman who should have the authority to deal with the charges against the Prime Minister and command respect and confidence from all[3]. But, he added, it was beset with difficulties in a large country like India. Interest in India was aroused by a report published in 1961 entitled "The Citizen and Administration: The Redress of Grievances". It was written by Sir John Whyatt, a former Chief Justice of Singapore, for "Justice," the British section of the International Commission of Jurists. It recommended a large extension of the system of the administrative tribunals to consider complaints against the discretionary actions of administrators, a large extension of the system proposed by the Franks Committee Report on Administrative Tribunals and Enquiries (1957) and the establishment of the British equivalent to an Ombudsman to look into complaints of maladministration. The Whyatt Report has been described as "one of the great non-state papers" and testifies to the efficacy of studies conducted by non-governmental organisations provided they are based on thorough research and cogent reasoning[4]. The result was the Parliamentary Commissioner Act in 1967.

It is unnecessary to trace the evolution of this institution or those of its counterparts elsewhere[5]. Three decades of study and experiment in India have helped enormously in defining the problems and the needs of the specific situation in our country and the tests of effectiveness which an Indian ombudsman must meet. The problem, broadly, is two-fold: maladministration and corruption. Abuse of power is implicit in both. There are five requirements which the Indian ombudsman must satisfy — accessibility to the ordinary citizen; jurisdiction wide enough to reach the most powerful executive in the land;

independence from executive power and influence; power fully requisite to the task; and sanctions which make the institution worthwhile.

It is trite to say that no office or institution can function in isolation from the rest of the society. It cannot but reflect its mores, strengths and failings. In India, the remark is not trite. It only describes a grave problem. The many Lok Pal Bills moved in Parliament in the last three decades and the Lok Ayukt Acts enacted in the States over the last two decades reveal dependence on two other institutions; neither of which is in good shape — the superior judiciary and the police force.

Unless the procedure for judicial appointments, recommended by the Law Commission, is reformed on the lines of the Bill moved in Parliament in 1990 by the then Union Law Minister, Dinesh Goswami, for the appointment of a National Judicial Commission, no Lok Pal will inspire much public confidence. Likewise it is imperative that the professional autonomy and integrity of the police force is ensured by implementing the reports of the National Police Commission.

In India, the State not only enjoys exclusive power to decide whether or not an inquiry is to be instituted on grave charges of maladministration or corruption on the part of its ministers and civil servants, but also vast powers on the disclosure of information. The rise of investigative journalism has alleviated the situation but the exposure of wrong has not ensured redress. Witness the scandals of recent years alone — HWD submarine, Bofors gun, Airbus deal, ABB loco deal, securities, sugar scam, Jain *Hawala* racket and telecom scandals.

But there is not the faintest sign of any serious move by the Government of India to establish a Lok Pal at the Centre nor have the opposition parties pressed seriously for the establishment of the institution although it is nearly three decades since a high-powered body recommended its establishment.

The Administrative Reforms Commission (ARC), headed by Morarji Desai, was set up by the Government of India on January 5, 1966. It is highly significant that its first major action was the *Interim Report on Problems of Redress of Citizens Grievances* which was submitted on October 20, 1966. It recommended the setting up of two institutions, the Lok Pal at the Centre and the Lok Ayukt in each State.

After an able and concise survey of the working of the Ombudsman in other countries, the report said: "The following would be the main features of the institutions of Lok Pal and Lok Ayukt:
- They should be demonstrably independent and impartial.
- Their investigations and proceedings should be conducted in private and be informal in character.
- Their appointment should, as far as possible, be non-political.
- Their status should compare with the highest judicial functionaries in the country.
- They should deal with matters in the discretionary field involving acts of injustice, corruption or favouritism.
- Their proceedings should not be subject to judicial interference and they should have the maximum latitude and power in obtaining information relevant to their duties.
- They should not look forward to any benefit or pecuniary advantage from the executive Government."

It would be true to say that the report set the basic pattern for all similar legislation that has been proposed or enacted since, though some departed from certain essentials. The Lok Pal would have the same status as the Chief Justice of India and be appointed by the President on the Prime Minister's advice after consultation with the Chief Justice of India and the Leader of the Opposition. He "would be free to choose his own staff "and would "have the powers of a court with regard to the calling of witnesses, documents, etc." The investigations would be in private. He would report to the Legislature. The Lok Ayukts would have similar status, powers and functions.

The Report made an important point which has been overlooked in all subsequent discussions for reasons not difficult to understand; it said that "for the Lok Pal to be fully effective and for him to acquire power, without conflict with other functionaries under the Constitution, it would be necessary to give a constitutional status to his office, his powers, functions, etc.,". That, it added, was no reason for the delaying, the legislation. "The Lok Pal, we are confident, would be able to function in a large number of cases without the definition of his position under the Constitution. The constitutional amendment and any constitutional modification of the relevant statute can follow."

There is, however, another consideration besides the ones the ARC mentioned. The entire edifice of the Lok Pal can be brought down by a mere ordinance, as the Press Council was in 1975 during the

Emergency. As in the case of the Election Commission and the Comptroller and Auditor General, it is highly essential that similar provisions are made by a constitutional amendment to endow the institution of the Lok Pal with constitutional status and the holder of the office with the security of tenure leaving it to Parliament to legislate the details. Since, however, there was never any real earnest at the Centre in this matter, the thought of constitutional amendment never troubled anyone's mind.

Appended to the report was a draft Bill running into thirteen clauses. It covered "Ministers" as well as "Secretary." The Prime Minister was not excluded. The Lok Pal's main function was to "investigate any action by these persons *suo moto* or a written complaint by a person (i) who claims to have sustained injustice in consequence of maladministration in connection with such action, or (ii) who affirms that such action has resulted in favour being unduly shown to any person or in accrual of personal benefit or gain to the Minister or to the Secretary, as the case may be."

It, thus, covered cases of both maladministration as well as corruption. There followed many exceptions and exemptions where he had no discretion — action in respect of which the person had a remedy before a tribunal or a court of law unless, in the latter case, the Lok Pal was satisfied that it was "not reasonable to expect him to take or to have taken such proceedings." He was endowed with discretion not to investigate if he was of the view that "a remedy for the injustice alleged to have caused thereby exists".

Eight other matters, as well as existence of legal remedies, were excluded from the Lok Pal's jurisdiction: "(a) Action taken in a matter certified by a Union Minister as affecting the relations or dealings between the Government of India and any foreign government or any international organisation of States or governments. (b) Action taken under the Extradition Act, 1962 or the Foreigners Act, 1946. (c) Action taken for the purpose of investigating crime or protecting the security of the State including action taken with respect to passports. (d) Action taken in the exercise of power in relation to determining whether a matter shall go to a court or not. (e) Action taken in matters which arise out of the terms of contract governing purely commercial relations of the administration with customers or suppliers, except where the complainant alleges harassment or gross delay in meeting contractual obligations. (f) Actions taken in respect of appointments, removals, pay, discipline, superannuation or other personnel matters. (g) Grant of honours and awards. (h) A decision made in exercise of his discretion by an administrative authority unless the elements involved in the exercise of discretion are absent to such an extent that no discretion has been exercised at all." Several of these were adopted in State Laws and the Central Bill of 1971.

Information or documents could be withheld from disclosure if the Cabinet Secretary certified that it "(a) might prejudice the security or defence or international relations of India (including India's relations with the Government of any other country or with any international organisation), or the investigation or detection of crime, or (b) which might involve the disclosure of proceedings of the Cabinet or any Committee of the Cabinet."

Additionally, a blanket power to suppress material was conferred: "A Minister may give notice in writing to the Lok Pal with respect to any documents or information specified in the notice or any class of documents so specified that in the opinion of the minister the disclosure of the document or information or of documents or information of that class would be contrary to public interest and where such a notice is given, nothing in this Act shall be construed as authorising or requiring the Lok Pal or any officer of the Lok Pal to communicate to any person any document or information specified in the notice or any document or information of a class so specified."

The Official Secrets Act was extended to the Lok Pal and his staff. Publication of "proceedings relating to an investigation" was punishable by the Supreme Court "as if it were a case of contempt before that court."

It was only a beginning. The report recorded: "The problem was thrown up in bold relief and in its full impact on the citizens in the very first round of our discussions with the Ministers of the Central Government and the Congress President; its importance, urgency and dimensions have been increasingly impressed upon us by the large volume of both official and non-official opinion which we have had the opportunity of consulting so far. The Commission was so impressed by both the unanimity and the strength of the popular demand on this subject that it decided to devote itself to this problem rather than form a separate group for the specific purpose of devising a scheme to enable the citizen to seek redress for an administrative injustice. The more the Commission considered this issue, the more was it convinced that the problem brooked no delay."

Thirty years later, one sees little interest in the establishment of a Lok Pal by the government or by the Opposition. Although as many as five Bills for this purpose were moved in the Parliament, none of them could reach the statute book. The first step for the establishment of the institution came with the introduction of the Lok Pal Bill in the Lok Sabha on May 9, 1968 to implement the recommendations of the Administrative Reforms Commission (ARC). The Bill was referred to a Joint Committee and was later passed by the Lok Sabha on August 20, 1969. But while it was pending in the Rajya Sabha, the Lok Sabha was dissolved and the Bill consequently lapsed. The Bill, as passed by the Lok Sabha, was reintroduced in the Lok Sabha on August 11, 1971. This also lapsed on the dissolution of the Fifth Lok Sabha.

The new Government which came to power in March 1977 introduced a Bill on Lok Pal in the Lok Sabha on July 28,1977. The 1977 Bill was considered by a Joint Committee of the two Houses of Parliament. The report of the Joint Committee incorporating certain amendments in the Bill was placed before the Lok Sabha on January 20, 1978. However, before the Bill could be considered and adopted by the Parliament, the Sixth Lok Sabha was dissolved and that Bill lapsed. No Bill on the subject was considered by the Lok Sabha (1980-84). Yet another Lok Pal Bill was introduced in the Lok Sabha on August 26,1985[6]. However, this new Bill was withdrawn by the Government itself on specious grounds in November 1988.

The National Front Government introduced the Lok Pal Bill, 1989 in the Lok Sabha on December 29, 1989 within days of assuming office. It lapsed with the dissolution of the Lok Sabha in 1991. The four Bills of 1971, 1977, 1985 and 1989 varied greatly in their ambit and scope. (The 1971 Bill was similar to the one of 1968.) To give an overview at the outset, the 1971 and 1985 Bills excluded the Prime Minister from their purview while the 1977 and 1989 Bills did not.

The 1971 Bill alone covered both grievances in respect of "maladministration" and allegations of misconduct. The 1977 Bill was confined to allegations only but it defined the term "misconduct" widely to cover improprieties as well as corruption. The 1985 Bill omitted grievances altogether and restricted the Lok Pal's jurisdiction to offences "punishable under Chapter IX of the Indian Penal Code (offences by or relating to public servants, such as bribery) or, under the Prevention of Corruption Act, 1947." In the joint note of dissent dated November 1988 on the withdrawal of the Bill by the Government, the Opposition members pointed out that "of various versions of the Lok Pal Bill presented till then, the 1985 Bill seemed to us the most anaemic in content and the most restricted in scope."

While the 1989 Bill contained certain improvements on earlier Bills, its jurisdiction clause was the narrowest. It covered only offences "punishable under the Prevention of Corruption Act 1988." Even offences punishable under the Penal Code were excluded.

On August 3, 1995, the Minister of State for Personnel, Mrs. Margaret Alva, informed the Rajya Sabha that the Government had already circulated the two draft Bills on Lok Pal of 1985 and 1989 to all political parties seeking their views. Forty-nine MPs were requested to send their suggestions to bring about a consensus on the Lok Pal Bill. Only five of them had responded till July 28. They were Chaturanan Mishra (CPI), E. Ahmed (Muslim League), Jaswant Singh (BJP), Chimanbhai Mehta (IND) and Ms. Dil Kumari Bhandari (SSP). She recalled that the Prime Minister Mr. P.V. Narasimha Rao had assured the House that the office of the Prime Minister as well as those of the Chief Ministers would be brought within the purview of the Bill. She also mentioned that Jaswant Singh had even suggested that the matter be left to the next Lok Sabha[7].

Mrs. Alva's allusion was to the Prime Minister's statement in the Rajya Sabha on December 15, 1994 that he was not averse to the inclusion of the Prime Minister's office within the scope of the Bill. On December 6, 1995, Mrs. Alva revealed in the Lok Sabha that the Union Home Minister, S.B. Chavan, had held discussions with the political leaders on this subject the day before. She added that the proposed Bill did not envisage any separate investigative machinery for the Lok Pal set up to enquire in high places. Mr. Saifuddin Chaudhary (CPM) said that there was no need for a Lok Pal if the Prime Minister was exempt from his jurisdiction[8]. (As a senior correspondent, Pushp Saraf rightly pointed out, Mrs. Alva "was speaking a half-truth when she stated that the poor response to her efforts to evolve a consensus was one of the reasons for the delay in bringing forward the legislation." The government was none too serious about it either[9].)

Meanwhile, several States went ahead with establishing their own version of the ARC's model. There is no uniformity in the width of their jurisdiction, independence or effectiveness. It is doubtful if any of them can be said to have caught the public imagination or carved a place for the Lok Pal in the consciousness of the ordinary citizen. Even so, that is no reason for writing them off as useless. Their work is conducted away from public gaze. The annual reports do not provide the details and receive little publicity. Citizens' bodies can activate the office and also help citizens to file complaints. There is, moreover, the incontrovertible fact that heads have rolled in a few cases thanks to the labour of some Lok Ayukts, and, in some others, Chief Ministers have been dragged before the Lok Ayukt.

Two recent cases illustrate this. It has been estimated that every third member of the Madhya Pradesh government, headed by Digvijay Singh, and including the Chief Minister himself, is facing charges before the Lok Ayukt.[10] Copies of complaints to the Lok Ayukt are freely published in the Press.

The Madhya Pradesh Lok Ayukt's 13th Annual Report for the year 1994-95 was released to the press on December 12, 1995[11]. But apparently it was not tabled in the State Assembly[12]. As many as three Ministers were indicted according to reports in *The Hindu* and *The Telegraph*. The Deputy Chief Minister, Subhas Yadav, was indicted for corruption. The Minister of State for Higher Education, Mukesh Nayak, was censured as being "incompetent to hold the office of an independent minister".

In another case relating to the allotment for setting up a petrol pump on government land to Devendra Kumar Sadho, brother of Ms. Vijaya Lakshmi Sadho, Minister for Tourism, Culture, Science and Technology, Public Enterprises and Implementation of 20-point Programme, the Lok Ayukt observed that Sadho's application for the allotment of land at a concessional rate should have been rejected because there was no policy or order permitting allotment of land at concessional rates to anyone for commercial purposes. "Even assuming that in future the Cabinet may approve of such a policy, it will be highly improper to begin implementing a policy for the benefit of a close relative of a Minister," the Report pointed out.

Another case figuring in the Lok Ayukt's Report related to the former Minister of State for Forest, Environment and Mineral Resources, Dayal Singh Tumrachi, against whom a probe was conducted for giving abortive appointments as forest guard to two persons. Tumrachi's resignation was later sought and accepted by the Chief Minister on the recommendation of the Lok Ayukt.

In this case, the Lok Ayukt had said in an earlier Report that "if a minister bypasses the Secretariat and sends his order or direction directly to the officer by whom it is to be complied with, he cannot throw on the shoulders of that officer the responsibility of examining the legality or otherwise of his order or direction. If such an order or direction is carried out and it turns out to be illegal, the minister will have to own full responsibility."

Apparently, this is the only case in which the Chief Minister acted on the recommendation of the Lok Ayukt. The ombudsman is essentially an officer of the legislature to whom he reports. His effectiveness depends considerably on the people's consciousness of their rights and that of their representatives in the legislature.

Experience in the States can help considerably in drafting legislation for the Lok Pal at the Centre. The State laws fall into two broad patterns. Most sought to follow the Lok Pal model. Three preferred to innovate like, Uttar Pradesh, Kerala and Tamil Nadu.

The States of Orissa, Uttar Pradesh and Maharashtra were the first to create the institution. The Orrisa Lok Pal and Uttar Pradesh Lok Ayukt Act, 1970, received the assent of the President of India on February 8, 1971, whereas the Maharashtra Lok Ayukt and Uttar Pradesh Lok Ayukt Act, 1971 was assented by the President on December 10,1971. Two years later, the Bihar Lok Ayukt Act, 1973, and the Rajasthan Lok Ayukt and U.P Lok Ayukt Act, 1973, were brought on the statute book. The Bihar Lok Ayukt Act received the assent of the President on January 16, 1974. Appreciating the importance of this institution, a few other States followed suit. The Uttar Pradesh Lok Ayukt Act, 1975, received the assent of the President on September 7, 1975 and was enforced with effect from July 12, 1977. The Madhya Pradesh Lok Ayukt Act, 1981, received the assent of the President on September 16, 1981. About two years later, the State of Himachal Pradesh enforced the Himachal Pradesh Lok Ayukt Act on June 1, 1983 and the Andhra Pradesh Lok Ayukt Act, 1983 was enforced with effect from November 1, 1983[13]. The Karnataka Lok Ayukt Act, 1984 replaced the Karnataka Lok Ayukt Ordinance 1 of 1984. It received the President's assent on January 16, 1985. The Acts of Andhra Pradesh, Bihar, Maharashtra, Rajasthan and

Uttar Pradesh do not cover the Chief Minister while those of Himachal Pradesh, Karnataka and Orissa do.

The three State innovations are the Utter Pradesh Public Men Inquiries Ordinance promulgated on October 21, 1967 by the Charan Singh Government; the Order of the Kerala Government, dated December 20, 1969, for "setting up of an interim machinery to enquire into allegations against public men", (replaced by the Kerala Public Men Prevention of Corruption Act, 1983), and the Tamil Nadu Public Men (Criminal Misconduct) Act, 1973. They merit far greater attention than they have received. There will, however, be a certain overlap between the function of a Lok Ayukt and those of a Commission of Inquiry, especially if the Kerala model described later in this chapter is followed.

It is proposed to discuss the salient features of the four Central Bills of 1971, 1977, 1985 and 1989, and then the two categories of State laws in order to formulate the basic principles to which any legislation for an Indian ombudsman should confirm to make the institution worthwhile.

The Lok Pal and Lok Ayukts Bill, 1971 sought to give effect to the recommendation of the ARC insofar as they relate to matters within the purview of the Union Government. Except for modifications of a formal nature, the Bill was identical with the Lok Pal and Lok Ayukts Bill, 1969, which was passed by the Fourth Lok Sabha on August 20, 1969. In its scope, the Bill differed from the draft Bill proposed by the Commission in two major respects. It did not extend to public servants in the States. Secondly, it did not confine itself to ministers and secretaries alone. In other words, the bill sought to provide a statutory machinery to enquire into complaints based on actions of all union public servants including ministers but excluding the Prime Minister.

Its definition of "public servant" was, apart the odious exemption of the Prime Minister, comprehensive. It included ministers, officials of government, local authorities in any Union territory, public corporations, government-owned companies and registered societies under government control.

Two classes of cases were covered. One related to "maladministration." This was defined to mean "action taken or purporting to have been taken in the exercise of administrative functions in any case, (1) where such action or the administrative procedure or practice governing such action is unreasonable, unjust, oppressive or improperly discriminatory; or (2) where there has been negligence or undue delay in taking such action, or the administrative procedure or practice governing such action involves undue delay."

The other category was defined in the term "allegation". It meant any affirmation in relation to a "public servant" that he "has abused his position as such to obtain any gain or favour to himself or to any other person or to cause undue harm or hardship to any other person, (ii) was actuated in the discharge of his functions as such public servant by personal interest or improper or corrupt motives or (iii) is guilty of corruption, or lacks of integrity in his capacity as such public servant."

The Lok Pal was to be appointed by the President, after consultation with the Chief Justice of India and the Leader of the Opposition, for a five-year term. Lok Ayukts were to be appointed in consultation with him to assist him in performing his duties under his "administrative control." They would all enjoy the security of tenure. Neither the Lok Pal nor a Lok Ayukt could be removed except on the ground of proven misconduct or incapacity after an inquiry by a sitting of a former Judge of the Supreme Court and an address by both Houses of Parliament adopted by a special majority.

The powers of a civil court for production of documents or summoning of witnesses were conferred by Clause 11(2). Only two classes of information or documents were exempt, cabinet proceedings or such as might "prejudice the security or defence or international relations of India (including India's relations with the government of any other country or with any international organisation), or the investigation or detection of crime." The "public interest" carte blanche clause of the ARC Bill was reproduced.

If an "allegation" was proved, the finding was communicated to "the competent authority", e.g. the Prime Minister in the case of a minister — for action which he was to report to the Lok Ayukt within three months. The term was one month in cases of maladministration in respect of both the public servant concerned and "the competent authority." If the Lok Pal was satisfied with the result, the case was closed. If not, he would report to the President who was bound to lay it before Parliament. He was free also to make available to the public the facts of the cases disposed of.

Investigations were to be conducted in private treating the identities of the complainant and the public servant confidential as a rule. They could be held in public if the Lok Pal so desired.

The exemption Clause (8) aroused controversy. Some topics were excluded for obvious reasons; *viz.*, if the complainant had any legal remedy though even here the Lok Pal could waive the bar or matters referred for inquiry with his consent, under the Public Servants Inquiries Act, 1850, or the Commissions of Inquiry Act, 1952.

But the list in the Third Schedule [read with Clause 8 (1) (a)] was of a different kind. It read thus: "(a) Action in a matter certified by a Secretary as affecting the relations or dealings between the Government of India and any foreign Government or any international organisation of States or Governments. (b) Action taken under the Extradition Act, 1962, or the Foreigners' Act, 1946. (c) Action taken for the purpose of investigating crime or protecting the security of the State including action taken with respect to passports and travel documents. (d) Action taken in the exercise of powers in relation to determining whether a matter shall go to a court or not. (e) Action taken in matters which arise out of the terms of a contract governing purely commercial relations of the administration with customers or suppliers, except where the complainant alleges harassment or gross delay in meeting contractual obligations. (f) Action taken in respect of appointments, pay, discipline, superannuation or other matters relating to conditions of service of public servants but not including action relating to claims for pension, gratuity, provident fund or to any claims which arise on retirement, removal or termination of service and (g) Grant of honours and awards."

When, in 1973, Jayaprakash Narayan launched his crusade against the fast rising spiral of corruption in the country, he trenchantly criticised these provisions of the bill in an article in his journal[14]. J.P. wrote "If the Lok Pal Bill and the Maharashtra Ayukt Act, which is claimed to be patterned after the former, were carefully scrutinised, it would be discovered that the action of these vital officers is severely limited and hemmed in by the restrictive provisions. It is in many ways a case of giving by one hand and taking away by the other... a fertile and well-known source of corruption at the State level, which embraces MLAs, local party functionaries and even ministers, is the matters of transfers, postings and promotions of subordinate and higher government servants of all departments. Not only is this a source of corruption, but it also occupies most of the ministers. The remedy for this also is institutionalization of the system." J.P.

contrasted the lethargy on this measure in contrast to "spectacular" activity on some others.

As Union Home Minister in the Janata Party Government, Charan Singh showed the same enthusiasm on this subject as he had done a decade ago as Uttar Pradesh's Chief Minister. His Lok Pal Bill, 1977 did not include grievances in respect of maladministration for which separate legislation was intended. Its prime concern was to combat corruption, "misconduct by a public man". Both terms were widely defined; "Public man" was defined to include any member(s) of the Council of Ministers for the Union, MPs and Chief Ministers. "Public servant" was given the same meaning as in Section 21 of the Penal Code.

"Misconduct" received the widest definition possible in Clause 3 (1): "A public man commits misconduct — (a) if he is actuated in the discharge of his functions as such public man by motives of personal interest or other improper or corrupt motives; or (b) if he abuses or attempts to abuse his position as such public man to cause harm or undue hardship to any other person; or (c) if he directly or indirectly allows his position as such public man to be taken advantage of by any of his relatives or associates and by reason thereof such relative or associate secures any undue gain or favour to himself or to another person or causes harm or undue hardship to another person.

"Explanation: For the purposes of this clause, 'associate' in relation to a public man includes any person in whom such public man is interested; or (d) if he fails to act in any case otherwise than in accordance with the norms of integrity and conduct which ought to be followed by the class of public men to which he belongs; or (e) if any act or omission by him constitutes corruption" as made punishable under Chapter IX of the Penal Code or under the Prevention of Corruption Act, 1947.

The jurisdiction was also wide: "(1) subject to the other provisions of this Act, the Lok Pal may inquire into any matter involved in, or arising from, or connected with, any allegation of misconduct against a public man made in a complaint under this Act. (2) No matter in respect of which a complaint may be made under this Act shall be referred for inquiry under the Commissions of Inquiry Act, 1952, except on the recommendation or with the concurrence of the Lok Pal." Allegations against civil servants were outside the purview of the Bill. Any person other than a public servant could make a complaint to the Lok Pal alleging misconduct against a public man in the manner prescribed.

For the rest, the provisions of the 1971 Bill were drawn upon with certain changes. For example, instead of the Leader of the Opposition, the presiding officers of both Houses of Parliament were to be consulted in the appointment of the Lok Pal. As in the 1971 Bill, he would have his own staff, but "as may be prescribed" by Rules made by the President (i.e., the Government). He could secure the services of any officer or agency of the Central or State Government or "of any other person or agency."

The Lok Pal was to enjoy the security of tenure of a judge of the Supreme Court. His sanction was the same report to the competent authority and eventually to the President. There was a special provision regarding the Prime Minister. The "competent authority" to deal with him was the Council of Ministers. Clause 18 required him to report to it "without delay" any complaint made against him to the Lok Pal which the latter had transmitted to him for his comments as well as the report of the Lok Pal on the complaint. This can be a meaningful check only if the Council of Ministers functions as such and not if it is an instrument of what Richard Crossman called the Prime Ministerial Government which the country witnessed under Prime Ministers Indira Gandhi and Rajiv Gandhi.

It was in a badly battered shape that this Bill emerged in the Report of the Joint Committee of Parliament presented on July 20, 1978. Chief Ministers were totally omitted from its purview. Legislators were given special treatment. The definition of "misconduct" was greatly restricted in Clause 3 of the revised Bill: "A public man, other than a legislator, commits misconduct —

"1. (a) if he is actuated in the discharge of his functions as such public man by corrupt motives; or (b) if he abuses, or attempts to abuse, or knowingly allows to be abused, his position as such public man for securing for himself or for any of his relatives or associates any valuable thing or pecuniary advantage; or (c) if any act or omission by him constitutes corruption.

2. "A legislator commits misconduct if he abuses, or knowingly allows to be abused, his position as such legislator for securing for himself directly or indirectly any valuable thing or pecuniary advantage."

There was nothing vague about the original definition. The definition of the misconduct in the original Bill was fully adequate. As well as including corruption, as made punishable under the Penal Code and the Prevention of Corruption Act, it covered failure on the part of a public man "to act in any case otherwise than in accordance with the norms of integrity and conduct which ought to be followed by the class of public men to which he belongs." This was not "too wide" and no reason was advanced for dubbing it so at all. It was more "amenable to different interpretations" than the word "reasonable" which is used to restrict the fundamental rights embodied in Article 19 and is otherwise commonly used in legal parlance without much difficulty.

Section 45 of the Army Act 1950 makes it an offence for any officer, junior commissioned officer or warrant officer to behave "in a manner unbecoming of his position and the character expected of him." Section 35 of the Advocates Act, 1961 renders an advocate liable to disciplinary proceedings, if he has been guilty of professional or other misconduct. These expressions have not been defined by the Acts because they are not susceptible to precise definition. On the other hand, the norms of conduct expected of an advocate or of an army officer are fairly well known. So, indeed, are those expected of a public man, thanks to the various Commissions of Inquiry.

It is illustrative of the difference between the approach of the framers of the bill and the joint committee that while the original bill included within "misconduct" any conduct on the part of a public man in the discharge of his functions which is actuated by "motives of personal interest or other improper or corrupt motives", the Committee deleted "personal interest or other motives" and confined the scope to "corrupt motives" alone. Thus, for all practical purposes, abuse of power, gross impropriety and the like were made completely exempt from the Lok Pal's jurisdiction.

The original definition, besides being comprehensive, was realistically flexible in that it covered violations of norms "which ought to be followed by the class of public men to which he belongs". This would have endowed the Lok Pal with ample discretion in applying the correct norms to members of parliament who, unlike other public men, wield no executive authority. Undoubtedly, the concept of misconduct cannot be the same for an MP as for a minister.

The Bill took good care of that, but the Committee deleted a salutary provision and proceeded to tackle a problem of its own creation.

Instead of the Union Council of Ministers, "the competent authority to the Lok Pal's Report on the Prime Minister, was one who is virtually a single appointee of his, *viz.*, the Speaker of the Lok Sabha, as in the case of any Member of Parliament."

The procedure for the Lok Pal's appointment was improved by empowering the presiding officers of both Houses of Parliament to consult leaders of various parties. It, however, speaks for the approach of the Committee that it took away from the Lok Pal completely the discretion whether or not to hold an inquiry in private or in public. If a legislator was involved, the inquiry had to be *in camera*.

The Lok Pal Bill, 1985 was far worse than either of its predecessors of 1971 or 1977. Introduced in the Lok Sabha on August 26, 1985, it was unceremoniously dropped by the Government itself in November 1988 on the ground that it did not cover grievances, a flaw by no means fatal and one which was of its own making. The remit was the narrowest possible. The Lok Pal was empowered by the Clause 8(1) to "inquire into any matter involved in, or arising from, or connected with, any allegation made in a complaint". This had to be read with the definition Clause 2(b) which defined "complaint" as one alleging that a "public functionary has, while holding any of the offices mentioned in Clause (e), committed any offence punishable under Chapter IX of the Indian Penal Code or under the Prevention of Corruption Act, 1947." If that was all, the Bill was utterly redundant. These statutes were enforceable by the court of law and the police, any way. The sanctions provided in the Criminal Procedure Code, 1973 could have been relaxed to facilitate the filing of a private complaint, a right which the Supreme Court had ruled in 1984 belonged to a citizen.[15]

"Public functionary" was, in turn, narrowly defined to cover only ministers. The Prime Minister was excluded as were civil servants and officials of State corporations. The only concession was the inclusion of Parliamentary Secretaries. The sole "competent authority" over all of them was the Prime Minister.

There was a retreat from previous Bills all along the line. The Chief Justice of India was to be consulted in the appointment of the Lok Pal. His security of tenure was diluted. Address by both the Houses of Parliament was dispensed with. The only safeguard was the inquiry by the Chief Justice of India or any of his colleagues chosen by him. The

Executive's say in the appointment of his staff was made more explicit ("as the President may determine"). Not that it was absent in earlier bills ("as may be prescribed", i.e. by rules made by the President).

As in previous bills, any person other than a public servant could file a complaint. Since the remit was only to enforce two penal statutes, the possibility of a conflict between police investigation and the Lok Pal's inquiry was inherent in the situation. Clause 13 empowered the Lok Pal to direct the police to defer the investigation, unless it was made pursuant to an order of any court.

There was one change in favour of openness. A provision to Clause 14 (4) empowered the Lok Pal to question the certificate issued by a Secretary to the Government that a document or information is of the exempted category (defence, etc.) order disclosure, examine it "in private for scrutiny" and "declare the certificate to be of no effect." This is noteworthy.

Clause 21 contained a draconian provision penalising disclosure of the identities of the parties or the particulars of the complaint before it is dismissed or the case is closed. It was made triable by the Lok Pal himself summarily and liable to a six months' prison term or a fine of Rs. 10,000 or both. Appeal lay only to the Supreme Court. There was no requirement of *mens rea*. The liability was absolute.

If the Lok Pal was dissatisfied with the action taken by the "competent authority" (the Prime Minister) on his findings, he had no power to submit a special report to the President.

The Note of Dissent dated November 29, 1988 signed by some members of the Parliamentary Committee protesting against the withdrawal of the Bill recorded in detail the time and the labour expended over it: "The Committee had visited 23 different States and Union Territories"[16].

Barring some changes, the thirty-three clauses of the National Front Government's Bill of December 29, 1989 were an exact verbatim reproduction of the thirty-three clauses of the 1985 Bill. One would have expected it to draw from the salutary features of the 1971 and 1977 Bills and combine them into one. It chose a different model.

Three departures from the 1985 Bill were in the liberal direction. Most notably, the inclusion of the Prime Minister within the sway of the Lok Pal. Secondly, in the event of his findings that any of the allegations against the Prime Minister have been "substantiated either wholly or partly," his report went to the Speaker of the Lok Sabha to be laid before the House within ninety days of its receipt [Clause 16(3)]. In contrast, Janata's Lok Pal Bill, 1977 provided that the report went to the Prime Minister himself who was enjoined to place it "without delay before the other members of the Council of Ministers." Thus, what the Janata Bill reduced to a private affair was made a matter of national concern to be dealt with publicly by the Lok Sabha and the nation at large.

Lastly, the 1985 Bill provided that the President shall after consultation with the Chief Justice of India, appoint, as Lok Pal, "a person who is or has been, or is qualified to be, a judge of the Supreme Court." The last category can include any advocate of ten years practice. The 1989 Bill restricted the qualification to two categories alone, *viz*., serving or retired judges of the court.

Besides, all the previous bills provided for a single-member institution. In 1989, a three-member Lok Pal was proposed too be set up with a Chairman and two other members and all three were to be either serving or retired Supreme Court judges.

Yet, all that this high-powered body could be asked to do was to probe charges of offences under the Prevention of Corruption Act, 1988 — and no more. This narrow limitation was a hangover of the 1985 Bill which ignored precedents completely.

In one respect, the remit of the 1989 Bill was narrower than that of its model of 1985, in that, unlike the latter, it was confined to offences under the Prevention of Corruption Act, 1988, omitting those under Chapter IX of the Penal Code.

Clause 21 of the 1989 Bill was a replica of Clause 21 of the 1985 Bill. This provision did not figure either in the 1971 or the 1977 Bill. There is everything to be said for the confidentiality of proceedings before the Lok Pal. But it is indefensible to provide for summary trial by the very person who is aggrieved and for offences to be widely defined excluding the elements of intention, public harm or prejudice to the proceedings. Such a provision is a threat to press freedom and is clearly violative of the fundamental right to freedom of speech and expression embodied in Article 19 (1) (a) of the Constitution of India.

Any legislation that will be drafted for adoption by the new Lok Sabha must take cognizance of these bills. There has been ample discussion in the past. Only policy decisions are required to combine the best elements of the 1971 and 1977 Bills and, indeed, to profit by the experiments in the various States.

The Maharashtra Lok Ayukt and Upa-Lok Ayukt's Act, 1971 was based entirely on the Central Bill of 1971. The first Lok Ayukt appointed under the State's law was a former Chief Justice of the Bombay High Court, Justice S.P. Kotval. His Annual Report for the first year (October 25, 1972—October 24, 1973) listed the flaws in the statute. The report is, therefore, of enormous help. Jayaprakash Narayan wrote his article, in *Every Man*, after a full discussion with Justice Kotval.

The Report noted: "It is to be regretted that in several cases notwithstanding that a complaint had merit or justice on its side, the Lok Ayukt or Upa-Lok Ayukt have had to refuse to investigate because of technical grounds such as want of jurisdiction under Section 8(1) (A) or because another remedy is theoretically open to the complaint, [Section 8(1) (b)], without going into the merits of the case."

Not all the limitations were unwarranted. Those listed in the Third Schedule — itself a replica of the Third Schedule of the 1971 Bill minus matters exclusively of Union concern — were open to serious objection. The police enjoyed "complete immunity" because of two limitations: "action taken for the purpose of investigating circle" and "action taken in the exercise of powers in relation to determining whether a matter shall go to a court or not". Even if the police refuse to act on a complaint for improper reasons, the Lok Ayukt's jurisdiction is barred; for, "action" includes "failure to act". Of the 903 complaints received in the year, 101 were against the police department.

Next as to Clause (c) of the Third Schedule, it refers to action taken in matters which arise out of the terms of a contract governing purely commercial relations of the administration with customers and suppliers. This will exclude from the jurisdiction of the Lok Ayukt and the Upa-Lok Ayukt the scrutiny of the implementation of all contracts of the public works department, of the excise department, all lease and licence, (e.g., contracts for building, grant of licences for liquor shops), the exploitation of forest produce or contracts for removal of lac or tendu leaves, etc. The exception contemplated in the clause does not materially affect the above limitation. The exception is "except where the complainant alleges harassment or gross delay in meeting contractual obligations." The report added: "the Lok Ayukt and Upa-Lok Ayukt have no separate investigating agency of their own for conducting investigations under the Act." He had requested the Anti

Corruption Bureau of the State Government to investigate a complaint against a minister "but the experience of the Lok Ayukt in this respect has not been happy. In important cases especially against a minister, investigation has either not been made or inordinately delayed".

It was not possible to utilise the service of "any person or agency", besides that of the State, "without financial sanction and creation of posts under Section 13 (3) (1)", which required the government's approval. The Union refused to lend the services of the CBI.

Justice Kotval made detailed comment, advisedly. First, because the Central Bill was on the anvil and was open to modification. "Secondly, after the Maharashtra Lok Ayukt and the Upa-Lok Ayukt Act was passed, other States have undertaken similar legislations but they have not adopted its provisions and have instead considerably modified them, particularly provisions like Section 8 or the Third Schedule. In fact, very recently on the 27th March, 1973 the State of Rajasthan passed the Rajasthan Lok Ayukt and Upa-Lok Ayukt Act, 1973 (Act 9 of 1973), and it is in respect of the very points which we have made that the Rajasthan Act has modified its own statute and made it more effective. We would point out the following features in respect of the Rajasthan Act: — (a) the definition of grievance in Section 2 (d) of the Maharashtra Act has been omitted. The result is that the distinction sought to be drawn in the Maharashtra Act between an allegation and a grievance has been abolished as unnecessary. [*This is not a matter for praise. It is a blemish* (emphasis author)] (b) there is no provision like section 8(3) of the Maharashtra Act in the Rajasthan Act so that the bar imposed on investigating grievances in respect of public servants mentioned in Section 2 (k) (1V) of the Maharashtra Act has been taken away. (c) most important of all, there are no provisions in the Rajasthan Act imposing limitations such as laid down in Section 8(1) (a) and (b) of the Maharashtra Act and the whole of the third schedule has been omitted."

He reported an encouraging public response and recommended that full publicity be given to the new remedies provided to the citizen. The Second Annual Report (1973 —74) noted that a copy of the previous report had not been laid before the legislature though a year had elapsed since its submission.

On June 17, 1977 Justice S.P. Kotval was obliged to make a special report to the Governor because Chief Minister S.B. Chavan had failed to act as "competent authority" on the Lok Ayukt's findings against two Ministers, H.G. Vartak and N.K Tirpude. The episode is instructive of what can befall the institution if the government proves obstructive.

The report was sent to Mr Chavan on July 1, 1976. He replied negatively and only through the Secretary to the Chief Minister on December 23, 1976. The Lok Ayukt re-read the papers and wrote again to the Chief Minister on April 14, 1977 but received no reply. Instead, Chavan spoke to the press on June 16, 1977.

State laws vary. The Karnataka Lok Ayukt Act, 1984 includes the Chief Minister, ministers, MLAs, civil servants as well as officials of State Corporations, companies, registered societies, co-operative societies, universities and local authorities. The "competent authority" in the case of the Chief Minister was the Governor "acting in his discretion". The Lok Ayukt could be appointed only after consultation with the Chief Justice of the High Court, presiding officers and leaders of opposition in both houses of the legislature. The qualification was raised to one who had held the office of a judge of the Supreme Court or that of the Chief Justice of a High Court. These were all highly commendable; but the Bill took over the Third Schedule (of exception) whole-sale.

The Andhra Pradesh Lok Ayukt & Upa-Lok Ayukt Act,1983 — which had received the Governor's assent on October 11, 1982 and that of the President on August 25, 1983 — excludes the Chief Minister but is, in a sense, more extensive than the Karnataka law. A sitting judge of a High Court can be appointed to the office.

The Karnataka Act maintains the distinction between "allegation" defined to include failure "to act in accordance with the norms of integrity and conduct" — and "grievance" of injustice or hardship through maladministration.

The Andhra Pradesh Act is confined to probe into any "allegation" of abuse of position, improper motivation, corruption or "lack of integrity". There was no provision comparable to the third schedule to the Central Bill of 1971.

Most State laws are variants on the 1971 model. The three innovations are real exercises in creativity and original thinking. The Uttar Pradesh Public Men Inquiries Ordinance, 1967, followed by a Bill the same year which lapsed, sought in essence to establish an Independent Commission of Inquiry as well as an independent directorate of prosecution. It covered ministers, legislators, and office holders of local bodies. Any one could prefer an "accusation" of "misconduct" against them; "misconduct" was not defined but the word has been construed in judicial decisions and in reports of commissions of inquiry.

It provided for the appointment of a chief investigator of the status of an Inspector General of Police and an investigating establishment under him. Any person could send to the governor a petition for instituting an inquiry into an accusation made by him. The governor had to prefer the accusation to a high court judge for preliminary scrutiny. He could make such a reference *suo moto* as well. In making the preliminary inquiry, the judge could ask for the assistance of any minister or officer of the State governor or of the chief investigator. He could also give the person against whom an accusation has been made an opportunity to explain any matter. In case he came to the conclusion that the accusation was reasonably substantiated, he had to refer it to the governor. The chief investigator had then to investigate into the matter and send his report confidentially to the governor. The governor could then refer the report to the Commission of Inquiry under this very law, consisting of one or two judges who then report their findings to the governor, and also pronounce them in public. If punishment was recommended, the chief investigator would pursue the prosecution.

The validity of the Tamil Nadu Public Men (Criminal Misconduct) Act, 1973 was upheld by the Supreme Court in *M. Karunanidhi* vs *Union of India & ANR. (1979) 3 S.C.C. 431*. Though it was repealed in 1977, it merits consideration as an innovative measure. It covered ministers and other public men including the Chief Minister and legislators. The Act created a separate offence called "criminal misconduct", which could be inquired into by a commissioner of inquiries with an additional commissioner of inquires to be appointed by the governor on the advice of the Chief Justice. The commissioner was to be of the status of a high court judge and the additional commissioner of a district judge. The term of the commissioner and additional commissioner was three years. Any one could make a complaint within the limitation prescribed (within five years from the date on which the criminal misconduct was alleged to be committed or within one year from the date on which the public man ceased to be such public man, whichever was latter). The commissioner could employ his own agency or depend upon other departmental agencies.

He could suggest prosecution under the Criminal Law (Amendment) Act 1952. The law was explicit. If prosecution was recommended, "the public man shall be prosecuted and tried under Section 6 of the Criminal Law (Amendment) Act, 1952."

"Criminal misconduct" was defined to include acceptance of illegal gratification as well as abuse of position to obtain any valuable thing or pecuniary advantage.

The most successful of the State innovations was the Kerala Order of 1969; more successful, ironically, than the Kerala Public Man (Prevention of Corruption Act, 1983). The order was simplicity itself. It covered the Chief Minister as well as the MLAs proving once again the spurious character of objections to their inclusion. It defined "misconduct" to include corruption, favouritism, nepotism, "abuse of position" or "any act of omission" in the official capacity which *inter alia* is actuated by "improper" motives. Any citizen could set the machinery in motion. The government was bound to refer the complaint to a serving or retired high court judge. If he found that "a *prime facie* case has been made out of that further investigation is necessary, he will report to the government accordingly."

The order effectively surmounted the first obstacle. For the practice has been for the head of the government to decide whether or not a complaint against himself or one of his colleagues disclosed a *prime facie* case to warrant the setting up of a commission of inquiry under the Act of 1952; in other words, to sit in judgement of his own case, virtually.

The order, in truth, only formalised a practice which had come into vogue in the State largely because of the balance of political forces and high public awareness and ready recourse to inquires into charges against ministers which explain the several commissions of inquiry before the order was made. Its success was due also to the judge who worked the order.[17]

The order was replaced by the Kerala Public Men (Prevention of Corruption) Act, 1983 which, in turn, was repealed by the Kerala Public Man's Corruption (Investigations and Inquiries) Act, 1987. It was passed by the State assembly on December 13, 1987. Three annual reports were submitted under the 1983 Act, from 1985 to 1987. Sadly, the legislation got enmeshed in litigation and political strife.

The 1983 Act covered the entire range of "public man" from the Chief Minister and MLA downwards in the widest amplitude to include office bearers of a registered trade union.

Corruption was defined to cover receipt of illegal gratification as well as the abuse of position. The definition was far narrower than in the order of 1969. A three-member commission was to be appointed by the governor "in consultation with", rather than on the advice of, the Chief Minister and the Chief Justice of whom two were to be retired or serving high court judges. The commission was to make a preliminary investigation and subsequently, if a *prima facie* case was found, a detailed one. Its report went first to "the government" and the next to the Governor if it was not satisfied with the action.

Like the Tamil Nadu Act, prosecution was mandatory if the Commission so recommended. It could also recommend that the public man vacate his post. But it was open to the government to reject this recommendation within 3 months of receipt of the report failing which the act obliged the public man to "resign his office if he was Chief Minister, Minister or MLA. In other cases, he was "deemed to have to vacate his office".

Another innovation to empower the Commission (Section 16) was to call for a special property statement in the prescribed form from any public man who was under investigation. Preliminary investigations alone were to be in private and were confidential.

The 1987 Act introduced the concept of "competent authority" for action "the governor acting in his discretion", in the case of the Chief Minister. The definition of "public man" was expanded to cover the office bearers of political parties, private schools and colleges and so was that of "corruption". Yet, it fell short of the 1969 order in that acquisition of pecuniary gain was made an ingredient in the offence of abuse of power as distinction from "improper motive", generally. However, a new offence was added — possession by himself or any member of his family or any one else on his behalf of "pecuniary resources or property disproportionate to his known sources of income."

The three-member Commission was retained. So was its two-stage procedure but with an addition which is highly questionable. Existence of "other remedies" could, in the Commission's discretion, justify a decision not to proceed further. Full powers to issue search warrants are conferred on the body.

Reports are to be submitted to "the government" and "the competent authority" is enjoined to intimate the action taken. If it is not satisfied with it, the Commission makes a special report to the governor. The power to order the public man to vacate his office was retained and strengthened by excluding the government's discretion to reject the recommendation. Only office bearers of political parties and trade unions are exempted from this. What is more, the Commission itself is empowered to initiate, rather than merely recommend, prosecution. It is, however, not spelt out as to how and by whom such a prosecution is to be conducted. It is essential that the Commission should be endowed with a judicial personality.

Rather than leave it to the Commission to call for property statements, the act obligates some public men, chief ministers, ministers, MLAs, etc. to submit it "a statement of his assets and liabilities and those of the members of his family" once in two years (Section 25).

The act evoked a mixed reaction.[18] An important change was that the Act of 1987 empowered the Governor to appoint members of the Commission only "on the advice tendered by the chief minister in consultation with" the Chief Justice and the leader of the opposition. This was invoked to challenge the appointment of the members, in the High Court on March 13, 1990[19].

This resume, which is illustrative and neither definitive nor exhaustive, demonstrates the obsolescence of the 1971 model and also exposes the spurious character of objections to the inclusion of the head of government or the legislators. If the offices of the Lok Pal and the Lok Ayukt are to have any meaning, these exclusions must be abandoned for good.

A good test is that the institution should be able to resist the indifference and even scorn of the executive of the kind to which, for instance, the Rajasthan Lok Ayukt has been subjected[20].

No uniform pattern should be imposed on the States. They should be free to innovate. The Model Bill prepared for and presented at the 3rd All India Lok Ayukts Conference in 1991 can, at best, serve as a guide. However, both at the Centre and in the States, the institution must conform to certain minimal requirements in order to meet the tests mentioned in this paper. These are:

(1) The offices of the Lok Pal and the Lok Ayukt should have a constitutional status, as recommended by the Administrative Reforms

Commission (ARC). As in the case of the Election Commission (Article 324 of the Constitution), the details can be laid down by the appropriate legislature (Article 327). But the legislature should not be left free to abolish the office itself or curb its authority.

(2) The constitutional provision should define the functions, the procedure for appointment to the office, the ambit of jurisdiction and the powers. This would make the minimal requirements mandatory. To this extent, uniformity will also be introduced.

(3) The functions should be to inquire into any "grievance" of "maladministration" as well as any "allegation" of "misconduct" by a citizen or *suo moto*. It is extremely important that both should be considered at one place as the 1971 Bill provided in contrast to the Bills of 1977, 1985 and 1989. Often, evidence of corruption comes to light when a grievance of maladministration is inquired into.

(4) The definition of "maladministration" in the 1971 Bill [Clause 2 (g)] is adequate but not so the definition of "allegation" [Clause 2 (a)] as pointed out in the paper. Even so, it is far better than the definition of "complaint" in the 1985 Bill and especially in the 1989 Bill [Clauses 2(b) and 2(c) respectively]. The definition of "misconduct" in Clause 3 of the 1977 Bill is adequate.

(5) Whether the Lok Pal should be a single member or multiple member is a matter of opinion. Given the amplitude of his jurisdiction, a multiple member body would be more appropriate.

(6) The procedure for appointment should be analogous to that appointment of judges of the Supreme Court and the High Courts as laid down in the Constitution 67th Amendment Bill, 1990 moved in the Lok Sabha on May 18, 1990 (it lapsed on the dissolution of the Lok Sabha later in the year). It provided for a National Judicial Commission, to recommend the appointments, comprising the Chief Justice of India and other judges. In the case of the Lok Pal, the appointing body should comprise the Prime Minister, the Chief Justice of India, the presiding officers of both the houses of Parliament and the leaders of the opposition in the Lok Sabha. A similar body should appoint the Lok Pal in the States.

(7) The Lok Pal should be a former judge of the Supreme Court or a former Chief Justice of a High Court. No one should be appointed to the office who is merely "qualified to be" a judge.

(8) The Lok Pal and Lok Ayukt should respectively have jurisdiction at the Centre and in the State over every "public man" as

defined in Clause 2(g) of the 1977 Bill as well as every "public servant" as defined in Section 2 (c) of the Prevention of Corruption Act, 1988; this is wider than the definition of "public servant" in Section 21 of the Penal Code. Specifically, the definition of "public man" should include both the chief executive as well as legislators (the Kerala Act of 1987 also provides a good guide to the definition of "public man.")

(9) The institution should have an independent staff of its own. As discussed in the paper on Commissions of Inquiry, an independent investigation agency should be set up on whose services the Lok Pal, Lok Ayukts and Commissions of Inquiry can freely draw upon.

(10) The institution should have a juridical personality. It should have the power to launch prosecution without the sanction of the government and to order a public man or public servant to vacate office. In the latter case, the order would be amenable to writ jurisdiction anyway. It would be fair to provide an appeal to the Supreme Court.

(11) The Lok Pal's jurisdiction should be confined to the Union's functionaries. The ARC's draft bill covered Ministers and Secretaries at the Centre as well as in the States (Clauses 2 and 7). The 1977 Bill included Chief Ministers in the definition of "public man". The 1971 Bill was confined to central ministers alone, bar the prime minister. So were the 1985 and 1989 bills (the latter included the Prime Minister). It would only be fair to have a clear demarcation of the Lok Pal and the Lok Ayukt.

(12) Public support is indispensable to success. The staff should assist the underprivileged who approach the Lok Pal or Lok Ayukt. NGO's and Public Interest Groups make people aware of the existence of the institution and help them to file the complaints. The proceedings of the institution should be opened to the public.

Notes & References

1. Justice William O. Douglas, United States vs. Wunderlick, *342 U.S 98* (1951).
2. *The Times*, May 27, 1992.
3. R.K. Dhawan, *Public Grievances and the Lok Pal,* Allied, 1981. p. 209.
4. Frank Stacey, *The British Ombudsman*, Oxford, 1971, p.22.

5. See Frank Stacey, *Ombudsman Compared*, Oxford, 1978 for the studies of the Swedish, Danish, Norwegian, Canadian and the British ombudsman and also of the French *mediateur*.
6. Lok Sabha Secretariat, *Lokpal*, New Delhi pp. 5-6.
7. *The Hindu*, August 4, 1995.
8. *The Hindustan Times*, December 7,1995.
9. *Indian Express*, December 10, 1995.
10. *The Hindu*, September 30,1995.
11. *The Hindu*, December 13,1995.
12. *The Telegraph*, December 19,1995.
13. Justice T.S. Mishra, *Lok Ayukt and Public Interest*, a Paper read at a Workshop at Patna on October 5, 1986.
14. *Everyman's*, September 1, 1973.
15. A.R. Antulay vs Ramdas Nayak & Anr. (1984) 2 SCC 500. See also *ibid*. p. 184 on the ruling that a legislator is not a "public servant "as defined in Section 21 of the penal code. Earlier in the same case (1982) 2 SCC 463 the court had ruled that in deciding whether or not to accord sanction for prosecution of a chief minister, the governor must use his individual judgement.
16. The text was published in *Indian Express*, December 20, 1988.
17. See A.G. Noorani, *Minister's Misconduct* (Chapter 7) on Azhimathi in Kerala, Vickers 1973.
18. See K.P.Nair's article in *The Hindu* of December 9, 1987 for an able comparison of the 1987 Bill with the Act of 1985.
19. *The Hindu*, April 16, 1990. See also K.P. Nair's article in *The Hindu*, March 18, 1990.
20. *The Statesman*, January 7 and 8, 1996.

9
Commissions of Inquiry
A. G. Noorani

India is, perhaps, the only democracy whose constitutional, legal and political systems do not ensure accountability to law by men at the helm of the nation's affairs despite having a Constitution which is based on the rule of law. The void in politics, stemming from the failure to evolve an effective party system and the absence of democratic functioning within the parties among other things, is outside the scope of this paper which is concerned with the legal and constitutional aspects of the problem.

Some of the drawbacks are common to all parliamentary democracies. In actual practice, the executive controls the legislature, and not the other way around as theory ordains. One of the most eloquent and best-known critiques of this distortion was delivered on October 14, 1976 by Lord Hailsham in the Richard Dimbleby Lectures on BBC: "The checks and balances which in practice used to prevent abuse have now disappeared," he warned. An "elective dictatorship is a fact and not just a lawyer's theory. Party discipline has become more strict. The power of whips has increased. Backbenches count increasingly for little"[1].

Hailsham said "All other free nations impose limitations on their representative assemblies. We impose none on ours." In contrast, India's Constitution does impose precise limitations on its legislatures but the polity has none of the other checks which operate in other democracies and is not sustained by a culture of autonomy. For example, in India, both the police and the prosecution machinery are firmly under executive control despite judicial pronouncements on the independence of the police[2].

It needs to be emphasised, at the very outset, that this flaw alone can vitiate any institution that may be devised to ensure accountability, be it the Commission of Inquiry or the Lok Pal. Both depend on the police. As two authorities on constitutional law, Geoffrey Marshall and Barry Loveday, point out: "The impartiality of the police is one of the main components of the rule of law. In recent times impartiality has been seen as guaranteed by the doctrine that all police officers have a degree of independence guaranteed by the law that is enjoyed by no other central or local executive officer."[3]

This is certainly not true of India. Interestingly, while British works on constitutional law invariably discuss the legal status of the police force, Indian works on the subject do not. Nor does India have any of the other checks such as an informed and assertive public opinion, well-organised political parties and a powerful Press although there has been considerable progress in these fields of late. The result is that a disproportionate burden has fallen on the judiciary.

As the debates in the Constituent Assembly show, the framers of the Constitution of India were well aware of the rise in corruption among ministers, civil servants, and the society in general. On one occasion, December 31, 1948, Dr. B. R. Ambedkar urged disclosure of assets by ministers at the time of assumption as well as demission of their office[4]. But no institutional checks were devised.

Corruption in public life goes back to the days when the freedom movement was in full swing. On a complaint by the Governor of Bengal, the Private Secretary to the Viceroy, G. F. de Montmorency, wrote to the Home Member of the Viceroy's Executive Council, Sir James Crerar, on August 16, 1924 about "actual payments made to members of the Legislative Council of Bengal to vote with the Swaraj Party."[5]

The premier political party, the Indian National Congress, tended to treat corruption as a party matter and the approach of its leaders was often politically selective[6]. The most striking instance of this is the Party's treatment of the Bihar Molasses Scandal. The Congress President, Dr. Rajendra Prasad, sent a colleague, Shankarrao Deo, to Bihar "to look into the matter."[7] Prasad complained to Home Minister Vallabhbhai Patel, on January 17, 1949 about Prime Minister Jawaharlal Nehru's omission to institute an inquiry[8]. The tendency persisted for over a decade after Independence. A party inquiry in 1958 exonerated the Chief Minster of Punjab, Pratap Singh Kairon, of charges of corruption[9].

One case in particular, that aroused much disquiet was "the Jeep Scandal" in which grave charges were levelled against India's High Commissioner to the U. K., V. K. Krishna Menon. It was dealt with first by a Sub-Committee of the Congress Parliamentary Party which reported on April 9, 1951, and next by the Public Accounts Committee in its Ninth Report. It recommended inquiry by a "high-level Committee consisting of one or two High Court judges." The Government of India refused to do so and declared the case to be closed on September 30, 1955.

In 1951, A. D. Gorwala, a civil servant with high reputation for integrity, sounded the tocsin. He had been asked by the Planning Commission to consider in different fields the question whether the present administrative machinery and methods were adequate and could meet the requirements of planned development. His report had a whole section entitled, *Integrity*.[10]

Now, nearly half a century later, the report still makes poignant reading. Gorwala wrote: "Parliamentary government is in its infancy in the country. Accordingly, this is the proper time to lay down and observe conventions, so that with the passage of years they may consolidate into traditions which those who come hereafter will accept instinctively knowing that, based as they are on the wisdom of their fathers, they will serve their turn well."

Recalling the Sanskrit proverb, "As the king, so the people," he stressed that it was the conduct of those at the top which shaped the country's development. By 1951, the situation in this regard had deteriorated enough for Gorwala to record the following:

"... during the past few years there have been various instances in which grave allegations of a specific nature have been made by responsible parties against persons occupying the position of Ministers of Government. Such allegations have on occasion been the subject of debates in the Legislatures. The ministry as a whole and the party which has put it in power having thrown their weight behind the minister complained against, the debates have either been inconclusive or have ended in a vote in his favour. Thereafter, the matter has generally been ended. Enquiries into the allegations have sometimes been made by senior all-India leaders of the principal political party; occasionally, their reports have been made public, but often they have remained secret. Some of the reports have exculpated those complained against and some have, in effect, condemned them. In any case, no action has been taken. It is not surprising that when grave allegations by responsible parties are made against people holding positions of high authority and they remain in power without being cleared of the accusations, the public feel that the influential always escape punishment."

Gorwala, therefore, urged that "arrangements must be made that no one, however highly placed, is immune from enquiry if allegations against him are made by responsible parties and a *prima facie* case exists."

This is the crux of the matter; the initiation of an investigation into crime or an inquiry into charge of corruption or maladministration must not depend on the wishes of the men in power. If it does, it ceases to be government according to the rule of law.

Gorwala, obviously influenced by the Lynskey Tribunal in Britain which had found John Belcher, Parliamentary Secretary to the Board of Trade, guilty of grave misconduct (1948), remarked: "There is no reason why similar tribunals could not work satisfactorily in this country, considering the high standard of our judiciary. All facilities for directing investigation, obtaining evidence, examining documents, etc., would have to be placed at the disposal of the tribunal. The authority responsible for setting up the tribunal might, for the Central Government, be the President, and for State Government, the Governor acting in consultation with the President. They, in either case, on being satisfied that there was *prima facie* evidence, would appoint a tribunal. An alternative would be to vest the power of appointing such tribunals in the Supreme Court."[11]

This was, probably, the first official document to discuss corruption by politicians in power. The tendency hitherto was to treat the vice as an affliction of the civil services or businessmen. The Report of the Corruption Enquiry Committee appointed by the Congress Government in Bihar, on April 8, 1938, for instance, was confined to "the crying evils of bribery and corruption believed to be prevailing in the various public services of Bihar." The report, submitted on November 30, 1938, left corruption elsewhere alone.

The British model was emulated by Parliament in 1952 when it passed the Commissions of Inquiry Act 60 of 1952. Hitherto, Commissions of Inquiry were appointed under executive order. Their remit generally concerned police firings or railway and other accidents. The Act was not intended specifically to provide a standing machinery for investigation into charges of misconduct against ministers or civil servants but simply to be a ready mechanism for inquiries with statutory powers "to enforce the attendance of witnesses and the production of documents." The first Commission of note to be appointed under the Act was the Press Commission on October 3, 1952.

The Act left the appointment of a Commission at the sole discretion of the Government or the Lower House of the Legislature, Central or State; in other words, the party in power. Section 3 (1), as originally enacted, read thus: "The appropriate Government may, if it is of opinion that it is necessary so to do, and shall, if a resolution in this behalf is passed by the House of the People or, as the case may be, the Legislative Assembly of the State, by notification in the Official Gazette, appoint a Commission of Inquiry for the purpose of making an inquiry into any definite matter of public importance and performing such functions and within such time as may be specified in the notification, and the Commission so appointed shall make the inquiry and perform the function accordingly."

Two features of the Act stand out. One is that the appointment of members of the Commission was also left to the discretion of the Government [Section 3 (2)]. There was no provision for consultation with the Chief Justice of India or the High Court and the Leader of the Opposition. The other is that the scope of the remit was defined in words of the widest amplitude: "definite matter of public importance." The Central Government was free, as the "appropriate Government" defined by Section 2 (a), to appoint a Commission to make an inquiry into any matter relating to any of the entries enumerated in any of the lists of topics for legislation in the Seventh Schedule to the Constitution. The power of the States was confined to List II or III.

A significant change was made by Section 2 of the Commissions of Inquiry (Amendment) Act 19 of 1990 in Section 3 of the Act of 1952. For the words "the House of the People or, as the case may be, the Legislative Assembly of the State" were substituted with the words "each House of Parliament, or as the case may be, the Legislature of the State."

This would enable an opposition-dominated Rajya Sabha or Legislative Council in a State to appoint a Commission of Inquiry even against the wishes of the Government. However, its composition would, nonetheless, be determined by the Government, not to forget the dependence of Commissions of Inquiry on the official machinery.

Article 44 of the Basic Law of the Federal Republic of Germany enables one-fourth of the members of the Bundestag (the Lower House of Parliament), to institute an inquiry. Article 44 is instructive and reads thus:

> "(1) The Bundestag shall have the right, and, upon the motion of one-fourth of its members the duty, to set up a committee of investigation which shall take the requisite evidence at public hearings. The public may be excluded.
>
> "(2) The rules of criminal procedure shall apply *mutatis mutandis* to the taking of evidence. The privacy of posts and telecommunications shall remain unaffected.
>
> "(3) Courts and administrative authorities shall be bound to render legal and administrative assistance."

The Commissions of Inquiry Act, 1952 endows Commissions with the powers of a civil court to ensure attendance of witnesses, requisition of documents and receipt of evidence on affidavits, etc. (Section 4). The Act was reviewed by the Law Commission of India in its Twenty-Fourth Report in December 1962.

In 1971, the Act was amended by the Commissions of Inquiry (Amendment) Act 79 of 1971 to empower Commissions to utilise the services of Government officers or investigation agencies under a newly inserted Section 5A which reads thus:

> "1) The Commission may, for the purpose of conducting any investigation pertaining to the inquiry, utilise the services;
>
> "(a) in the case of a Commission appointed by the Central Government, of any officer or investigation agency of the Central Government or any State Government with the concurrence of the Central Government or the State Government as the case may be; or
>
> "(b) in the case of a Commission appointed by the State Government, of any officer or investigation agency of the State Government or Central Government with the concurrence of the State Government or the Central Government, as the case may be."

The officer or agency is empowered to summon witnesses, requisition records etc., and report to the Commission. As Section 5A(5) says: "The Commission shall satisfy itself about the correctness of the facts stated and the conclusions, if any, arrived at in the investigation report submitted to it under Sub-Section (4), and for this purpose the Commission may make such inquiry (including the examination of the person or persons who conducted or assisted in the investigation) as it thinks fit."

Thus, the Commission may not employ a private investigation agency or individual. The appointment depends on "the concurrence" of the Government. In practice, the Commissions of Inquiry depend on the CBI or the State police.

The Amendment Act of 1971 also added provisions for the protection of the reputation of persons likely to be prejudicially affected and obligates the Commissions of Inquiry to give them "a reasonable opportunity of being heard." Sections 8 B and 8 C confer detailed rights of participation on such persons.

The Amendment Act enjoined "the appropriate Government" to lay the Commission's Report before the Lok Sabha or the State Assembly, as the case may be, "together with a memorandum of the action taken thereon within a period of six months of the submission of the report by the Commission to the appropriate Government" [Section 3 (4)]. This provision has been honoured more in its breach than in its observance.

For two decades from 1958 onwards, the Commissions of Inquiry Act, 1952 served as a fairly effective instrument for investigation into charges of corruption, abuse of power and the like; in each case, however, because the government established it whether of its own free volition or under force of circumstances.

The first notable Commission of Inquiry to be appointed under the Act to inquire into a public scandal was the one comprising the Chief Justice of Bombay, M. C. Chagla, on the Life Insurance Corporation of India's (LIC) purchase of shares in certain companies controlled by Haridas Mundhra. It was appointed on January 7, 1958 and submitted a report on February 13, 1958. This record of despatch has not been equalled. There was no evidence on affidavit. All the witnesses deposed orally on oath in open proceedings. They included Feroze Gandhi, MP; T. T Krishnamachari, Union Finance Minister; H. M. Patel, Principal Secretary to the Finance Ministry; H.V.R. Iyengar, Governor of the Reserve Bank and G. R. Kamat, Chairman of the LIC. M. C. Setalwad, Attorney General, appeared for the government but acted independently and made no attempt to act as defence counsel for the Minister. He performed the same role as tradition ordains for the Attorney General in Britain and as was performed by Sir Hartley Shawcross before the Lynskey Tribunal in 1946. In the circumstances, there was no counsel for the Commission.

Another noteworthy feature was that the Commission was not asked to probe into charges in a memorandum or, for that matter, debates in Parliament on a particular day. The Commission was required to inquire into three main questions: "(i) Whether the purchases were in accordance with normal business principles or practices; (ii) the propriety of the purchases and (iii) the person or persons responsible for the purchases."

Justice Chagla, however, took the unusual course of first personally examining the witnesses first, leaving it to the Attorney General to "supplement the evidence in any manner that he thinks proper." In this, he was clearly wrong. A grave error was perpetrated when, on January 28, Haridas Mundhra's application for legal representation was rejected by the Commission though he had been summoned to give evidence and grave charges had been levelled against him earlier in the proceedings. The Attorney General also opposed Mundhra's plea[12].

Justice Chagla found that there was clear acquiescence on the part of the minister in the role played by Patel with regard to the transaction of June 24, 1957 and the lack of repudiation by the minister supported Patel's case that the minister had approved of the transaction in Bombay.

Having rejected Krishnamachari's version on the basis of the evidence, Chagla stated the legal position as follows: "In my opinion, in any case, it is clear that constitutionally the Minister is responsible for the action taken by his Secretary with regard to this transaction. It is clear that a Minister must take the responsibility for actions done by his subordinates. He cannot take shelter behind them. Nor can he disown their actions. The doctrine of ministerial responsibility has two facets. The Minister has complete autonomy within his own sphere or authority. As a necessary corollary he must take full responsibility for the actions of his servants."[13] T. T. Krishnamachari resigned from the Union Cabinet.

As late as June 3, 1960, the Congress Working Committee passed the following resolution: "Whereas complaints are received occasionally about misuse of authority by responsible Congressmen, it is advisable to have a permanent machinery to examine the merits of such complaints. For this purpose, the President is authorised to appoint a Panel out of which he may nominate one or more persons, wherever he considers such action necessary, to inquire into such complaints and to report to him." The Act of 1952 was not even mentioned.

Nor was it invoked when, in 1963, charges were levelled against Union Minister for Mines and Fuel, K. D. Malaviya, in the Serajuddin affair. Instead, Prime Minister Nehru referred them to a sitting judge of the Supreme Court, Justice S. K. Das, rejecting the advice of the Attorney General, C. K. Daphtary, for a full inquiry. He told the Lok Sabha on May 7, 1963: "There is going to be no judicial inquiry as such. This matter essentially is a matter for the Prime Minister to decide on the advice of eminent persons. It will naturally be a quasi-judicial inquiry because there is a Supreme Court Judge. It is not a normal judicial inquiry, it is not that with judicial procedures and all that. It will be upto him to decide of course."[14]

On August 17, 1963, the results of the inquiry were announced in the Lok Sabha. Two of the six charges were upheld. The report was not published. Malaviya resigned from the Cabinet. He expressed great dissatisfaction with the procedure followed by the Judge. So did the Opposition. The procedure satisfied nobody. Such an approach to inquiries set a tradition of stalling on inquiries even when they were called for on the facts. Nehru's note recommending an inquiry dated October 25, 1963 to President S. Radhakrishnan on the Kairon case, was written in the wake of certain strictures on Kairon by the Supreme Court.[15]

A memorandum of charges against Kairon had been presented to the Congress President, U. N. Dhebar, as far back as May 4, 1958, but nothing came of it. Another was presented to his successor on August 14, 1960 with similar results. Only the Supreme Court's strictures against the Chief Minister of Punjab for not responding personally and on sworn affidavit to charges made against him forced the Centre's hands.

On November 1, 1963, the Government of India appointed a Commission of Inquiry, consisting of Justice S. R. Das, a former Chief Justice of India, "to inquire into the allegations made against Kairon by Devi Lal and others in a memorandum presented to the President of India on the 13th July, 1963." The inquiry was held on the basis of affidavits and not oral evidence. The report recorded: "The Commission took the view that where the affidavits taken and read together were reasonably clear and unambiguous and the Commission was able to hold, without any reasonable doubt, that a *prima facie* case had not been made out in respect of one or more of the charges, the persons making or supporting such charges could not be permitted to have another opportunity to adduce fresh evidence or to cross-examine the person charged on the off-chance of being able to make out a case which in legal parlance may be said to be sufficient to go to the jury. Likewise if a *prima facie* case had been out in respect of one or more of the charges the person charged could not be permitted to claim another opportunity to clear himself by adducing fresh evidence or cross-examining the persons making the charges. The Commission was of the opinion that where the affidavits were so evenly balanced that it could not come to a firm conclusion then and then only could the Commission say that it was necessary to record oral evidence."

The Commission accepted that its inquiry had neither prosecutor or plaintiff, no accused or defendant. "There is no list of charges to be adjudicated upon... its function is only to inquire."[16] But, in effect, the Commission converted itself into a court trying specific charges in the memorandum and cast the onus of proof entirely on the memorialists. It rejected their submission that "it was the duty of the Commission to collect all available evidence by the exercise of its own powers."[17] The Commission ruled "that an individual must be presumed to be innocent until the contrary is proved beyond reasonable doubt by dependable evidence freely given and publicly ascertained or by the irresistible probabilities of the case."[18] The two are not identical. The former is the standard of proof required in a criminal case and the latter is required in a civil suit. Several charges were upheld. Kairon resigned once Prime Minister Lal Bahadur Shastri published the report in view of Kairon's reluctance to resign.

The Das Report was published on June 11, 1964. Shortly before that, on March 31, 1964, the Committee on Prevention of Corruption set up by the Government of India in 1962 submitted its report. The Committee was headed by K. Santhanam and its members were Santosh Kumar Basu, MP., Tikaram Paliwal, MP.; R. K. Khadilkar, MP.; Nath Pai, MP.; Shambu Nath Chaturvedi, MP.; L. P. Singh, Director, Administrative Vigilance Division and D. P. Kohli, Inspector General, Special Police Establishment. The terms of reference dealt mainly with government servants. Only one term of reference was general enough to bring ministers within its ambit, *viz.*, "to suggest measures calculated to produce a social climate both amongst public servants and in the general public in which bribery and corruption may not flourish." The Committee considered the aspect of ministers in the chapter entitled, *Social Climate*.

The Committee's assessment of the "climate" was no different from Gorwala's a little over a decade earlier. It said:

> "There is a widespread impression that failure of integrity is not uncommon among Ministers and that some Ministers who have held office during the last 16 years have enriched themselves illegitimately, obtained good jobs for their sons and relations through nepotism, and have reaped other advantages inconsistent with any notion of purity in public life. The general belief about failure of integrity amongst Ministers is as damaging as actual failure....
>
> "It is a pity that neither the Congress authorities nor the great leaders who took over the Government of India realised that importance of evolving a suitable machinery and procedure for preventing and dealing with such corruption."[19]

The Committee proceeded to make two recommendations in this regard. One was a code of conduct for Ministers. The other was a defined procedure for investigation into charges against them:

> "...If a formal allegation is made by any ten members of Parliament or a Legislature in writing addressed to the Prime Minister or Chief Minister, through the Speakers and Chairmen, the Prime Minister or Chief Minister should consider himself obliged, by convention, to refer the allegations for immediate investigation by a Committee as has been suggested later in this Section. This would be in addition to the responsibilities of the Chief Ministers of States to take note of minister and chief allegations made in the Press or which otherwise come to their notice. In respect of such allegations also the Prime Minister and the Chief Ministers should be free to refer the matter to the proposed Committee.....
>
> "We consider that the appropriate course would be for the President to constitute on the advice of the Prime Minister a national panel. Whenever allegations against a Minister require to be inquired into an *ad hoc* Committee should be selected out of this national panel by the President. The Committee may consist of three persons one of whom at least should have held or should be holding a high judicial office. It should be the duty of the Committee to ascertain whether there is a *prima facie* case. The Committee should have the power to direct the Central Bureau of Investigation, in suitable cases, to investigate and report. If the Committee wishes to make any inquiries otherwise than

through the Central Bureau of Investigation it should be given all the necessary facilities and assistance including free access to all documents, files, etc., without being hampered by any claim of privilege. On the completion of the inquiries either through the Central Bureau of Investigation or otherwise, the Committee should consider the available material and advise as to further action, if any, that may be necessary. It may advise that a regular case be registered for investigation with a view to prosecute the Minister concerned or a Commission of Inquiry be appointed under the Commissions of Inquiry Act, 1952. If the Committee makes such a recommendation the Minister should resign as a matter of convention and should remain out of office till the completion of the proceedings. If the Minister is found guilty of the allegations or is found to have been corrupt he should be dismissed and should also become ineligible for becoming a Minister or for holding any elective office. The necessary legal instruments for giving effect to this provision should be brought into existence. Until such time as the necessary legislation is made, there should be convention which would give effect to this provision."[20]

The core of the second recommendation is the initiation of an inquiry at the request of any ten legislators regardless of the wishes of the Government in power; initially "by convention" and eventually, under a "legal instrument." The *ad hoc* Committee's function and duty would be "to ascertain whether there is a *prima facie* case." This would effectively deprive governments of the standard pretext which has been almost invariably advanced whenever memoranda of charges are delivered viz., that they do not disclose a *prima facie* case. The Committee would be assisted by the CBI. If a *prima facie* case is disclosed, it could advise either registration of a case for investigation or appointment of a Commission of Inquiry.

It is a matter of opinion whether a Committee of three persons, one of whom should have held or should be holding a high judicial office, is necessary for so limited a function. It is very much the duty of the police, in law, to act on any information about commission of an offence laid before it and to investigate into it diligently and expeditiously. As for the appointment of a Commission of Inquiry, as will be pointed out at the conclusion of this survey, an effective arrangement can be arrived at so as to activate either a Commission of Inquiry or the Lok Pal and leave it to either to pronounce on the charges. The governing test would not be the existence of a *prima facie* case but, as the Salmon Commission put it, "a nation-wide crisis of confidence" which warrants the appointment of a Commission. In other cases, the charges should be inquired into by the Lok Pal.

The Commissions of Inquiry that followed tended, by and large, to follow the precedent set by the Das Commission and inquire into specific memoranda of charges. They did not act as inquisitorial bodies.

Justice N. Rajagopalan, a former Judge of the Supreme Court, was appointed on a Commission of Inquiry set up by the Government of Jammu & Kashmir on January 30, 1965. Its terms of reference were in two parts. One concerned "the nature and extent of the assets and pecuniary resources" of Bakshi Ghulam Mohammed, members of his family and named relatives in October 1947, when he became Minister, and in October 1963, when he resigned as Chief Minister of the State.

The second part of the terms of reference directed the Commission to inquire whether, during the same period, Bakshi Ghulam Mohammed and members of his family and other relatives "obtained any assets, pecuniary resources or advantages or other benefits by Bakshi Ghulam Mohammed abusing the various official positions held by him or by the aforesaid members of his family, his other relatives and persons exploiting with his consent, knowledge or connivance the various official positions held by him." In making this latter inquiry, however, the Commission was asked to consider only the thirty-seven specific allegations listed in the Second Schedule to the terms of reference.

The Commission relied on affidavits and official records. The State Government adduced such evidence in support of the charges but did not lead any oral evidence to explain contradictions although it was afforded an opportunity to do so. The standard which the Commission adopted was proof so "overwhelming" as to rule out "any alternative innocent explanation." The onus of proof rested on the government. A good many charges were upheld.

Bakshi had been arrested on September 22, 1964, in order to prevent him from moving a motion of no-confidence against the G. M. Sadiq Ministry, and was released in December 1964. Despite the adverse findings in the Commission's Report submitted on June 30, 1967, he was given the Congress (R)'s ticket for the Lok Sabha elections in 1971.

Meanwhile, in 1967, the State Government persuaded the State Legislature to adopt an amendment to the Representation of the People Act disqualifying persons found guilty by the Commissions of Inquiry. Since there is no corresponding provision in the Central law on the subject, viz. the Representation of the People Act, 1951, the result was that Bakshi could be an MP but not an MLA. He could aspire for the Prime Ministership of the country, which was well beyond his reach, but he was effectively barred from ever becoming the Chief Minister of the State, which was well within his reach then.

Despite a CBI Report dated November 15, 1964 recommending "further inquiries" into charges levelled by the Opposition against the former Chief Minister of Orissa, Biju Patnaik — who had resigned as such in 1963 — and his successor, Biren Mitra, no Commission of Inquiry was appointed. Instead, the charges were examined by a Sub-Committee of the Union Cabinet. It found "improper use of authority by leaders of the Government" but opined against the setting up of a Commission of Inquiry.

It was only after the General Elections of 1967 when a non-Congress Ministry came to power that a judicial inquiry was set up. On October 26, 1967, the Singh Deo Ministry appointed H. R. Khanna, who was then a Judge of the Delhi High Court, as the Commission of Inquiry to inquire into charges against Patnaik, Biren Mitra and thirteen other Ministers, including Sadasiba Tripathi, Leader of the Opposition. Justice H. R. Khanna submitted his report on January 15, 1969. The Commission found Patnaik and Biren Mitra guilty of some grave improprieties.

The terms of reference required the Commission to inquire into the conduct of named persons between June 23, 1961 and March 8, 1967 from which "it appears" to the State Government that they had "committed various acts of misconduct, misappropriation", etc. The Commission observed that "as the precise particulars are missing, the respondents cannot be said to have notice of the factual allegations they have to meet and rebut." It cited the provisions of the Code of Civil Procedure on civil suits and the Code of Civil Procedure on the particulars required in a valid charge. The State Government thereupon filed the particulars as directed by the Commission which upheld certain charges and rejected others. Again, this was more a trial than an inquiry.

In a related case, a former Judge of the Supreme Court, Justice J. R Mudholkar, was requested by the Chief Minister of Orissa, R. N. Singh Deo "for a preliminary verification" of charges made in a memorial to the President on June 26, 1967 alleging acts of corruption and improprieties against Ministers who held office between 1947 and 1961. The Chief Minister's letter of May 3, 1966 outlined the remit to Justice Mudholkar who proceeded thereafter to style himself as "Special Judge for Inquiries." In his report dated September 26, 1968, Justice Mudholkar found a *prima facie* case against Harekrushna Mahtab on various counts.

On January 8, 1971, the Orissa Government appointed Sarjoo Prasad, a former Chief Justice of Rajasthan and Assam High Courts but then a practising advocate at the Supreme Court, as Commission of Inquiry only hours before the Singh Deo Government fell as a result of Mahtab's withdrawal of support to it.

Sarjoo Prasad took oral evidence. The memorialists made themselves scarce, "may be due to changes on the political stage," the Commission remarked. The State Government filed detailed particulars in support of charges, some of which were upheld in a Report dated May 25, 1972.

A similar course was adopted in the Bihar inquiries. Justice T. L. Venkatarama Aiyar, a former Judge of the Supreme Court, was appointed to a Commission of Inquiry on October 1, 1967 by the United Front Ministry of Bihar to probe into allegations of abuse of power and corruption against six former ministers of the State belonging to the Congress. The Commission directed the State "to file a statement specifying the charges" against them. The inquiry was held on affidavit evidence.

It ruled that "the burden is undoubtedly on the State to establish the charge beyond all reasonable doubt." The Report upheld several charges.

The United Front Ministry fell on January 25, 1968 when the Assembly passed on a no-confidence motion against it. A new Ministry was formed by the Soshit Dal headed by B. P Mandal with the support of the Congress Party. Mandal and others of the Dal had defected from the Front earlier in August 1967. Mandal's ministry did not last long. On March 18, 1968, it succumbed to a motion of no-confidence, but not before it had appointed, on March 12, another Commission of Inquiry to inquire into charges against the Ministers of the United Front Ministry. Justice Mudholkar conducted the inquiry. Here, again, "formal charges were formulated by the State against the respondents and filed before the Commission". It ruled that a "notification (under Section 3 of the Act) which permits an inquiry to be made into the conduct of an unnamed person would rob it of definiteness. It must, therefore, be characterised as *ultra vires*."

Kerala is a classic case of the use of the Commission of Inquiry as a political weapon. The High Court struck down on January 20, 1970 the notification appointing one such Commission on the ground of *mala fide*[21].

One Commission of Inquiry, headed by Justice S. Velu Pillai, was appointed by a resolution of the State Assembly on October 17, 1969 in respect of four ministers. His remit comprised "the allegation of corruption and favouritism raised on the floor of the House and those submitted to the Hon'ble Home Minister by some Hon'ble Members of this House."

The Commission held: "A vast area of accusations made in the Assembly was left uncovered by the statements of the parties in the inquiries (the memorialists). I did not conceive it to be proper or within my province in holding an inquiry of this nature, fact-finding though it be, to act as an investigator myself or to devise a machinery to investigate the truth of those accusations. At the same time, I could not simply shut my eyes to them, for want of pleading as in a civil action. Such accusations had of course to be tested; for this purpose, as no material was furnished by members of the public pursuant to the public notification and to the individual letters addressed, I had to rely for the most part on government files." In law, the Commission is very much required "to act as an investigator itself." The standard of proof adopted was the same as in a criminal trial — proof beyond reasonable doubt.

The Interim Probe Machinery Order of December 12, 1969 enabled any citizen to set in motion the process of accountability. Once, Justice R. Sankaranarayana Iyer found that a *prima facie* case existed against P. K. Kunju, following the procedure laid down in the Order, Justice Velu Pilai was appointed as Commission of Inquiry by the State Government in 1970. He was asked to ascertain "the extent of debts" of Kunju when he became Minister and "the portion of the debts repaid" by him when he was Finance Minister, "the sources of funds," and a specific charge of nepotism.

A. N. Mulla, was a former Judge but a practising counsel when he was appointed as Commission of Inquiry on October 18, 1969 to inquire into charges made against M. N. Govindan Nair and T. V. Thomas in two memoranda. Oral as well as documentary evidence was received.

Justice P. Govinda Menon was appointed as Commission of Inquiry on December 16, 1970 to inquire into the charges levelled against B. Wellingdon in the Kerala Assembly on three specified days. The report was submitted on March 24, 1972.

Thus, all the Commissions of Inquiry that inquired into charges of corruption or misconduct against ministers followed the precedent set by the Das Commission in 1964 and functioned as courts of law trying specific charges rather than following an inquisitorial procedure.

After an interval of eight years, the Central Government appointed on October 16, 1971 what proved to be a precursor to a series of Commissions of Inquiry against ministers of State governments run by political parties who were opposed to the ruling party at the Centre. Kairon's was the last case of a Central Commission of Inquiry against a member of the ruling party. This time it was against former ministers of Punjab, including P. S. Badal, former Chief Minister, in respect to charges made in memoranda and letters to the President plus "further allegations... that may be referred to the Commission by the Central Government." The Government did not produce any evidence, however.

Initially, Justice D. S. Dave, former Chief Justice, was appointed to conduct the inquiry, but he was unable to proceed much further. On January 20, 1973, Justice L. N. Chhangani, a former Judge of the Rajasthan High Court, succeeded him. He made plain his rejection of the standard of proof adopted hitherto by pervious Commissions, *viz.*, one of proof beyond reasonable doubt. But he did not propound his alternative in clear terms beyond saying that "the approach in such inquiries should be non-doctrinaire, pragmatic, realistic and imaginative rather than doctrinaire, mechanical or wooden."[22] As in Kerala, the Commission's work was hampered by the indifference of the memorialists once the Commission was set up.

Into the same genre falls the Sarkaria Commission. It was quintessentially an off-shoot of the Emergency. Memoranda against the Chief Minister of Tamil Nadu, M. Karunanidhi and his colleagues had been submitted to the President as far back as November 1972.

Prime Minister Indira Gandhi sought his explanations that month. He responded in December 1972. By 1973, the process of rejoinders by memorialists and replies thereto was over.

On January 31, 1976, President's Rule was imposed in the State. On February 3, the Government of India appointed Justice R. S. Sarkaria, a sitting Judge of the Supreme Court, as Commission of Inquiry to inquire into allegations contained in the memoranda submitted to the President in 1972 and on December 1, 1975. On April 12, 1976, the Commission invoked Section 5A of the Act and sought the assistance of the investigating agencies of the Centre and the State.

The Commission ruled that "the task of the Commission is essentially inquisitorial." The memorialists are not "*dominus litis*. They cannot stop the enquiry by abandoning their allegations" before the Commission.

There is grave doubt as to the correctness of the Commission's rejection of the respondent's plea for oral examination of deponents of affidavits, especially on matters on which affidavit evidence is intrinsically inadequate; for example, charges of receipt of illegal gratification. Karunanidhi and most of the other respondents withdrew from the Commission as had the Punjab Ministers from the Chhangani Commission.

Similar problems arose in the Commissions set up in the post-Emergency days on how to ensure the rights of persons charged with misconduct and summoned to appear before the Commission and the fairness of procedure generally so as to command public confidence in its proceedings and the findings in its report. The most famous of these, the Shah Commission, had to suffer the ignominy of having its proceedings in respect of the prime respondent, Mrs. Indira Gandhi, and her colleague, Mr Pranab Mukherjee, declared "void and ultra vires" on December 20, 1979 by Justice T. P. S. Chawla of the Delhi High Court for non-compliance with the statutory safeguards (Sections 8 B and 8 C) of the Act based on principles of natural justice. Although the judgement ranged far and wide on a host of issues, on the crucial issue of observance of those safeguards from the very inception, it was, with respect, clearly right[23].

On May 28, 1977, the Government of India appointed a Commission of Inquiry consisting of J. C. Shah, a retired Chief Justice of India "to inquire into the facts and circumstances relating to specific instances of subversion of lawful processes and well-established conventions, administrative procedures and practices, abuse of authority, misuse of power, excesses and / or malpractices committed during the period when the proclamation of Emergency made on 25th June 1975 under Article 352 of the Constitution was in force or in days immediately preceding the said Proclamation." Also included were acts of misuse of powers of arrests or issue of detention orders; atrocities on detenues; use of force in the implementation of the family planning programme and the demolition of houses during this period. The Commission utilised the services of investigation officers of the Government. The Commission submitted its First Interim Report on March 11,1978; the Second on April 26, 1978; and the Third and Final Report on August 6, 1978.

The Commission received over 48,000 complaints and a mass of official records. The inquiry was held in two stages as laid down in a ruling on September 29, 1977. At the first stage the Commission would consider whether on a "preponderance of probability that it is necessary to probe further into the matter ..." if so, it would at the next stage hold an inquiry and apply Sections 8 B and 8 C of the Act which read thus:

"8 B. If at any stage of the inquiry, the Commission: -
(a) considers it necessary to inquire into the conduct of any persons; or (b) is of opinion that the reputation of any person is likely to be prejudicially affected by the inquiry. The Commission shall give to that person a reasonable opportunity of being heard in the inquiry and to produce evidence in his defence: provided that nothing in this section shall apply where the credit of a witness is being impeached.

"8 C. The appropriate government, every person referred to in Section 8 B and, with the permission of the Commission, any other person whose evidence is recorded by the Commission:—
(a) may cross-examine a witness other than a witness produced by it or him;
(b) may address the Commission; and
(c) may be represented before the Commission by a legal practitioner or, with the permission of the Commission, by any other person."

Case summaries were read out in public proceedings involving individuals and testimony recorded before Sections 8 B and 8 C were applied. As will be pointed out, there is a better procedure for ensuring fair play.

The Commission of Inquiry to probe into charges against three Chief Ministers set up during this period, followed precedent. In response to a Memorandum of Charges against the Chief Minister of Andhra Pradesh, J. Vengala Rao, presented to the Prime Minister on April 6, 1977, the Government of India appointed on May 19, 1977 a Commission of Inquiry consisting of Justice J. R. Vimadalal, a former Judge of the Bombay High Court. It was well-known that he had been transferred to the Andhra Pradesh High Court in 1976 as a punishment for his rulings in cases of detention. Honest and able as the Judge was, one would have thought that he was not the best judge for such a task though he did conduct the proceedings fairly.

He rightly rejected proof beyond reasonable doubt as the rigid standard to be adopted but applied the test of "preponderance of probability, though, what should be the extent of that preponderance must...depends upon the gravity of the consequences of its finding ..." on a particular issue. On the standard of proof, his discussion remains the most instructive. With the exception of two charges relating to Sanjay Gandhi's visit, all the others were rejected. The Commission was appointed though no *prima facie* case existed in respect of those charges. But it helped to allay public disquiet and resolve a "crisis of confidence." The Government of India led no evidence, the task was left entirely to the memorialists. The Commission had its own counsel and an investigation team comprising police officers.

On May 23, 1977, the Government of India appointed a Commission of Inquiry consisting of Justice A. N. Grover to inquire into the charges made in a memorandum presented to the Prime Minister on April 11, 1988 against the Chief Minister of Karnataka, Devraj Urs. Excluded were matters covered in the terms of reference of a Commission of Inquiry, consisting of Justice Mir Iqbal Hussain, a former Judge of the Karnataka High Court, set up by the State Government on May 18, 1977. Justice Grover had resigned as Judge in April 1973 on being superceded along with Justice J. N. Shelat and K. S. Hegde for the appointment of the Chief Justice of India. Under the circumstances, it was not a wise appointment. His First Report was submitted on January 10, 1978 and the Second and Final Report... On two points, the Final Report contains highly relevant observations. One relates to the need for an independent investigation agency for

Commission of Inquiry and the other to the use of investigation reports under Section 5A of the Act. They should not preclude inquiry by the Commission itself. The Government of Karnataka's challenge to the validity of the Commission's appointment was rejected by the Supreme Court.[24]

On June 14, 1977, Justice P. Jaganmohan Reddy, a former Judge of the Supreme Court, was appointed as Commission of Inquiry to inquire into "all matters" relating to specified transactions of the Government of Haryana when Bansi Lal was its Chief Minister in order to ascertain whether any impropriety was committed. A Director of Investigation with staff was appointed. Three reports were submitted on November 30, 1977; March 23, 1978 and June 23, 1978. Like Justice Grover, Justice Jaganmohan Reddy also stressed the "need for a permanent investigating agency to serve the Commission of Inquiry." He suggested an alternative, "a separate wing be added or attached to the investigating agency with permanent staff for conducting investigation to assist the Inquiry Commissions." He also opined against inquiries by Commissions once criminal proceedings had begun.

The Commission of Inquiry on Maruti Affairs, set up on May 30, 1977, consisted of a sitting Judge of the Supreme Court, Justice A. C. Gupta. The core issue was whether "undue favour" was shown to the three Maruti concerns floated and run by Sanjay Gandhi. The matters for inquiry were clearly specified. The report submitted on May 31, 1979 is a model of brevity, impartiality, and thoroughness. A large number of witnesses were examined and a mass of documents perused by the Commission.

Of a fundamentally different kind was the inquiry conducted in 1979 by Justice C. A Vaidyalingam, a retired Judge of the Supreme Court, into charges against the families of Prime Minister Morarji Desai and Home Minister Charan Singh. He was not appointed as Commission under the Act of 1952 but styled himself a "Special Judge." His authority, such as it was, derived from the two letters to him dated April 27 and May 2, 1979 by the Union Home Minister, H. M. Patel. His remit was "to go through the debate on the motion adopted in the Rajya Sabha on August 10, 1978 and advise the Government whether any *prima facie* case in respect of any of the charges referred to in the debate which pertain to the period after the present Government took office is established against the family members of the Prime Minister and those of the then Home Minister, Charan Singh, so as to justify a formal inquiry under the Commissions of Inquiry Act." None of the MPs who levelled charges during the debate assisted the inquiry despite "repeated requests." No one paid any attention to the Report, dated January 25, 1980, on its publication, either. It was a wholly irregular and futile exercise.

The '80s saw Commissions of Inquiry completely discredited as a credible mechanism for accountability. It was all over in a period of five years. It began on February 17, 1982 with the appointment of the Kudal Commission to inquire into "the working and activities, including publications and sources and misuse of funds" of four named Gandhian bodies including the Gandhi Peace Foundation. It was headed by Justice P.D. Kudal who had a long and controversial record as a Congress politician before his appointment as Judge of the Rajasthan High Court.

Justice Ranganath Misra's conduct of the Commission of Inquiry into the Delhi riots in 1984 added to the disillusionment.[25]

The political inquiry was not an altogether new phenomenon, though a sitting Judge of the Supreme Court, Justice K. K Mathew, was appointed as Commission of Inquiry on February 10, 1975 to inquire into the explosions at Samastipur on January 2, 1975 which resulted in the death of the Union Minister, L. N. Mishra. He declined to answer the main query as to "the facts and circumstances pertaining to the explosion." But he went out of his way to devote a whole Chapter (V) on "the extent of the right to dissent in our democracy." It was a thinly veiled attack on Jayaprakash Narayan and the movement he had launched in Bihar against corruption. (The Chapter ended with a recommendation for the establishment of a Lok Pal.)

Justice Mathew's appointment as Chairman of the Second Press Commission and the Law Commission. His Report as Commission of Inquiry on the Chandigarh question, under the Punjab Accord of July 24, 1985, did much to wreck the accord.

Justice M. P. Thakkar was a sitting Judge of the Supreme Court when he was asked to conduct an inquiry into Mrs. Indira Gandhi's assassination. The Commission of Inquiry was formally constituted on November 20, 1984. The report was published in 1989 after extracts from it appeared in the Press.

Justice Thakkar simply abdicated his task and refused to hold an inquiry. Having done that, he proceeded to do something worse — he aired freely, wild suspicions and asked the Special Investigation Team to chase them. This is what he said: "The Commission cannot itself hold an inquiry into the facts and circumstances of the matter which will be more in the nature of a trial." His own "observations" were "made on the basis of the material gathered in the course of the investigative exercise which precedes an inquiry proper and not on the basis of an inquiry." This was so far the simple reason why he had declined to hold an inquiry. Thakkar asserted categorically that "this report is based on the pre-inquiry investigative exercise and not an inquiry under Section 8 B of the Commission of Inquiry Act, which is neither feasible nor practicable. The rest has to be done by the investigative agency." All the same, he freely displayed some "needles of suspicion."

The rest was accomplished by Justice Thakkar and another sitting Judge of the Supreme Court, Justice S. Natarajan, as Commission of Inquiry on the engagement of the Fairfax Group Inc. in the United States by the Finance Ministry. It was appointed on April 6, 1987 and the report was submitted on November 30, 1987. It rushed to examine Bhure Lal, Director of Enforcement, on May 5 even before it had acquired a staff (May 7), its offices (May 25), or its counsel (June 3). It "began functioning," the Report records, on June 4. Bhure Lal was not given time to engage any counsel. His examination was violative of Sections 8 B and 8 C of the Act. There were other violations of the law.

The Thakkar-Natarajan Report was a blatantly political document. On December 14, 1987, V. P Singh, former Union Finance Minister, revealed in the Rajya Sabha how these judges were selected for appointment on the Commission. A Union Minister, P. Shiv Shankar, brought along a list of the desirables to the office of Prime Minister Rajiv Gandhi out of which the two Judges were selected. Well before that, public disenchantment with Commissions of Inquiry was complete. When the Bofors Scandal broke out in 1987, hardly anyone demanded the setting up of a Commission of Inquiry. The demand was for a Joint Committee of Parliament (JPC).

The Government and the Opposition could not agree neither on its terms of reference nor its powers. In consequence, the opposition declined to participate in the JPC that was set up by the motion adopted by the Lok Sabha on August 6 and by the Rajya Sabha on August 12, 1987. The JPC's Report was presented to both Houses of Parliament on

April 26, 1988. It was a command performance. It rejected all the charges against the government as well as Bofors and was exposed to increasing ridicule with the publication of each installment of the Bofors papers in *The Hindu*, shortly thereafter.

Far more successful was the Joint Committee to enquire into Irregularities in Securities and Banking Transactions set up by a resolution of the Lok Sabha on August 6, 1992 and the Rajya Sabha the next day. To no small extent the success was due to the personality of its Chairman, Ram Niwas Mirdha. The report, submitted on December 11, 1993, necessarily represented a compromise arrived at among the JPC's thirty members.

In varying degrees of severity, four Union Ministers, several senior officers and a number of public sector undertakings were criticised. The Committee's warning of the consequences "if a system be devoid of the moral quotient" was widely noted. It appeared all too clearly from the Action Taken Report (ATR), which the government submitted to Parliament on July 25, 1994, that it had not accepted the JPC's recommendation in several key areas. Revised paragraphs of the ATR were submitted by the government in December 1994 in order to silence criticism.

The JPC was in truth a retrograde move. The Commissions of Inquiry Act, 1952 is modelled on a British statute, the Tribunals of Inquiry (Evidence) Act, 1921, which was subjected to a careful review by the Royal Commission on Tribunals of Inquiry (1966) headed by Lord Justice Salmon (Cmnd. 3121; HMSO, London). The Commission noted that from the middle of the 17th century until 1921, the norm was inquiry by a Select Parliamentary Committee and occasionally by a Commission of Inquiry.

In 1912 in the UK, there occurred what became known as the Marconi Scandal involving several including Lloyd George and Rufus Isaacs. A select committee of fourteen members, excluding the Chairman, was appointed "to investigate those rumours." It split along party lines in 1913; so did the House of Commons. When, in 1921, grave charges were made against officials of the Ministry of Munitions, Parliament enacted the Act of 1921.

By 1966, there had been four major inquiries in post-war Britain of which three were under the Act — the Lynskey Tribunal (1948), the Parker Tribunal (1957) on improper disclosure of information on the bank rate, and the Radcliffe Tribunal (1962) on a spy scare. The

Denning Inquiry (1963) into the Profumo affair was not set up under the Act nor was the recent Scott Inquiry on arms to Iraq. There had been considerable criticism of the damage to reputations of individuals by the proceedings of the Tribunals.

The Royal Commission said:

> "We recommend that no Government in the future should ever in any circumstances whatsoever set up a Tribunal of the type adopted in the Profumo case to investigate any matter causing nation-wide public concern. For the reasons we have stated, we are satisfied that such a method of inquiry is inferior to, and certainly no acceptable substitute for, an inquiry under the Act of 1921....
>
> "We are strongly of the opinion that the inquisitorial machinery set up under the Act of 1921 should never be used for matters of local or minor public importance but always be confined to matters of vital public importance concerning which there is something in the nature of a nation-wide crisis of confidence. In such cases we consider that no other method of investigation would be adequate." (Para 27 of the Report, p.16).

Its observations on the essentially inquisitorial nature of the Tribunal's work are noteworthy. "The Tribunal directs the inquiry and the witnesses are necessarily the Tribunal's witness. There is no plaintiff or defendant, no prosecutor or accused; there are no pleadings defining issues to be tried, no charges, indictments, or depositions. The inquiry may take a fresh turn at any moment. It is, therefore, difficult for persons involved to know in advance of the hearing what allegations may be made against them." (Para 30; p. 17).

The Commission propounded safeguards which are essentially the same as those in Sections 8B and 8C of the Act of 1952. One point of difference deserves to be noted. The person summoned as witness "should have the opportunity of being examined by his own solicitor or counsel and of stating his case in public at the inquiry" (Para 32; p. 18). He should have the right "in the first instance" of being examined by his own counsel before he is examined or cross-examined by others (Para 57; p.24). Also, immediately after the opening speech by counsel for the Tribunal, counsel for the witnesses should be permitted to make brief speeches giving their version to the Tribunal and thus to the public.

Section 1 of the Act of 1921 permits appointment of a Tribunal only in pursuance of a resolution by both Houses of Parliament "for inquiring into a definite matter described in the Resolution as of urgent public importance." The Royal Commission opined that no Tribunal should be set up to probe into "a nebulous mass of vague and unspecified rumours."

The terms of reference of British Tribunals are far less precise than those of the Indian Commissions. The Lynskey Tribunal was appointed "for inquiring into a definite matter of urgent public importance, i.e. whether there is any justification for allegations that payments, rewards or other considerations have been sought, offered, promised, made or received by or to Ministers of the Crown or other public servants in connection with licences or permissions required under any enactment, regulation or order or in connection with the withdrawal of any prosecution and, if so, in what circumstances the transactions took place and what persons were involved therein."

Among the questions it considered was "whether there were allegations of the nature set out in our appointment." In other words, the Tribunal itself ascertained and defined the allegations and proceeded to consider them. This is in glaring contrast to Indian Commissions which are provided precise charges as if they are trial courts.

The Lynskey Report said:

"The first question we had to decide was one of procedure. A Tribunal appointed under the Act of 1921 is itself responsible for the collection of evidence, taking statements from witnesses, presenting their evidence then resting its accuracy and finally finding the facts. In a simple case it might be convenient for the Tribunal itself to carry out these responsibilities, but where there are a number of transactions to be investigated it would not merely be inconvenient but physically impossible within a reasonable time for the Tribunal to undertake these tasks.

"The services of the Treasury Solicitor, Sir Thomas Barnes, G.C.B., C.B.E., and his staff were placed at our disposal. We also had the assistance of Superintendent A. J. Thorp and other officers of the Metropolitan Police. The Treasury Solicitor with the assistance of the police interviewed all persons whom they thought might be able to give useful information to the Tribunal, and statements were taken from them. These statements were then placed before us and we directed what further inquiries should be made and eventually decided which witness should be called to give evidence before us."(Cmnd. 7616; HMSO, London; p. 1.)

The Radcliffe Tribunal was asked to inquire into possible breaches of security as well as allegations that the First Lord of the Admiralty and his Service Chiefs knew of a spy other than the one who was detected and "any other allegations which have been or may be brought to their attention, reflecting similarly on the honour and integrity" of ministers and civil servants. The report records that in order to find out "what was being said," the Tribunal drew on "Parliamentary criticism and press criticism." (Cmnd. 200q; HMSO, London). This is why the Press accused Prime Minister Harold Macmillan of launching a witch hunt against it. Every newspaper report on the matter was scanned. Much of the Press criticism was exposed to be false. The leading newspapers were represented by a counsel before the Tribunal.

Apply this to allegations of misconduct against ministers in India, and the limitations of the Commissions of Inquiry become obvious. They are self-imposed since Section 3 of the Indian Act of 1952 is not much different from Section 1 of the British Act of 1921. The Das Commission set a wrong precedent. Justice J. R. Mudholkar opined in his Report on the U.P. Ministers that "the conduct of an unnamed person cannot lawfully be inquired into." (p. 281 of the Report).

The Supreme Court ruled in the case of the Bihar Ministers that "if the charges were vague or speculative suggesting a fishing expedition we would have paused to consider whether such an inquiry should be allowed to proceed." These remarks are clearly obiter.[26]

In the *State of Madhya Pradesh* vs. *Arjun Singh & Ors.* {(1993) 1 SCC 51 at p. 54; (para 8)}, the Court said that the State Government was free to appoint any Commission of Inquiry after "applying its mind to any fresh or further material placed before it" and added: "Such formation of opinion depends on the subjective satisfaction of an appropriate Government but should be based on an objective or real material and not merely on some vague allegations or hearsay evidence or to make fishing inquiry." These too were, in the context, obiter. The Court has had no occasion yet to consider fully the model on which the Act of 1952 is based nor the manner in which it has worked. Commissions of Inquiry in India need to be set firmly on the track of inquisitorial work if they are to perform their tasks properly.

The Commissions of Inquiry Act, 1952 was reviewed by the Law Commission in its 24th Report submitted on December 26, 1962. It did not deal with the issues that have arisen recently. A Joint Committee of Parliament reported on November 9, 1970 on the Commissions of Inquiry (Amendment) Bill, 1969 which was enacted in 1971. The Committee strongly opined against leaving it to the Government to discontinue a Commission "before it has completed its task " (Para 14).

Suggestions

In the light of the foregoing, it is suggested that:

(1) There should be a comprehensive review of the Commissions of Inquiry Act, 1952 in the light of experience gained since its enactment. This review should be undertaken by a Committee that commands public confidence and it should particularly consider the abuse of the Act by governments and also its violation by the Commissions of Inquiry.

(2) No Commission or Committee of Inquiry should be appointed except with statutory sanction. The S. K. Das, Mudholkar and Vaidyalingam inquiries were highly irregular.

(3) A Committee of Parliament, other than those established under the Rules of Procedure of each of its Houses, such as the Public Accounts Committee, is ill-suited to undertake inquiries of the kind undertaken by the Commissions of Inquiry, e.g., the JPCs on Bofors or Securities and Banking transactions.

While in Britain, the Ministers, Lloyd George and his colleagues, were grilled by the select committee, the Indian JPC cannot summon ministers and is hopelessly dependent on the Speaker under the Rules of Procedure of the Lok Sabha. He appoints its Chairman (Rule 258), determines disputes as to the relevance of a witness or a document (Rule 270) and on "Procedure or otherwise." He can also issue directions to regulate the procedure and organise the committee's work (Rule 283). A Parliamentary Committee is intrinsically susceptible to political influence.

(4) There is now a new "culture of appointments" as reflected in the Press Council Act, 1978 and all the four Lok Pal Bills. The Government no longer has the sole discretion on appointments of persons in high judicial or quasi-judicial positions. The Supreme Court only upheld the Special Courts Bill, 1978 when the Government

agreed to its suggestion that the presiding Judge would be a sitting Judge of a High Court and he would be appointed with the concurrence of the Chief Justice of India [In re: the Special Courts Bill, 1978; (1979) 1 SCC 380].

It is of vital importance that suitable amendments should be made to Section 3 (2) of the Act and the Government's unfettered power of appointment of members of a Commission of Inquiry be curtailed by requiring consultation with the Leaders of the Opposition in both the Houses of Parliament, their presiding officers and the concurrence of the Chief Justice of India.

(5) Likewise, the unfettered power of refusal to appoint a Commission of Inquiry should be abolished. It is highly desirable that one-third members of the legislature should have the power to move for the establishment of an enquiry, on the lines of Article 44 of Germany's Basic Law. It is necessary to assuage public concern once there is a "crisis of confidence", quite regardless of the existence of a *prima facie* case, as is the practice in Britain demonstrated, most notably in the Radcliffe inquiry.

The solution suggested, tentatively, is to allow executive and legislature to have their way in the decision to appoint Commissions. Neither is likely to abuse the power since the composition of the Commission will be subject to the concurrence of the Chief Justice of India, besides other consultative checks.

(6) There should be a separate, independent investigation agency to serve the Commissions of Inquiry, the Lok Pal and the Lok Ayukts.

(7) The inquisitorial character of Commission of Inquiry should be restored.

(8) Justice J. R. Mudholkar suggested in his Report on the United Front Ministers that the representation of the People Act, 1951 should be amended to disqualify from candidature *inter alia* anyone found guilty of corruption and the like by a Commission of Inquiry. Such a provision exists in Section 24 F of the Jammu and Kashmir Representation of the People Act, 1957. However such a provision should be inserted in election law only if the Act of 1952 is so amended as to render abuse of its provisions by the Government and arbitrariness by Commissions of Inquiry well nigh impossible.

(9) Sections 8 B and 8 C of the Commissions of Inquiry Act, 1952, should be recast in the light of the observations in the Salmon Report.

(10) The two institutions, Lok Pal and Commission of Inquiry, should be so meshed together, apart from a common investigative staff, that the Lok Pal could *suo moto* set in motion procedures for the establishment of a Commission of Inquiry if a public scandal has surfaced, e.g., the Bailadila, the Bihar fodder scam and the Orissa party funds scandals.

(11) The Centre's right to appoint Commissions of Inquiry against Chief Ministers was challenged by Mr. M. Karunanidhi in 1971[23](vide the writer's, Ministers' Misconduct, pp. 392-394 for the text of Mr. Karunanidhi's letter of December 14, 1972 to Prime Minister Indira Gandhi) and by Mr. Devraj Urs in 1977. The constitutional position is not free from doubt. Entry 45 in the Concurrent List in the Seventh Schedule to the Constitution empowers both the Union and the States to legislate on "Inquiries and statistics for the purposes of any of the matters specified in List II or List III." It is a concurrent power. Justice Kailasam, in his dissenting judgement, opined that Entry 45 should not be construed to give the Union power to appoint Commissions of Inquiry against Chief Ministers. It militates against the federal principle, he ruled. The best course is to amend the Act to bar the Union from instituting such inquiries unless the conduct of the State Ministers has been of such a magnitude as to make the scandal a matter of national or inter-State concern, e.g. the fodder scam in Bihar. This proviso should be written into the Act in clear terms. Certainly, the practice of the Centre receiving memoranda of charges against Chief Ministers, demanding explanation from them and setting up a Commission of Inquiry to probe into them is violative of the federal principle and is liable to abuse; indeed, it has been abused and should be abandoned. The Lok Ayukts should deal with the charges and, in any case, one-third members of the State Assembly should be able to have a Commission of Inquiry set up.

The Sarkaria Report noted (page 65; para 2. 22. 24 and 25) that one "startling result" from the Supreme Court's construction of Entry 45 in List III would be to empower the States also to appoint Commissions of Inquiry against Union Ministers. It, however, opined that the potentiality of abuse of the power "is no ground for amending the constitution." It suggested two safeguards against abuse of the power by the Union — a resolution passed by both Houses of Parliament and prior approval by the Inter-State Council set up under Article 263. These safeguards should be written into the Act, it said.

Neither safeguard is altogether satisfactory although both can serve as deterrents. The best course is to define in the Act, precisely enough, the gravity of the matter which can warrant a probe, while excluding it explicitly merely because memoranda have been submitted to the Union against Ministers in a State. It must be "a matter of national concern which has created a crisis of confidence."

(12) Finally, it is highly important to formulate guide lines for protecting the rights of the accused if a Commission of Inquiry and a trial concerning the same matter proceed simultaneously. The Madon Commission on the Bhiwandi riots (1970 - 72) was able to avoid any conflict by not compelling the accused to depose. Contrary to the impression in some minds, a trial should not prevent the setting up of a Commission of Inquiry. As Justice Y.V. Chandrachud observed in his Report of October 20, 1970, as Commission of Inquiry on the death of Deen Dayal Upadhyaya: "The scope of this inquiry is wider than the scope of the sessions trial. I must determine why the murder was committed — a question that has wider ramification than the question before the session court; namely, whether the accused before it were guilty... I can conduct a probe into the real truth."

James Hamilton, Assistant Chief Counsel to Senator Sam Ervin's Committee on the Watergate affair recorded in his book *The Power to Probe* that Senator Ervin believed that "exposing the true nature of the scandal to the country was even more crucial than convicting a few high administration officials for their crimes."[27]

Justice K. K. Mathew opined to the contrary and in error in his Report on the death of Mr. L. N. Mishra as a result of the explosion in Samastipur in 1975. He refused to probe into the circumstances of the death on the ground that a trial was in progress.

One fundamental consideration must be borne in mind as it concerns the very nature of such inquiries. They are set up in the belief that their findings will form public opinion and lead to action. In his definitive work *Trial By Tribunal*, Prof. G.W. Keeton observed that "the function of this fact-finding organisation was found increasingly to establish what the facts are, and to leave the final verdict on the propriety of what has been done to public opinion." This essential character of Commissions of Inquiry should be retained. The follow up to their Reports should be left the Lok Pal or Lok Ayukt.

Notes & References

1. *The Times*, October 15, 1976.
2. Vide Second Report of the National Police Commission, Government of India, August 1979, para 15-40, p.30.
3. Vide their essay 'The Police: Independence and Accountability' in Jeffrey Jowell and Dawn Oliver, *The Changing Constitution*, Oxford University Press, Third Edition, 1994, p. 295.
4. Constituent Assembly Debates, Vol. 7, pp. 1187.
5. Salil Kumar Nag, *Evolution of Parliamentary Privileges in India till 1947*, Sterling, 1978, p. 212.
6. Vide G. Rudrayya Chowdari, *Prakasam: A Political Study*, Orient Longman, 1971, pp. 158-86 on the Congress High Command's treatment of T. Prakasam's acceptance of purses of money presented to him and Durga Das (ed.), *Sardar Patel's Correspondence* 1945-50, Navajivan Publishing House, Ahmedabad, Vol. 2, pp. 243-50.
7. See Durga Das (ed.) (No. 6 above) Vol. 9, p.51. vide pp. 512-520 for the text of a draft unsigned report to the Congress President on the scandal.
8. *Ibid*, p. 51.
9. A. G. Noorani, *Ministers' Misconduct*, Vikas, 1973, p.44.
10. See A. D. Gorwala, 'Report on Public Administration,' *Planning Commission*, pp. 12-27.
11. *Ibid*, p.16.
12. 'Mundhra Inquiry: The Full Story', *Free Press Journal*, Bombay, 1958.
13. *Ibid*, p.80.
14. Lok Sabha Debates, Vol. 18, April 25 to May 7 1963, 4th Session, 3rd Series, col, 14211.
15. S. Pratap Singh vs. State of Punjab, A.I.R. 1964, Supreme Court 72.
16. 'Report of the Commission of Inquiry', New Delhi, June 11, 1964 p. 18.
17. *Ibid*, p. 12.
18. *Ibid*, p. 285.
19. 'Report of the Committee on Prevention of Corruption,' Government of India, Ministry of Home Affairs, 1964, pp. 101-102.
20. Ibid, pp. 102-103.
21. P. K. Kunju vs State of Kerala & Ors. A.I.R. 1970 Kerala 252, for details of other such commissions, see A. G. Noorani, *Ministers' Misconduct* (No. 9 above), Ch. 7 on Azhimathi in Kerala.

22. *Report of the Commission of Inquiry into the allegations against certain former Ministers of Punjab*; Mr Justice D. S. Dave, Mr. Justice
L. N. Chhangani, New Delhi; pp. 184-185. This report was submitted on April 26, 1975. Another followed on September 30, 1975.
23. Smt. Indira Gandhi vs. Shri S.C. Shah, ILR(1980) 1 Delhi 552. Vide Kiran Bedi vs. Committee of Inquiry (1989) 1 SCC 494 for an authoritative and detailed exposition of the law on the subject.
24. State of Karnataka vs. Union of India (1977). Of the seven members of the Bench, Justice P. S Kailasam alone held 4 Supreme Court cases 608, that it was not open to the Centre to appoint a Commission of Inquiry against a Minister in a State Government. He raised points on the federal aspect which deserve closer examination than they have received.
25. For detailed analyses, see A. G. Noorani, *Indian Affairs: The Constitutional Dimension*, Konark, 1990, pp. 338-353 and 362 - 366.
26. K.B. Sahay & Ors. vs. Commission of Inquiry & Ors., A.I.R. 1969, S.C. 258.
27. James Hamilton, *The Power to Probe*, Random House, New York, 1976, p. 129.

10
Prevention of Corruption
Towards Effective Enforcement

C.V. Narasimhan

Corruption in public life and services has grown to alarming proportions in recent years. It marks the performing style of all politicians in power, actively abetted by unscrupulous businessmen and aided by acquiescent bureaucrats. It is presently experienced by all sections of the people. *Mamool* payments are extorted by most of the government functionaries in the field even for discharging their normal duties and providing services to which the public are legitimately entitled. In public perception, every government department now seems to function as a conduit for the regular upward flow of bribe money to the top political levels.

At the time of Independence in 1947, the country inherited a power-oriented administrative system left by the British Raj. The people at large were used to a *maa-baap* government on whose benevolence they depended for their existence and progress in any sphere of activity. That the government in present times is actually an instrument of their own creation through the Constitution is not conceptually perceived by the people. Since their overall attitude to the government has remained the same as it was during the British Raj, it has become natural and easy for the elected representatives after Independence to play a similar role as the British administrators did and make capital out of the system.

Classification of Anti-Corruption Measures

Measures for tackling the problem of corruption may be broadly classified under three heads: (i) preventive, (ii) punitive and (iii) promotional. Preventive measures will include electoral reforms and administrative reforms which would render the transaction of all government business more transparent and accountable to the people. Punitive measures will relate to laws, rules and the mechanism for effective investigation, court trial, departmental disciplinary action and other means to deter the corrupt functionaries. Promotional measures will cover encouragement of value-based politics, inculcation of moral and ethical principles among the younger generation in schools and colleges and the build-up of a kind of social ostracisation of corrupt people by the society. This paper primarily deals with the punitive aspect in some detail.

Prevention of Corruption Act: MPs and MLAs Not Covered

A special law to deal with corruption was first enacted in 1947 in the form of Prevention of Corruption Act. It defined certain categories of public functionaries as 'Public Servants' under the Act, and spelt out the punishment for different acts of bribery and corruption by such public servants. All personnel in service under the Central Government and the State Governments, all employees of public sector undertakings under these Governments, all ministers in the Government at the Centre and in the States, all judges and magistrates and other judicial officers and all employees of municipalities and corporations and other statutory civic bodies came under the definition of 'public servant' under this Act. It was comprehensively amended in 1988 to include some more public functionaries under the definition of 'public servant' for the purpose of the Act. For example, all employees of universities were brought under the purview of this Act in 1988. However, a matter of great significance is that while ministers fall under the definition of public servant as per the Act, MPs and MLAs do not unless they happen to hold an office or occupy a position in government and get remunerated for it. In other words, the people's representatives, viz. MPs and MLAs as such do not come under the purview of the Prevention of Corruption Act, even in its amended form in 1988. This is a very significant omission. An attempt had been made earlier in 1972 to include MPs and MLAs in the definition of 'public servant' in the Indian Penal Code Amendment Bill 1972, but a Joint Committee of Parliament rejected the proposal.

Santhanam Committee

In the early years after Independence, the Government's keenness to root out corruption was reflected in several administrative measures that were taken to discipline the conduct of public servants and effectively monitor their performance by the hierarchical command structure in each department. The Santhanam Committee set up by Parliament in 1962 examined this matter and made a number of recommendations for strengthening the vigilance and anti-corruption machinery in the Government. In the late '50s and early '60s, the Delhi Special Police Establishment had successfully investigated some cases involving high functionaries. The Government dealt with the reports of these investigations promptly and effectively, and a climate was brought about which was conducive to the containment of corruption in all public services; but this did not last long.

Political Corruption

The late '60s and early '70s witnessed a qualitative change in the political life in the country. Politics emerged as an alluring avenue leading to positions of enormous power and patronage. Enforcement of regulatory measures in commerce and industry by the issue of a variety of permits, licences, certificates and so on at various stages and levels led to increased corruption all around, particularly at the political level where ministers could and did take decisions deliberately favouring or disfavouring parties for a consideration. The phenomenon of political corruption thus came into being. The electoral process also lent itself to manipulations by muscle power and money power and thereby enlarged the volume of political corruption.

Assumptions Behind the Existing Scheme of Anti-Corruption Measures

The existing scheme of anti-corruption work is based on three assumptions:
(i) Functionaries at the topmost level in the Government are sincere and keen on putting down corruption.
(ii) Supervisory officials in the administrative system at the middle and top levels will themselves be motivated by the status of their office to check corruption at the lower levels and at the cutting edge of the administration.
(iii) Special measures devised for the expeditious conduct of court trials and departmental proceedings against corrupt officials will ensure quick and severe punishment which would deter corruption.

The above assumptions were valid in the early years after Independence. The Santhanam Committee's Report further enlarged and strengthened the anti-corruption measures based only on these assumptions. Unfortunately, the recent decades have witnessed the collapse of all the three assumptions. Firstly, political corruption at the level of ministers has grown to monstrous proportions. No one believes that the leaders of any political party are sincere and keen in rooting out corruption. Secondly, when ministers themselves become corrupt, the senior officers in their departments are rendered weak and ineffective to check and put down corruption among the subordinate officers who have political linkage. A few officers of high integrity and strong commitment to the national good try to remain aloof from this quagmire of corruption and restrict and content themselves by merely being correct in what they personally do, record and advise in the files. They have no power to override or annul *mala fide* decisions taken at the minister's level despite the factually correct and administratively fair and just notings and advice recorded in the files. The prolonged continuance of such a state of affairs in the Government has resulted in a number of officers, even at senior levels, succumbing to the situation and joining the political game of moneymaking and sharing the spoils. Thus, the entire administrative structure in the country has been considerably weakened, and is unable to render efficient public service as far as the common people are concerned. Lastly, court convictions and punishments in departmental disciplinary proceedings in respect of corrupt officials have been relatively few, considering the wide spread of corruption as perceived by the people. Even these few convictions and punishments are badly delayed owing to procedural blocks and legal wrangles. The slow moving criminal justice system has ceased to have any deterrent effect on the potential bribe-takers. In this way, all the three earlier assumptions are no longer valid. Any effective mechanism for anti-corruption work in present times will, therefore, have to include new institutional measures which will draw their strength and support from the Constitution itself, either directly or indirectly.

Genesis of CBI

During the years of the Second World War (1939-45), the scope for corruption in the Central Government increased enormously with the handling of large contracts for construction works and supplies connected with defence. It was then that the Government of India set up, for the first time, a special investigating unit in the War Department to handle all inquiries relating to corruption. This unit expanded later as the Delhi Special Police Establishment (DSPE), and was given a statutory basis by the enactment of the Delhi Special Police Establishment Act of 1946. After Independence, it developed as a specialised investigating agency under the Central Government primarily to deal with allegations of corruption pertaining to Central Government employees and also be available for assisting the State Governments in the investigation of specific crimes which may have inter-state ramifications or some other special features which make it desirable that the investigations be done by a Central agency rather than the State Police. In its expanded form, the Delhi Special Police Establishment was named the Central Bureau of Investigation (CBI), and has been functioning as such from 1963 under the control of the Central Government.

Powers of CBI

CBI derives its investigating powers from the DSPE Act, and can exercise them on its own authority within the limits of Union Territories and Centrally-administered areas only. Even here, investigating powers are limited to the specific offences that are notified by the Central Government under Section 3 of the Act. Offences relating to bribery and corruption have been notified by the Central Government in this context. As and when the CBI is required to investigate a case of murder, dacoity, kidnapping, abduction or such other offences unconnected with bribery and corruption, a special notification is issued to enable the CBI do such investigations.

Under Section 5 of the DSPE Act, the Central Government may empower the CBI to investigate the notified offences even in the limits of any State, but such empowerment can be ordered only with the consent of the Government of that State. This legal stipulation arises from the fact that the DSPE Act creates a police agency, and 'police' is in the State List in the Seventh Schedule of the Constitution. Item 80 of the Union List, which permits the extension of the powers of the police in one State to another State, also prohibits such extension without the consent of the second State.

In the first few years after Independence, there was no practical difficulty in the functioning of the CBI within the limits of the States also, because the same political party was in power in the States as well as at the Centre. The situation changed when different political parties got into power in the States. Some of them started withdrawing the consent given by the earlier State Governments whenever they felt that an investigation taken up by the CBI was politically embarrassing or uncomfortable for them. Such situations have so far been defused by mutual understanding. But the CBI's status as an investigating agency within a State continues to be unstable and dependent on the State Government's mercy. This is a serious handicap in planning any nation-wide network of investigating units for anti-corruption inquiries.

Enactment of New Law to Give Nation-Wide Jurisdiction to CBI

The above difficulty can be overcome if the Central Government legislates a separate law to put the CBI on a statutory basis. In fact, the name 'Central Bureau of Investigation' figures in Item 8 of the Union List in the Seventh Schedule and, therefore, Parliament can enact a law separately for the CBI. The new law has to project the CBI as an investigating agency only and not a police agency, as otherwise it will be hit by Item 2 of the State List, which refers to 'police'. In fact, there is no need to project the CBI as a 'police unit'. It has no role or responsibility regarding maintenance of public order or peace, regulation of traffic or a host of such 'law and order' duties of the regular police. The CBI is solely concerned with *investigations* of specific cases assigned to it under law. Therefore, it would be sufficient if the new law spells out specifically the powers of arrest, search, seizure, summoning and examining witnesses which are presently available to the police when they investigate a cognizable case, and confers these powers on the CBI to facilitate their investigations. We have an example in the Customs Act which confers on customs officers the power to arrest, search and seize in certain circumstances related to smuggling. Likewise, a comprehensive CBI Act can take care of all the requirements of investigation work of the CBI. The subject of 'promotion and maintenance of integrity and efficiency in public services' does not figure as a specific item in any of the Lists in the Seventh Schedule. Parliament can, therefore, legislate the new CBI Act in exercise of its residuary powers under Article 248. An independent statutory basis for the CBI is very necessary for any effective anti-corruption scheme to cover the nation as a whole.

The Estimates Committee of the Fourth Lok Sabha in its 78th Report had observed that 'it is necessary to give a statutory basis to the CBI in order to place it on a sounder footing'. In the follow-up action, a draft CBI Bill was prepared in 1990, but no progress could be made because it impinged on Centre-State relations. The Estimates Committee of the Tenth Lok Sabha noticed this impasse and recommended strongly in its 13th Report (1991-92) that this legislation should be taken up without further delay. The deadlock on the Centre-State aspect of the matter can be resolved if, as recommended earlier in this paragraph, the CBI is projected as an investigating agency and not a police agency. This matter has to be pursued urgently in the interest of effective anti-corruption work.

Anti-Corruption Bureaux in States

While the CBI functions as the investigating agency for anti-corruption work in respect of matters to which the executive power of the Union extends, the States have their separate anti-corruption bureaux (ACB) for handling vigilance and anti-corruption work with regard to State matters. The CBI functions within the framework of the DSPE Act, but the State ACBs are regular police units and derive their powers of investigation from the Police Act only. However, in both cases, the investigating agency functions under the superintendence of the Central Government or the State Government concerned. While Section 2 of the DSPE Act enables the CBI to exercise the powers available to regular police officers while investigating any specific case, it also lays down that the exercise of such powers will be subject to any order which the Central Government may make in this matter.

Whenever there is public pressure for an enquiry into the misconduct of a minister, the Central or the State Government usually resorts to the Commission of Inquiry Act to set-up a Commission to inquire into specific allegations made against the minister. A Commission of Inquiry is normally headed by a Supreme Court or High Court judge (either serving or retired). Though its proceedings are conducted more or less in the manner of a court, it is only a fact-finding body and not a court of trial and, therefore, it does not have power to award any punishment to a person against whom an allegation may get *prima facie* established during the inquiry. It merely presents a report about the facts ascertained during the inquiry and it is for the government concerned to decide the further course of action. If a person is to be prosecuted on the basis of facts brought out by the Commission, the matter is referred to the CBI or the State ACB for a regular investigation. Once again the process of examining all the witnesses in detail is gone through by the investigating agency, and then the matter is put before a regular criminal court for trial. At the trial stage, witnesses are examined for the third time and only then is the stage reached for the awarding of specific punishment to the accused if found guilty. All this takes a very long time, diluting the thrust of the entire exercise. The effect of quickly awarding a severe punishment to the guilty person is not achieved. Since the same set of witnesses are subjected to examination by different bodies at different stages separated by long intervals of time, the accused persons invariably tend to exert their influence and power to pressurise the witnesses in a variety of ways and make them prevaricate while giving evidence in the final stage in the court. Thus, the course of law and justice is thwarted and ultimately nothing worthwhile is achieved.

Not a single CBI case involving ministers has ended in a firm conviction in the court during the last 40 years. There are instances where cases against ministers have been withdrawn by the Government even at the stage of court trial, solely on the basis of fresh exculpatory statements obtained from important prosecution witnesses by the accused ministers themselves and presented before the Government, pleading for the withdrawal of the case on the ground that the prosecution was false and politically motivated.

The Commissions of Inquiry Act does not envisage a permanent Commission of Inquiry in office. It merely enables the Central and State Governments to appoint such a Commission as and when required. The Act itself does not provide for a permanent body to function as the investigating arm of the Commission. Under Section 5A of the Act, the Commission usually secures the services of investigating officers from the CBI or the State Police for a short term of deputation to assist the Commission in identifying the relevant witnesses and getting their preliminary statements recorded before the Commission itself starts formally examining them in open judicial proceedings. These investigating officers have ultimately to get back to their parent agencies under the Central or State Government after the Commission's work is completed. This circumstance makes it difficult for them to function with complete independence and objectivity while making inquiries under the Commission. They are naturally inhibited by the prospect of victimisation on their return to the government fold, if their inquiries result in the exposure of misdeeds of a powerful person in the political establishment. This is an important factor which detracts from the ultimate quality of a Commission's inquiry when the accused happens to be a political VIP.

Scope for Extraneous Interference with Investigations

In the present scheme of things, the CBI or the State investigating agency functions under the total control of the Central or State government concerned. Therefore, in all cases investigated by the CBI or the State investigating agency, the Government concerned has full scope even at the stage of investigation to acquaint itself with the details of evidence as and when discovered by the investigating agency. This circumstance affords ample scope for the Government, which in reality means the ruling party, to interfere at the stage of investigation itself and thwart the course of truth and justice to the detriment of public interest. Cases against VIPs are specially prone to such interference. The Bofors case is a typical example.

Working procedures within the CBI provide for a considerable amount of preliminary scrutiny and assessment of any information or complaint received by the CBI before a case is registered for regular investigation. The level at which this decision is taken within the CBI is determined by the rank of the official against whom the information or complaint is received. For example, cases against gazetted officers will require scrutiny at the level of DIG. Cases against heads of departments will be decided at the level of the Joint Director or Director. By and large, in the 1950s and 1960s, the CBI enjoyed full powers for taking such decisions within the CBI itself. As a matter of convention, the Director of CBI used to keep the Prime Minister / Home Minister informed after the registration of the case, if it involved a very high-ranking officer in the Government or a political VIP. In later years, some restrictive procedures have been formally laid down by the Government in regard to registration of cases by the CBI. Presently, these restrictions require prior clearance from the Government before the CBI can take up any case for investigation against an officer of the rank of Joint Secretary to Government and above. All such restrictions seem to be based on the powers given to the Government under Section 2 of the DSPE Act.

The State ACBs are also bound by similar restrictive provisions which are more or less of the same pattern in all the States. In Tamil Nadu, the State Directorate of Vigilance and Anti-Corruption cannot take up any inquiry against an All India Services officer without prior permission from the Government. Further, the Directorate does not have authority to scrutinise any file in the Government Secretariat except through the Secretary to the Government who may call for and scrutinise the file himself in the first instance and then decide whether the Directorate may be permitted to see it.

These restrictive procedures at the Centre and in the States in regard to anti-corruption work are detrimental to prompt and proper verification of vigilance information against top-ranking functionaries in the Government. This is a big drawback in the existing system, and has to be set right. In its 13th Report (1991-92), the Estimates Committee of the Tenth Lok Sabha had strongly urged the Government to do away with these restrictive procedures in regard to anti-corruption inquiries.

CBI Investigations: A Status Report

A critical analysis of the annual reports of the CBI from 1972 to 1992 reveals the actual volume, nature and ultimate effect of CBI investigations. Some significant features are noted below:

Collection of Information

The number of CBI cases started on regular complaints received by the CBI are relatively small as may be seen from the following figures:

	1972	1992
(i) No. of complaints examined during the year	6,650	6,520
(ii) No. in item (i) which led to CBI cases of regular investigation	477	229

About 70% of the cases registered by the CBI are based on information collected by the CBI's own staff. Viewed against the growing power of corrupt elements in administration and their potential to cause serious harm to anyone who may attempt to expose

Prevention of Corruption

their misdeeds, the reluctance of the victims of corruption to come up with formal complaints to the CBI is understandable. The responsibility, therefore, lies on the CBI to take the initiative of activating its own intelligence units and collecting information pertaining to corruption. The same observations apply to the State ACBs.

Volume of Cases Handled and Action Recommended

The volume of new cases taken up by the CBI year after year has more or less remained at the same level. In fact, the figures for 1992 show a slight decrease compared to 1972. But the volume of cases whose investigation was completed during the year has gone down. A majority of cases investigated by the CBI result in departmental disciplinary proceedings only. Relatively lesser number of cases are chargesheeted in the court. The figures are as follows:

		1972	1992
(i)	No. of new cases registered during the year	1349	1231
(ii)	No. of cases investigated and finalised during the year (including old cases)	1790	1412
(iii)	No. of cases in item (ii) prosecuted in court	384	505
(iv)	No. of cases in item (ii) referred for departmental action	887	652

Results of Court Trials

Disposal of CBI cases in the court has also shown a decline. The percentage of convictions has come down to 69% in 1992 compared to 85% in 1972. At the end of 1992, there were 4,148 cases pending trial compared to 1,362 at the end of 1972. Among the 4,148 pending cases, as many as 3,000 have been pending for over four years and some for over 15 to 20 years.

The relevant figures are furnished below:

		1972	1992
(i)	No. of cases disposed of in court during the year	352	237
(ii)	No. in item (i) which ended in conviction	300	164

	1972	1992
(iii) No. in item (i) which ended in discharge/acquittal	52	73
(iv) Percentage of conviction in court	85.2	69.1
(v) No. of cases pending in court at the end of year	1,362	4,148

Result of Departmental Action

The number of supervisory officers at the middle and senior levels, i.e., gazetted officers who have been either convicted in the court or punished in departmental disciplinary action as a result of CBI cases, is very small, taking the country-wide spread of government personnel and the perceived extent of corruption among them. Even among the gazetted officers who have been punished in the departmental action, the number among them who have been given severe punishment like dismissal/removal/retirement from service is very small. Out of 547 gazetted officers who were departmentally punished in 1992, there were only 62 dismissals. The relevant figures are furnished below:

	1972	1992
(i) No. of public servants convicted in court	194	85
(ii) No. in item (i) who were of gazetted rank	15	44
(iii) No. of public servants punished in departmental action	806	798
(iv) No. of item (iii) who were of gazetted rank	150	547
(v) No. in item (iv) who were dismissed/removed/retired from services.	8	62

Disproportionate Assets of Public Servants

The common man's perception of a corrupt official is based on the visible assets acquired by the corrupt official disproportionate to his known source of income. While it is usually difficult to get evidence from the victims of corruption about the specific instances in which they had been forced to give bribe, it is relatively easier to secure evidence from third parties about the assets acquired by corrupt officials over a long period. Under Section 13 (1) (e) of the Prevention of Corruption Act, the very possession of unaccountable assets by a public servant is a substantive offence by itself, irrespective of the other specific offences of bribery which may or may not be proved against him.

A case of disproportionate assets, if properly investigated and established, is a strong weapon to deal with corrupt officials. The record of the CBI in handling cases of this kind is not very encouraging. The number of such cases taken up by the CBI is very small, and most of the cases finalised by it have resulted only in the departmental disciplinary proceedings. Convictions in court have been very few, and even among those convicted, gazetted officers are much less. Even in departmental proceedings the ultimate result is not encouraging. Out of the 27 gazetted officers punished in 1992, there were only two dismissals. The rest got away with minor punishments. The relevant figures are furnished below:

Cases of Disproportionate Assets

		1972	1992
(i)	No. of new cases registered during the year	89	57
(ii)	No. of gazetted officers involved in the item (i)	44	34
(iii)	No. of items investigated and finalised during the year (including old cases)	94	77
(iv)	No. in item(iii) which were prosecuted in court	11	24
(v)	No. in item (iii) which were referred for departmental action	58	42
(vi)	No. of cases disposed of in court	6	5
(vii)	No. in item (vi) which ended in conviction	5	2
(viii)	No. of gazetted officers involved in item (vii)	2	—
(ix)	No. of cases decided in departmental action	40	44
(x)	No. in item (ix) which resulted in punishment	28	24
(xi)	No. of gazetted officers involved in item(x)	9	27
(xii)	No. in item (xi) who were dismissed / removed / retired from service	1	2

Set-up of Vigilance Officers

A fundamental principle projected by the Santhanam Committee is that the primary responsibility for maintaining integrity and rectitude besides efficiency of a department of the government rests squarely on the head of the department. Any outside organisation like the CBI can function only as a supporting agency by conducting investigations in specific cases. The preventive aspect of anti-corruption work has to be borne, in a large measure, by the head of the department and his staff down the line. In fact, vigilance work should be viewed as an integral part of the responsibility of every supervisory officer at every level. In 1955, the Central Government introduced a scheme of having a Chief Vigilance Officer (CVO) at the top level in each department assisted by vigilance officers (VOs) down the line at middle levels to assist the head of the department in providing guidance and maintaining a constant drive for the effective handling of all corruption complaints and disciplinary proceedings arising from such complaints. They are also required to monitor the actual functioning of the department, particularly at its cutting edge, constantly review the working procedures and streamline them from time to time to eliminate the scope for practice of corruption and the consequent harassment of people who come to transact work with the department.

Central Vigilance Commission

On the Santhanam Committee's recommendation, a Central Vigilance Commission headed by the Central Vigilance Commissioner (CVC) was set up by the Central Government by an executive decision embodied in a Resolution in the Ministry of Home Affairs dated 11 February 1964. The powers and functions of the CVC, as detailed in the Resolution include the following:

(i) To undertake an inquiry into any transaction in which a public servant is alleged to have acted for an improper purpose, or
(ii) To cause an inquiry to be made into:
  (a) any complaint that a public servant had exercised his powers for improper or corrupt purposes,

(b) any complaint of corruption, misconduct, lack of integrity or other kinds of malpractices on the part of a public servant including members of the All India Services even if such members are for the time being serving in connection with the affairs of a State government.

(iii) To call for reports, returns and statements from all ministries, departments, or corporate Central undertakings so as to enable it to exercise general checks and supervision over the vigilance and anti-corruption work in the ministries, departments, undertakings.

(iv) To take over under its direct control, such complaints, information or cases as it may consider necessary for further action which may be either:

    (a)   to ask the CBI to register a regular case and investigate it, or
    (b)   to entrust the complaint, information or case for inquiry
        (1) to the CBI, or
        (2) to the ministry, department, or undertakings concerned.

Central Vigilance Commissioner — Terms of Appointment

The Resolution further provides that:

"1. The CVC —

"(a) will be appointed by the President by warrant under his hand and seal;

"(b) will not be removed or suspended from office except in the manner provided for the removal or suspension of the Chairman or a Member of the Union Public Services Commission;

"(c) will hold office for a term of six years or till he attains the age of 65, whichever is earlier; and

"(d) on ceasing to hold the office of the CVC, shall not accept any further employment under the Union or a State government or accept any political public office.

"2. The CVC will be attached to the Ministry of Home Affairs, but in the exercise of its powers and functions, it will not be subordinate to any ministry or department and will have the same measure of independence and autonomy as the Union Public Service Commission.

"3. The CVO in ministries and departments will be appointed in consultation with the CVC, and no person whose appointment as CVO is objected to by the CVC will be so appointed.

"4. The CVC will have the power to assess the work of the CVOs and VOs and the assessment will be recorded in the character rolls of the officers".

CVC's Present Role

The first CVC was a former Chief Justice of a High Court and, therefore, its work started with the required judicial independence and objectivity. Subsequent appointees have been drawn from the IAS, with the appointment being made just when the officer was about to superannuate at the top level in administration. In actual practice, the CVC's role is now confined to tendering advice to departments on the action to be taken on CBI reports in regard to gazetted officers. The CVC also advises on the reports drawn up by the inquiry officers on the conclusion of departmental disciplinary proceedings arising from corruption cases against gazetted officers. The CVC makes an overall review of the preventive work turned out by the CVOs and VOs in different departments and gives them necessary directions. Very rarely has the CVC given directions to the CBI for regular investigation of any sensational case which might have been slurred over otherwise.

Annual Report of the CVC

The Resolution also provides for submission of an annual report by the CVC to the Ministry of Home Affairs about its activity, drawing particular attention to any recommendation made by it which had not been accepted or acted upon. A copy of this report, together with a memorandum explaining the reasons for non-acceptance of any recommendation of the Commission, has to be laid by the Ministry of Home Affairs before each House of Parliament. In the actual working of the CVC, this provision has not had any significance because the CVC's annual reports have not drawn any significant interest or attention from the Members of Parliament.

Enactment of New Law for the CVC

A qualitative change in the impact of the CVC and the entire setup of CVOs can be brought about only when the CVC is set up statutorily with adequate provisions to ensure its functional independence and judicial orientation. The procedure for the appointment of the CVC may involve the Leader of the Opposition also on similar lines as adopted for the appointment of the Chairman and Members of the National Human Rights Commission. A person who is qualified for appointment as a Supreme Court judge alone shall be appointed CVC.

The new Act for the CVC should also provide for an investigating wing under the CVC's control, more or less on the lines provided for the National Human Rights Commission. The powers exercisable by the members of the investigating wing for making effective enquiries which will include searches, seizures and arrests should also be spelt out in detail separately in the same Act.

State Vigilance Commission

CVC should also be involved in the process of selection and appointment of the Director, CBI. Similar arrangements may be brought into being in the States also. Just as the Protection of Human Rights Act has provisions which enable the States to constitute State-level Human Rights Commissions with duties and responsibilities within the State, the new Central Vigilance Commission Act may also have provisions for the constitution of the State Vigilance Commission with a corresponding role for directing and supervising vigilance and anti-corruption work within the State. This will include monitoring the work of the State ACBs also on the same lines as proposed for the CVC in regard to the CBI.

Ombudsman

Public grievances arising from maladministration were sought to be redressed by an authority called Ombudsman which was first conceived in Sweden in 1809 as an autonomous, independent inquisitorial authority to inquire into complaints of transgression of law by administrative authority in the course of handling administrative affairs, illegality or delays in reaching decisions, discourtesy or rudeness, unfairness, bias, incompetence, high-handedness, mistakes, failure to respond, furnishing misleading statements, etc. Similar institutions of Ombudsman with some modifications regarding powers and responsibilities were established in Finland in 1819, Denmark in 1953, New Zealand in 1962, Norway in 1963, United Kingdom in 1966 and Australia in 1976.

Legislation for Lok Pal

On the recommendation of the Administrative Reforms Commission in 1966, a Lok Pal Bill was introduced in our Parliament in 1968-69 to set up an Ombudsman-type of body but it lapsed with the dissolution of the Lok Sabha. The Bill, in a revised form, was again introduced in 1977 but that also lapsed. The Bill was introduced for the third time in 1989 but even that has not taken shape.

Some States like Orissa, Maharashtra, Rajasthan, Bihar, Uttar Pradesh, Andhra Pradesh, Karnataka, Madhya Pradesh, Gujarat and Himachal Pradesh have statutorily set up inquiry authorities similar to Lok Pal to look into certain types of complaints of maladministration in the State, but all the enactments suffer from the same drawback viz., non-availability of a truly independent and unbiased investigating agency to aid the inquiry authority.

A New Lok Pal Bill

There has been a lot of talk lately of introducing a fresh Lok Pal Bill. A mere rehash of the old drafts of the Bill will not do to meet the needs of present times. The new Lok Pal Bill should include the following ideas, concepts and arrangements:

(i) The Lok Pal should be set up as a standing judicial body in the nature of an ombudsman at the Centre with responsibility for making inquiries into complaints of corruption and misconduct against all Central ministers (including the Prime Minister), Members of Parliament and top level bureaucrats in the Government.

(ii) The Lok Pal may be a multi-member body with all its members including the Chairman, being persons who are working or had worked or are qualified for appointment as judges of the Supreme Court.

(iii) The appointment of the Chairman and members of the Lok Pal shall be decided by the President in consultation with the Chief Justice of India, after obtaining the recommendations of a committee on the lines prescribed in Section 4 (1) of the Protection of Human Rights Act (1993) for the appointment of Chairperson and members of the National Human Rights Commission. The significance of this committee is that it includes the Leaders of Opposition in the Lok Sabha and the Rajya Sabha besides the Prime Minister. This will eliminate any possible political bias in the appointment process.

The Lok Pal shall be assisted by a permanent secretariat of its own, separately funded in the same manner as presently followed for the Comptroller and Auditor General of India.

Investigating Wing and Prosecuting Wing for Lok Pal

The Lok Pal shall be statutorily provided with an investigating wing and a prosecuting wing which will be filled with personnel, specially selected by the Chairman of the Lok Pal, with due regard to their background of impeccable honesty, professional efficiency and integrity. They may be drawn from the existing cadres of investigating agencies and prosecuting agencies at the Centre and in the States, but they shall be permanently seconded to the Lok Pal and shall not be required to return to their parent units while in service. Their pay and allowances shall be duly protected from any possible victimisation by *mala fide* administrative action in the government machinery at a later stage.

It shall be competent for the President, and the President alone, acting within his discretion and judgement, to examine the reports of inquiry by the Lok Pal and decide on the further course of action thereon, which may include:

(a) launching of prosecution in court against those found *prima facie* guilty of criminal offences, or
(b) debarment of those found guilty of any misconduct from standing for election to Parliament or State Assembly or any statutory body for any specified period as may be provided in the Lok Pal Act.

Prosecution for criminal charges which arise from the Lok Pal's report shall be directly launched and handled in court by the prosecuting wing of the Lok Pal only.

Viability of Separate Staff for Lok Pal and CVC

The proposal to have a separate investigating wing and prosecuting wing for the Lok Pal or CVC set-up raises the question whether it will be practicable to have investigators and prosecutors function within such a small closed system for their entire career. The answer may be found in the existing set-up of the CBI itself which has about 800 investigating officers and 200 prosecutors. About 75% of the CBI staff are drawn on deputation from the State police, and after the deputationists prove their mettle in CBI work, they are permanently absorbed in the CBI and get the normal career benefits within the CBI. Those who do not make the grade, are sent back to their parent State. This system has worked well in the CBI, and can be adopted for the staff of the Lok Pal or CVC also without difficulty. Even though their number may not be large, a suitable hierarchical career structure can be designed for them. They may also be made eligible for higher level posts in the Ministry of Law, as a kind of career facility. The scheme of having separate investigating and prosecuting staff permanently attached to the Lok Pal or CVC is viable and workable.

Integration of CVC and Lok Pal

The statutory arrangements proposed above envisage a Lok Pal to look after inquiries into corruption at high levels including the political executive, and a CVC to monitor vigilance and anti-corruption work done by the CBI and the set-up of VOs in all government departments. Since the essential and ultimate objective is the same for both, it would be best to integrate the two institutions and have a common legislation which would make the CVC a member of the Lok Pal itself and perform the tasks proposed for the CVC as above. A common secretariat, investigating wing and prosecuting wing can serve both, in the integrated set-up. This would facilitate better coordination and development of legal expertise in the long run.

Lok Pals in States

The State-level Lok Pals should be similarly set up statutorily in each State or for a group of States by Central legislation, with jurisdiction to inquire into complaints of corruption and misconduct against top-level bureaucrats in the State government and State ministers including chief ministers. Appointment of the State Lok Pals shall also be made by the President only. Procedural arrangements applicable to the Lok Pal shall, *mutatis mutandis*, apply to the State Lok Pals.

Commissions of Inquiry Act to Continue

In view of the proposed comprehensive set-up of the Lok Pal/CVC at the Centre and in the States as statutory bodies to deal with complaints of high-level corruption, there will be no need to have *ad hoc* commissions appointed under the Commissions of Inquiry Act to deal with the same matter. However, the Commissions of Inquiry Act may continue to remain on the statute book to facilitate appointment of special commissions to inquire into any matter of public importance not involving corruption e.g., air crash, train smash or collapse of a public building or river dam resulting in several deaths, etc. The investigating and prosecuting staff of the Lok Pal/CVC may be deputed to assist such Commissions of Inquiry as and when they are set up.

Monitoring of CBI Cases by the Supreme Court or High Courts

In recent years, the CBI has had to take up some cases on specific directions from a High Court or the Supreme Court and report the result of the investigation to the Court. Though the number of such cases is not large, all have been very sensational and have, therefore, required concentrated and continuous attention from the CBI for thorough and expeditious investigation. In the recent *Hawala* Case, the Supreme Court has been practically monitoring the progress of investigation from time to time. In fact, the Supreme Court has been doing the type of supervisory work, which, in the normal course, the Director of CBI can and should do if he was under no pressure, direct or indirect, from the political executive in the Government. While an odd case may get such attention from the Supreme Court once in a while, it would not be a healthy dispensation for the Supreme Court or High Courts to take on such a supervisory role at the stage of the investigation itself. Investigation proceeds on the basis of information as well as evidence. Courts are used to dealing with evidence but not information. Assessment of information and its follow-up is a matter for intimate executive supervision. It does not seem appropriate for regular courts of trial and appeal to get involved in this fieldwork. We have to look for some other arrangement for ensuring cleanliness of investigation in the midst of polluting politics.

Monitoring of CBI Cases by CVC

In the existing scheme of things, there is ample scope for politically motivated interference from the Government side at the stage of investigation, because the CBI is part and parcel of the Government establishment. The very appointment of the Director of CBI and all other personnel down the line, their career prospects and several other service benefits are all within the domain of the Government only. It is this circumstance that operates against the professional independence of the CBI. This handicap has to be remedied. However, we cannot possibly conceive of the entire CBI organisation functioning autonomously outside the Government and being answerable only to courts, because such an arrangement might encourage excesses by the CBI field staff down the line. Further, the Government has its own primary responsibility to ensure honesty and integrity of its personnel, and it requires an organisation like the CBI under its own control and direction to handle the normal anti-corruption work for which the Government is responsible. The intervention of an outside institution like the Lok Pal or CVC is called for only in regard to high-level corruption or other sensitive cases which are prone to draw political interference. For normal anti-corruption work, we must have the existing CBI set-up continue under the Government's administrative control, at the same time eliminating the scope for Government interference with the professional independence of the CBI to conduct its investigations. One possible arrangement for this purpose could be to empower the proposed judicially oriented CVC to monitor the progress of the CBI investigations on such selective basis as it may decide, to ensure thoroughness and correctness of the investigations. The CVC may prescribe its own norms for identifying the types of cases which require such monitoring. The law relating to the Lok Pal or CVC set-up may also provide for any person to make an application to the CVC for including any particular case in the monitoring list, even though it may not fall within the norms laid down by the CVC. The point is whether such a case should be decided by the public interest involved and the scope for extraneous interference with the course of investigation. Since the proposed CVC will be made up of persons who are either sitting or retired or qualified to be judges of the Supreme Court, this arrangement would obviate the need for the Supreme Court's interference in such cases in future.

Prior Sanction for Prosecution

There are provisions in some laws which stipulate that the prosecution of a public servant in a court for an alleged offence committed by him, while acting or purporting to act in the discharge of his official duty, requires prior sanction from certain specified authorities. Under Section 197 Cr.P.C., a public servant, not removable from office except with the sanction of the Central or State Government, cannot be prosecuted for such an offence without prior sanction from the Central Government or the State Government concerned. Under Section 137 of the Customs Act, prior sanction from the Central Government will be required for the prosecution of any Customs officer of and above the rank of Assistant Collector of Customs for any alleged offence committed by the officer under the Act. In the case of officers below the rank of Assistant Collector of Customs, prior sanction for prosecution has to be sought from the Collector of Customs.

Under Section 19 of the Prevention of Corruption Act, prosecution of a public servant for an alleged offence under the Act requires previous sanction from the authority competent to remove him from office. If this requires the sanction of the Central or State Government, it has to be accorded under Section 19 by the concerned Government.

In the present scheme of things, if the CBI seeks sanction from the Central Government for prosecution under the Prevention of Corruption Act, the CBI report is routed through the Central Vigilance Commission (CVC) which advises whether it may be accorded or not. In most cases, the CVC's advice is accepted, but there have been instances where the Government had declined to accord sanction. Such decisions of the Government are based on their perception and appreciation of the evidence brought up by the CBI.

In very sensitive cases of high-level corruption involving political VIPs, the issue of sanction for prosecution assumes political overtones. The existing scheme of things gives scope for *mala fide* exercise of discretion and judgement in either sanctioning or not sanctioning prosecution.

The rationale behind such provisions in law which stipulate previous sanction for prosecution is that the officials in enforcement agencies require to be protected against malicious or vexatious prosecution in court which may be deliberately launched by professional criminals to wreak vengeance against them. Honest and upright officials have to be effectively protected against such malicious prosecutions under the Prevention of Corruption Act also, because it is not uncommon that false allegations are made and evidence is cooked up by dishonest and unscrupulous elements in the society whose activities are severely curtailed by such officers. While appreciating the need for such a protective clause in the Prevention of Corruption Act, we should also guard against the same clause being availed of by a corrupt executive in the Government to thwart the prosecution of a corrupt and favourite subordinate official. It is, therefore, necessary to have a statutory arrangement spelt out in the Prevention of Corruption Act itself to ensure that:

(i) the competent authority makes the order sanctioning or refusing to sanction prosecution, within a specified time limit, say one month, and

(ii) if the competent authority refuses to sanction prosecution, it shall state the reasons for refusal which shall be embodied in the order of refusal and it shall be open to the investigating agency to appeal against the order of refusal of the component authority to the Lok Pal whose decision thereon shall be final and binding on the Government concerned. Appropriate amendments to the Prevention of Corruption Act for this purpose have to be drafted along with the proposed legislation for the Lok Pal set-up which will include the Central Vigilance Commission.

Confiscation of Property Acquired through Corrupt Means

Provisions exist in the Criminal Law Amendment Ordinance of 1944 for attaching the properties acquired by a corrupt public servant when an alleged offence under the Prevention of Corruption Act committed by him is under investigation. This Ordinance continues to be law under Article 372 of the Constitution. The temporary attachment which can be ordered by the competent court under this Ordinance at the stage of investigation can be followed up by an order of forfeiture of the property to the Government if and when the accused person is convicted of the offence in the court. Under the existing provisions, this forfeiture is limited to the property procured by the convicted person by means of the offence for which he stands convicted. If the prosecution is for the offence of possession of *disproportionate* assets which is punishable under Section 13 (i) (e) of the Prevention of Corruption Act, the final order of forfeiture at the time of conviction can cover all the properties which are included in the disproportionate part of his assets. It would serve the cause of anti-corruption work better if the law is substantially amplified to cover properties acquired by a corrupt public servant in the names of his family members and relatives also. It is well-known that habitual corruption at high level results in acquisition of *benami* (proxy) property by the corrupt person in the names of others under his control. The Smugglers and Foreign Exchange Manipulators (Forfeiture of Property) Act of 1976 provides for an procedure for the investigation and ultimate confiscation of properties acquired by smugglers and foreign exchange racketeers not only in their own names but also in the names of their 'relatives' as elaborately defined in the Act. The Criminal Law Amendment Ordinance of 1944 may now be replaced by a more comprehensive Act to deal with properties acquired by public servants by corrupt or illegal means not only in their own names but also in the names of their relatives and others under their control. The new law may follow the pattern of the Smugglers and Foreign Exchange Manipulators (Forfeiture of Property) Act, 1976.

Comprehensive Assessment of Corruption Intelligence

Effective anti-corruption work requires a good intelligence back-up. It is intelligence that leads to evidence. Quite a lot of intelligence relating to corruption in services becomes available to different enforcement agencies like the Income Tax, Customs, Central Excise, Directorate of Enforcement, Intelligence Bureau and State CID. They function under different authorities and pursue their allotted tasks separately. The corruption aspect of the intelligence with them may get overlooked in this process. For example, the undeclared large assets of a public servant detected in an income tax raid may be pursued by them solely from the revenue angle of tax collection, whereas the corruption angle of possession of disproportionate assets can and should be pursued by the CBI. There is no institutional arrangement now for a coordinated assessment of intelligence with different agencies for effectively pursuing the corruption aspect. The *Hawala* Case is a typical example. We now have a Joint Intelligence Committee in the Cabinet Secretariat of the Central Government for a joint assessment of intelligence pertaining to national security. On similar lines, a small group under the Cabinet Secretary may be authorised to convene periodic meetings with representatives from the other enforcement agencies for pooling all the available intelligence pertaining to corruption. Follow-up action thereon can be taken up by the CBI.

Statutory Role for Civil Services

In the early years of Independence, it was a sort of working convention among civil servants that the ministers would decide policy matters while the civil services would deal with executive matters arising from policy implementation. The then political leadership also functioned according to this convention. In later years the ministers savoured the prestige and power behind executive orders which affect the service personnel in the entire system, and preferred to be (and have remained) the sole decision-makers in all matters, including postings and transfers of the lowest grade government servants. Such overriding powers at the level of political executive have facilitated enormous growth of all-pervasive political corruption, which is now perceived as the fountainhead of all other corruption. We have to seek a way out of this impasse which the civil services have got into.

Article 53 of the Constitution stipulates that the executive power of the Union shall be vested in the President and shall be exercised by him, either directly or through officers subordinate to him, in accordance with the Constitution. There is no reference to 'Minister' in this Article. But Article 77 requires the President to make rules for allocating among ministers the transaction of government business in various departments. It is from these business rules that ministers derive their statutory power to decide all matters arising in the government. It is this provision which enables a minister officially to overrule the secretary to the government in any matter, however right the secretary may be on record and however unjust and unfair the minister's decision thereon be. The time has now come for amending Article 77 to facilitate allotment of certain aspects of business to the Union Civil Services at the higher levels in the Government Secretariat also. The allotment may be so made as to reflect the working convention mentioned in the above paragraph. Article 166 which deals with the same matter in regard to the States should also be amended likewise. These amendments would go a long way in checking high-level political corruption.

MPs and MLAs to be Defined as 'Public Servant' in Law

MPs, MLAs and elected representatives in metropolitan councils, municipal corporations, municipalities, *panchayats* and such other statutorily-constituted local bodies should be included in the definition of 'public servant' in the Prevention of Corruption Act by a specific amendment for this purpose. These public functionaries should be required by law to submit to a prescribed authority, an annual statement of assets held in their names as also in the names of their parents or sons, daughters and other close relatives. These annual statements should be made available by the prescribed authority for scrutiny by any member of the public who makes an application for it.

Code of Conduct for MPs and MLAs

In the present-day realities of public life, the MPs and MLAs and their henchmen play a large role in promoting contacts at high levels. The lifestyles of many among them and their acquisition of large assets, both personal and *benami*, within a short period, do not inspire public confidence about their integrity or propriety of their financial transactions. It is their conduct that sets the standards for public life in the country. Recognising the need for evolving a Code of Conduct for the legislators to ensure their integrity and commitment to serve public interest, the Central Government started an exercise in 1975 to draft a code in consultation with the State Governments, but this was later given up in the atmosphere of 'Emergency'. It may be revived and a 'Code of Conduct' for MPs and MLAs brought into force without delay. A special committee designated as Ethics Committee may also be constituted in Parliament and each State Assembly to monitor the strict observance of the Code by all members.

Audit of the Accounts of Political Parties

Section 13A of the Income Tax Act which was introduced in 1979 states that all kinds of income of political parties registered with the Election Commission shall be totally exempt from income tax, provided the books of accounts are maintained and duly audited. In practice, all political parties get away with a total absence of accountability of their finance, and none of them is subjected to any assessment by the Income Tax Department. With their penchant for handling black money, all political parties revel in this 'no accounts and no tax' status and deliberately generate and sustain a permissive atmosphere which breeds corruption all around. In the recent case of 'Political parties election expenses and maintenance of accounts,' the Solicitor General admitted before the Supreme Court the Government's failure to enforce the I.T. Act provision relating to political parties. The judgement delivered by the Supreme Court on April 4, 1996 in this case would, hopefully, ensure strict enforcement of the relevant provisions in the Income Tax Act and the Companies Act to make all political parties maintain proper accounts of their income and expenditure from now on. This would go a long way in curbing political corruption.

A special cell should be set up either under the Comptroller and Auditor General or the Election Commission to conduct periodically a regular audit of the accounts kept by all registered political parties. A clearance from this Audit Cell must be made statutorily necessary for a political party to claim exemption for its income under Section 13A of the Income Tax Act.

Comptroller and Auditor General

Audit has an important role in the overall scheme of anti-corruption measures. An effective and independent audit system deters fraudulent practices in financial dealings in the government and the public sector.

Some important cases successfully investigated by the CBI in the past were based on information exposed in audit reports presented by the Comptroller and Auditor General (CAG). Effective prevention of corruption requires the CAG to be a person highly reputed for his integrity, professional competence and independence, and free from bias of any kind. The incumbents of this post in the early years of Independence were persons of impeccable integrity with a good background of audit work. In later years, senior IAS officers who had functioned as secretaries to the Government have been appointed as CAG on the eve of their retirement from service. Public confidence in the audit system and its credibility are badly eroded if an officer who had participated in deciding large-scale contracts for works and supplies on government account is later appointed as CAG to preside over the audit of such transactions. There is an immediate need to lay down formally in law a procedure for the appointment of CAG to ensure that a person with a high reputation for integrity and known for his professional competence and independence, with a good background of audit work alone fills the post.

Police Reform

Effective investigations and prosecutions under the Prevention of Corruption Act cannot be conceived in isolation from the overall scenario of general law enforcement in the country. Police is the primary agency of the State for law enforcement. In the present dispensation, the police system has become increasingly vulnerable to interference by extraneous persons. Police performance is perceived by the common people to be increasingly partisan and politically directed. This has seriously handicapped impartial, truthful and effective law enforcement. The National Police Commission (NPC), set up by the Central Government in 1977 with wide-ranging terms of reference for a complete overhaul of the police system to meet the aspirations and expectations of people in our democracy, has made several recommendations for police reform to secure an effective, impartial and honest police performance. A very important recommendation made by the NPC is to free the police from the exclusive control of the Government which always has a distinct political colour and direction at any given time, and put the police under the control of a multi-member State Security Commission which would be a statutory body presided over by the Chief Minister with members including the Leader of the Opposition in the State Assembly, a retired High Court judge and a few other eminent public men including academics of repute. Several other vital recommendations of the NPC follow from this basic recommendation of a State Security Commission to monitor police performance in the State. Any amount of focusing on radical measures in law and executive action for effective anti-corruption work will not be realistic unless the overall scenario of law enforcement in general becomes clear and bright. Witnesses examined by the CBI and State ACBs in corruption cases are sometimes threatened by musclemen at the command of the corrupt official concerned. The growing nexus between criminals and politicians has further encouraged this trend in recent years. Highhanded and intimidatory tactics adopted by corrupt persons to suppress the evidence against them can be defeated only if the police is effective in dealing with the aggressive and disorderly elements in the society. This requires a professionally competent police, free from extraneous interference. Immediate implementation of the NPC recommendations for police reform should, therefore, be viewed as a 'must' for effective anti-corruption work also.

Comprehensive Legislation for the Proposed Reforms

The reforms and changes suggested above can be brought about only by necessary amendments to the Constitution and the enactment of separate laws for the envisaged purposes. The establishment of Lok Pals at the Centre and in the States along with their investigating wings and prosecuting wings and the procedure for the transaction of their business have to be incorporated in a separate law to be passed by Parliament. The conduct of MPs and MLAs has also to be governed by a separate code drawn up by Parliament and State Assemblies. The appointment of Lok Pals at the Centre and in the States has to be made by the President himself, in exercise of his discretion and judgement, without having to consult the Council of Ministers. This would require an appropriate amendment to Article 74 of the Constitution.

Working Group for Drafting Legislation

A small working group under the lead of a retired Supreme Court or High Court judge held in high esteem should be immediately entrusted with the task of drafting a comprehensive Bill for the necessary amendments to the Constitution and the enactment of separate laws for the different purposes mentioned above.

Several ameliorative and welfare measures launched by the Government for the advancement of socially and economically backward classes are rendered ineffective by the creeping corruption in administration. The poor and uninfluential sections of the backward groups find that unless they pay bribes to the operating functionaries in the field, they will not get the full benefit of the welfare measures intended for them. Rural youth suffer most in this situation. Their economic distress and enforced idleness without adequate job opportunities, drive them to despair and some of them take to violent extremism. This phenomenon further weakens our social structure and tends to destabilise our society. Subjected to the constant play of such divisive and disruptive forces within itself, our society can hardly gather itself to remain as a strong unit and march towards economic prosperity. In such a situation, corruption cannot be viewed as a mere moral issue. It is a vital economic issue which saps the production potential of the nation and induces people to discard the path of hard work and take to shortcuts for achieving short-term individual gain. This ultimately brings down the quality of output in all fields of production. National economy gets disrupted. By corrupt means, the rich may become richer, but the poor become poorer, and the nation degenerates. The rising generation should realise that this will be the resulting scenario in the coming years if the canker of corruption is not effectively stopped and cured right now. The seriousness and urgency of the matter have to be understood by the youth of the country.

Summary of Recommendations

In conclusion, the recommendations and reform proposals made in this paper are summarised below:

(i) A new law may be enacted by Parliament to give statutory powers to the CBI to function as a central investigating agency on a nation-wide basis without having to secure the consent of State

Governments to make inquiries within the territory of State Governments.

(ii) The existing restrictive procedures prescribed for the CBI and the State ACBs for dealing with complaints of corruption against high-ranking officers in the Government may be reviewed and modified to give functional independence to these agencies for speedy verification of intelligence relating to high-level corruption.

(iii) The existing set-up of the Central Vigilance Commission (CVC) may be put on a statutory basis.

(iv) A Lok Pal may be set-up as a statutory body at the Centre for dealing with complaints of corruption against all Central ministers (including the Prime Minister), members of parliament and top-level bureaucrats in the governments.

(v) The Lok Pal may be a multi-member body, with all members including the Chairman being persons who are working or had worked or are qualified for appointment as judges of the Supreme Court.

(vi) Appointment of the Chairman and members of the Lok Pal may be made by the President by a procedure similar to the one adopted for the appointment of Chairman and members of the National Human Rights Commission, in which the leaders of the Opposition in the Lok Sabha and Rajya Sabha have an effective role in the appointment process.

(vii) The statutory set-up proposed for the CVC may be integrated with that of the Lok Pal by making the CVC one of the members of the Lok Pal. The charter of functions of the CVC may be defined as a part of the charter of the Lok Pal.

(viii) A separate investigating wing and prosecuting wing may be set up as a part of the establishment of the Lok Pal. Their services will be available for all inquiries and prosecutions launched by the Lok Pal.

(ix) The Central Lok Pal Act may also provide for a State Lok Pal/Vigilance Commission with a similar charter of functions in regard to all ministers (including the chief minister) and services in the State. The President shall be the appointing authority for the State level Lok Pal also.

(x) The existing Commissions of Inquiry Act may remain, since special commissions may still be required to inquire into matters of public importance other than those involving allegations of corruption. The investigating and prosecuting staff of the Lok Pal may be utilised to assist the Commissions of Inquiry also as and when they are set up.

(xi) CBI will continue to function under the administrative control of the Central Government and function as its primary investigating agency. Specific cases relating to high-level corruption may be notified by the Lok Pal/CVC from time to time for being monitored by the CVC even as the CBI proceeds with the investigation. This will eliminate the scope for *mala fide* interference by the Government or other extraneous sources in the investigation of sensitive cases involving VIPs, political or otherwise.

(xii) The definition of 'public servant' in the Prevention of Corruption Act should be amplified to include MPs and MLAs and all elected representatives in metropolitan councils, municipal corporations, municipalities, *panchayats* and such other statutorily-constituted local bodies. These public functionaries should be required by law to submit to a prescribed authority an annual statement of assets held in their names as also in the names of their parents or sons, daughters and other close relatives. The annual statements should be made available by the prescribed authority for scrutiny by any member of the public who makes an application for it.

(xiii) A Code of Conduct may be drawn up to govern the conduct of legislators to ensure their integrity and commitment to serve public interest. A special committee designated as Ethics Committee should be set up in Parliament and each State Assembly to ensure strict observance of this Code by all members.

(xiv) Section 13 A of the Income Tax Act should be strictly enforced to secure proper maintenance of accounts by all political parties. A special cell may be set up either under the Comptroller and Auditor General or the Election Commission to conduct periodically a regular audit of these accounts. A clearance from this audit cell may be made statutorily necessary for a political party to claim exemption for its income under Section 13 A of the Income Tax Act.

(xv) Articles 77 and 166 of the Constitution may be amended to facilitate allotment of certain aspects of business to civil servants also at the higher levels in the Government Secretariat. This would check whimsical, capricious or *mala fide* disposal of the Government business at the level of the political executive.

(xvi) A formal procedure may be laid down in law for the appointment of Comptroller and Auditor General to ensure that a person with a high reputation for integrity and known for his professional competence and independence with a good background of audit work alone fills the post.

(xvii) In regard to prior sanction for a prosecution under the Prevention of Corruption Act, existing provisions of Section 19 of the Act may be amended to ensure that:

(a) the competent authority makes the order sanctioning or refusing to sanction prosecution within a specified time limit, and

(b) if the competent authority refuses to sanction prosecution, it shall state the reasons for refusal which shall be embodied in the order of refusal, and it shall be open to the investigating agency to appeal against such an order to the Lok Pal whose decision thereon shall be final and binding on the government concerned.

(xviii) Any amount of focusing on radical measures in law and executive action for effective anti-corruption work will not be realistic unless the overall scenario of law enforcement in general becomes clear and bright. Immediate implementation of the NPC recommendations for police reform should, therefore, be viewed as a 'must' for effective anti-corruption work also.

(xix) The Criminal Law Amendment Ordinance of 1944 provides for attachment of properties acquired by a corrupt public servant when an alleged offence under the Prevention of Corruption Act committed by him is under investigation. This statute may be replaced by a more comprehensive Act to deal with properties acquired by public servants by corrupt or illegal means not only in their own names but also in the names of their relatives and others under their control. The new law may be modelled on the Smugglers and Foreign Exchange Manipulators (Forfeiture of Property) Act, 1976.

(xx) A small working group under the lead of a retired Supreme Court or High Court judge held in high esteem should be immediately entrusted with the task of drafting a comprehensive Bill for the necessary amendments to the Constitution and enactment of separate laws for the different purposes mentioned above.

People's Movement for Reforms

Legislation for the proposed reforms and changes would require the willingness of MPs and MLAs and political leaders of the country to accept the need for such reforms and changes and accordingly move them in Parliament and State Assemblies. Left to themselves, the political bosses, elected representatives and various government functionaries who are presently benefiting from the fast spreading corruption all round will not be inclined to adopt fundamental changes in the system which will at once reduce scope for corruption. The pressure for effecting changes has, therefore, to be built up by the people at large. Presently, there seems to be a wave round the world where the peoples of different countries are expressing their disgust at the wrong doings of unscrupulous politicians who have brought them to the sorry mess they are in. Italy, South Korea and Japan are examples where people's anger against corruption-ridden governments has displaced discredited rulers by new men who hold out the promise of cleansing public life. A people's movement is now called for in our country to fight the war against corruption and save the nation from disintegration. The younger generation in schools and colleges have a vital stake in this matter and should, therefore, deliberate and evolve a methodology for mounting pressure to bring about these reforms and changes in our system.

11
Corruption in India
A Strategic Agenda for Action

Samuel Paul

The essays in this volume provide a wide-ranging review of the problems and constraints of the public institutions, legal systems and processes, and behaviour patterns in our society that have contributed to the growing phenomenon of corruption. They have analysed the political and bureaucratic processes at work, and assessed the legal and institutional reforms needed to combat corruption. In all cases, the authors have highlighted directions for change and reform that government and society at large need to initiate and support in order to improve probity in public life. The approach presented here is not so much on individual sectors of the economy or on specific departments of the government, but rather on the overall legal, institutional and behavioural aspects of the government that are critical to corruption control. The focus is on the need to redesign and improve the underlying framework of our basic public institutions that serve all sectors, their structures and systems in order to achieve corruption control.

Our contributing authors have concluded their papers with concrete proposals for action, ranging from amendments to the laws and constitution of the country, to specific steps for improving the working of the public institutions with which citizens interact. Given the current public concern about corruption in the country, it is not surprising that similar proposals have emanated from other quarters too in recent months. The concreteness and specificity of our proposals, however, distinguish them from the more general statements that tend to be made on the same themes. Needless to say, even within the contributions to this volume, there are overlaps and occasional conflicts between some of the recommendations of the different authors. When experts examine a complex problem from different personal and disciplinary perspectives, this is perhaps unavoidable.

Some of our authors have proposed a major restructuring of the way in which the government functions, both at political and bureaucratic levels. Their proposals are perfectly valid given the urgent need to improve the efficiency and effectiveness of different public institutions and governmental functions. Such reforms will also create a favourable setting for tackling corruption. Thus improved recruitment, career development and reward systems in the civil service will go a long way in institutionalising a more efficient and responsive bureaucracy that will also be less corruption prone. Implementation of the National Police Commission recommendations (1977-1981) will, for instance, improve the morale and accountability of the police who are responsible for enforcing laws including those pertinent to corruption control. Systematic reforms of the laws, regulations and institutions are essential for the orderly progress of the country. There is no doubt that the quality of governance in our society will improve significantly as a result of administrative reforms.

Corruption, however, is a multifaceted and complex phenomenon; interventions on many fronts and the collaborative efforts of many people are required to control it. If we add the numerous proposals for action emanating from other quarters to the recommendations of this volume, the task may seem daunting to any government, or for that matter, to any society. From the standpoint of controlling corruption, focus on comprehensiveness may thus become counter-productive for several reasons. Firstly, when taken together, these reforms may cause such an overload on government that scarce public resources and attention would be spread thin. Secondly, all reforms are not equally critical to the control of corruption. An improvement in efficiency or quality by itself need not necessarily reduce corruption. Thirdly, more often than not, comprehensiveness in the arena of reform can make prioritisation extremely difficult. A more strategic approach that links together a select set of proposals covering both the institutional and behavioural dimensions of corruption control is therefore in order.

Accordingly, we shall endeavour to present the outlines of a strategic agenda for action to tackle corruption. The agenda is based largely on the specific recommendations contained in the essays. Where there are gaps, some new proposals have been added. Where recommendations are in conflict, an attempt has been made to present the relevant options and to assess their implications. Such a strategic agenda may give our policy makers and other key players a sense of the critical interventions necessary to combat corruption and a greater appreciation of the interrelationships between the parts.

The propensity for corruption in any society can be controlled only by systematically reducing the incentives and opportunities to engage in corrupt practices. An agenda for action to control corruption must identify the key interventions necessary to minimise such incentives and opportunities in the Indian society. Drawing upon the essays in this volume, we present four action areas as the essential building blocks for a national agenda for corruption control: (a) reform of the political process, (b) restructuring and reorienting the government machinery, (c) empowerment of citizens, and (d) creating sustained public pressure for change. The rationale underlying these themes does not need much elaboration. The political process needs reform at strategic points in order to create an enabling environment that is conducive to the control of corruption. Effective implementation of new initiatives will occur only through a restructuring and reorientation of key public institutions of the country and their bureaucracy. Pressure for these changes must also come from citizens who in turn need to be enabled to play this role through access to information and other means of empowerment. Finally, public pressure for change can be sustained only through the active intervention of civil society institutions such as the media and a variety of non-governmental organisations at both local and national levels.

Action on the recommendations presented here will call for initiatives and collaborative efforts by numerous players and organisations. In many cases, the recommendations are interrelated and will reinforce each other. By highlighting selected areas for action, and combining the institutional and behavioural dimensions of the reforms required, we are essentially underscoring their priority and mutual reinforcement, and their potential to trigger off other initiatives and behavioural changes in society that can also contribute to the control of corruption.

A. The Political Process: Strategic Interventions for Reform

Reform of the political process is the most sensitive area in our agenda and is of fundamental importance. It is not uncommon to find anti-corruption efforts at the micro level being subverted by corrupt political leaders at higher levels. The power over resources, information, patronage and decisions that the political leadership in India enjoys is so vast that it is imperative to set right the process by which they come to appropriate this power. This is not to expect that the qualities of political leaders and representatives could be rigidly specified or to ask for a different form of government. Even within the confines of the existing system of government, it should be possible to reform the process by which representatives get elected and rise to power. If this process can be improved at strategic points, it is possible that persons with greater integrity and commitment to public service will be attracted to the political arena. The objective then should be to get political parties to commit themselves to a set of practices, discipline and values which together can create an environment that is more conducive to the control of corruption. Thus, the leaders thrown up by political parties that are dependent largely on funds from big business or other interest groups will tend to be of a different orientation and value base compared to those whose election is financed by small contributions from the people at large or State funding without strings attached. The latter set of leaders, when elected, are likely to be less vulnerable to *quid pro quo* arrangements and co-option by powerful organised groups in society. If they are less corruption prone and are not motivated to build corrupt war chests, the pressures down the line to engage in similar practices can also be expected to decline. The financing of elections to political offices is thus a central issue from the standpoint of corruption control.

A similar case exists for improvements in the functioning and management of political parties. If parties are not governed by generally accepted norms of good management and are not transparent and accountable as public organisations ought to be, how can we expect them to lead the country and its government in terms of *efficiency, accountability and transparency*? Maintenance of audited accounts, compliance with income tax guidelines and public disclosure of information are practices that have to be insisted upon in order to make political parties more accountable and less susceptible to the pressures of corruption. When leaders brought up under this discipline assume power, their values and orientation, and the signals they give their colleagues and subordinates, are likely to be more supportive of corruption control than would be the case otherwise. Hence, the need to take a close look at the way our political parties are managed.

A third aspect of the political process that has a bearing on corruption is the code of conduct governing the behaviour of elected representatives and political appointees and related issues in terms of their compensation and privileges. When monetary compensation is limited, there is an understandable tendency to sell privileges. Incentives to engage in corruption are stronger when penalties for the abuse of power are weak and poorly implemented. Corrective action here may call for a modification of laws and regulations governing the conduct of elected representatives and other political appointees, and their treatment when charged with misconduct. An important area for reform pertains to defections or floor crossing by elected representatives which in many cases are believed to be the result of corrupt influences. The final authority for determining disqualification under the Anti-Defection Law may need to be vested in the Election Commission rather than in the Speaker of the House or Chairman of the Upper House.

Recommendations

1. We begin with a set of proposals for cleansing the national and State elections of money power. This is central to the reform of the political process. There is substantial agreement now among political parties and opinion leaders in the country on the need to use public funds to meet the election expenses of candidates. Reimbursement by government of the candidates' election expenses in parliamentary and State elections is a reform whose time has come. Candidates of recognised political parties as well as independent candidates under specified conditions should be eligible for such reimbursement from public funds. Such financing may be provided in kind (e.g., free but limited television or radio time) as well as in cash. Guidelines should be established to minimise election expenses. The recent parliamentary elections have demonstrated the feasibility of holding modest and orderly elections. Details of the proposed reform can be worked out once it is decided to introduce State funding of elections. According to reasonable estimates, State funding of election expenses will not impose an impossible burden on the exchequer.

2. State funding of elections should ideally be accompanied by a ban on donations to political parties and individual candidates by

business enterprises. Private financing has inherent risks of abuse that can never be fully eliminated even with the best of regulations. State funding of elections should be used to wean political parties away from any obligation to business groups. If, however, donations by business groups cannot be banned, the conditions for such donations should be specified and strictly enforced on both the donors and recipients. Political donations above specified limits may be made subject to approval at the shareholders' meetings of companies. All donations should be made known through the annual reports of companies.

3. Uncontrolled election expenditure has contributed substantially to corrupt practices. Several measures can be taken to keep election expenses within reasonable limits. Reduction in the campaign period, curtailment of permissible items of expenditure (e.g., transportation of voters), and strict enforcement of expenditure ceilings are steps that merit special attention. Ceilings should include expenditure incurred by all sources (viz., candidates, friends and well-wishers, and parties). Election accounts submitted by candidates should be cross-checked with those furnished by their political parties. The introduction of electronic voting machines can reduce the period of campaigning and thereby provide an important means of reducing expenditure for candidates as well.

4. There are several other steps which can be taken to reduce the scope for abuses and corruption in the conduct of elections. The use of electronic voting machines will partly eliminate rigging. Appointment of watch-dog committees in constituencies and polling stations may act as a deterrent to abuses and corruption. The use of heliographed, multipurpose photo identity cards (despite the recent problems in its implementation) will minimise impersonation. Considering the vital role of clean elections in the reform of the political process, they need to be given high priority as their benefits far outweigh the costs involved.

5. The Anti-Defection Act needs to be amended as follows to ensure that legislators are not bought and sold. Some of the suggestions made in this regard are: (a) no defection should be recognised in a legislature party unless it is the result of a split in the parent party; (b) a cooling-off period between leaving one party and joining another should be specified; (c) there should be a ban on taking office after defection to the ruling party.

6. The integrity of the political process is influenced greatly by the way politicians and political parties conduct themselves. Their organisational culture, discipline and integrity are seen by, and influence, everyone else. It is, therefore, essential to enact a law for regulating the functioning of political parties. This law should require political parties to (a) hold regular organisational elections to various levels; (b) maintain prompt and systematic accounts and submit audited accounts to the prescribed authority (e.g., the Election Commission or the Comptroller and Auditor General); and (c) comply with income tax regulations and guidelines. A clearance from the Audit Cell should be necessary for a political party to claim tax exemption under the Income Tax Act. The Election Commission may be given the authority to derecognise political parties if they fail to observe the proposed law. Greater transparency and compliance with the law by political parties will go a long way in reducing the scope for corrupt practices and other abuses in their day-to-day operations and, in the process, exert a positive influence on other public institutions.

7. A code of conduct needs to be adopted by Parliament to provide guidelines for the conduct of elected representatives and to take appropriate action when departures from accepted norms are observed. Such codes of conduct exist in other countries. Proposals for a code of conduct for legislators have been made in India too, notably by the late Mrs. Durgabai Deshmukh, but were never acted on. An Ethics or Conduct Committee under the chairmanship of the Speaker of the Lok Sabha or State Assembly will be necessary to monitor observance of the code and decide on the actions to be taken in case of violations. Elected representatives should also be required to declare on oath or affirm every year the assets held by them and their sources of income. These returns should be monitored by the Ethics Committee and appropriate action taken to ensure the integrity of legislators.

8. Elected representatives deserve to be compensated adequately so that they are able to devote their primary attention to public service. It is, also, in the fitness of things, that their monetary emoluments are increased to reflect the scale of their expenses from time to time. More rational compensation and benefits policies for elected representatives are desirable not only for the purpose of reducing the incentives and opportunities for corruption, but also for larger reasons of efficiency and effectiveness. At the same time, action can be taken to reduce or

eliminate their material and non-transparent privileges which lend themselves to easy abuse such as quotas for gas connections, petrol pumps, telephone connections and school admissions. The recent steps taken by the Government of India along these lines are commendable.

9. Though the Prevention of Corruption Act was substantially amended in 1988 to include more public functionaries under the definition of "public servant", Members of Parliament (MPs) and Members of Legislative Assemblies (MLAs) are not within the purview of this Act. Early steps need to be taken to bring MPs, MLAs, and all other elected representatives of local governments and such other statutorily-constituted local bodies within the purview of this Act.

10. The Criminal Law Amendment Ordinance of 1944 should be replaced by a more comprehensive Act to deal with properties acquired by public servants through corrupt or illegal means not only in their names, but also in the names of their close relatives and as *benami* (proxy).

11. There is considerable evidence in India of the close links between political corruption and criminalisation of politics. No person with a criminal conviction should therefore be permitted to contest in an election to the legislature. Legislators convicted for criminal offences during their tenure should be required to vacate their seats forthwith.

B. Restructuring and Reorienting Government Machinery

A proper functioning of the government and its institutional mechanisms is bound to reduce the scope for corruption in any society. The reality, however, is that the structures, systems and style of functioning of many of India's public institutions, and the orientation of the bureaucracy, have contributed directly and indirectly to the culture of corruption. Bureaucracy can be divided into two categories. One is primarily concerned with the planning and implementation of policies, programmes and the delivery of services. The other, consisting largely of specialised agencies, is concerned with monitoring the resources and processes utilised in these activities with a view to preventing abuses and enforcing the law. From the standpoint of corruption control, we identify four important areas for the restructuring and reorientation of both these parts of the bureaucracy. The focus here is not merely on streamlining their functioning, but more importantly on augmenting their integrity and impartiality. The interventions are strategic in the sense that once these reforms are in place, many other desirable changes in the functioning of public institutions and the behaviour of the bureaucracy may also follow.

The key reforms called for are deregulation and debureaucratisation, bounded discretion in decisio-making, realignment of the government's audit, intelligence and investigating agencies to achieve better corruption control, and the insulation of key appointments and personnel decisions from undesirable interference. Of these, deregulation of industry and commerce has already made notable progress since 1991. While not all observers are agreed on the details of these measures, most will concede that they have reduced the scope for corruption in government. The challenge now is to adapt this approach to other sectors and activities where opportunities for corruption are widespread. The focus of reform needs to shift to the State and local government levels where entrepreneurs as well as ordinary citizens are still heavily dependent on a variety of public services, approvals and licences. Deregulation on a massive scale is not necessarily a prerequisite for corruption control. The trick is to identify areas for intervention where the payoff in terms of corruption control is likely to be the highest. A strategic approach will require that the focus of reform should be on the more corruption-prone public agencies that also have the most interaction with people.

A second area for restructuring and reorientation pertains to the use of discretion in public decision-making. Administrative decisions on complex subjects may have to be based, for good reasons, on the use of discretion and judgement by public officials. However, non-transparency and lack of accountability in decision-making have created opportunities for collusion and corruption. Corruption control calls for discipline in this area through an explicit adoption of a set of guidelines for the use of discretion, and documentation of the specific reasons for discretionary decisions to be made available to the affected parties. For important categories of administrative decisions, the concerned authorities should be required to issue clear instructions on the use of discretion. These should also be made available to the public. These arrangements should include tribunals to decide on appeals pertaining to administrative decisions.

Thirdly, specialised public agencies with a watchdog function or which are directly concerned with the investigation of corruption cases and law enforcement need to be strengthened from the point of view of effectiveness and integrity. The scope for legislative and institutional reform and management improvements is substantial here. Information-sharing and coordinated work among these agencies are much needed steps. New mechanisms for reporting and sharing pertinent audit findings can be devised to aid investigative processes. The institution of Lok Pal which has been supported by all political parties should be given constitutional status and placed at the apex of a network of ombudsmen established at the level of the State governments and other major public authorities. This independent network should be accessible to all citizens who wish to register complaints about corruption and misconduct even against the highest public officials. It is of vital importance that the Lok Pal should be underpinned by an independent agency for investigation and prosecution.

The fourth area for reform concerns the process of making top level appointments to the sensitive and specialised public agencies referred to above and appointments and transfers in the higher levels of the bureaucracy. It is leaders who set the tone in their organisations and signal others on whether corruption and abuses will be tolerated or not. Credible and transparent approaches to the selection and appointment of persons to these positions will go a long way in attracting persons capable of resisting corruption and preserving their autonomy. In the bureaucracy, it is not only appointments, but also transfers that need to be insulated from arbitrary action. While selection, appointments, transfers and promotions in the entire bureaucracy deserve a close look, from a strategic perspective, the right place to start is at the top. These changes will call for a major reorientation in the thinking of the top echelons of the political and administrative levels.

Recommendations

1. A major review of the regulations governing the transactions of public agencies at the State and local levels with citizens and business enterprises must be undertaken with a view to eliminating their scope for creating incentives and opportunities for corruption. The initial

focus of the review should be on departments and agencies with which citizens interact on a regular basis such as the police, general administration, public distribution system, utilities dealing with electricity, water and telephones, and local bodies providing basic civic services. The need for reform is the greatest and maximum impact can be achieved at State and local levels. Clear guidelines should be provided to the public who seek services and approvals, while minimising the scope for officials to make case-by-case discretionary decisions and authorisations. Ensuring transparency and fairness is most difficult where the use of discretion and case-by-case approvals are involved. Where case-by-case decisions are unavoidable, stricter supervision, checks and clearer guidelines need to be put in place. Decision-making in more open forums and public access to information on such decisions are necessary. The objective of this reform is not to dilute the regulatory function of the government. Rather, it should improve the efficiency and effectiveness of regulation while making it less susceptible to corruption.

2. In all important areas of decision-making that entail the use of discretion, potential abuses can be minimised by issuing administrative instructions to guide the use of discretion. This is especially necessary where such decisions result in the allocation of substantial funds, entitlements or privileges such as contracts, building permissions and licenses. Instructions should state the policy in accordance with which discretion is to be exercised. Greater transparency and clarity on the reasons for decisions are measures that tend to minimise the scope for abuse of power and corruption.

3. There should be a provision for the public to challenge the decisions of administrative authorities in respect of matters like grant of exemptions and privileges. This can be facilitated through the creation of tribunals for hearing appeals against such decisions. Such tribunals should follow inquiry procedures for fact-finding rather than resort to dilatory adversarial proceedings.

4. The primary responsibility of the civil service to uphold the rule of law needs to be unambiguously reaffirmed. Political neutrality of the civil servant must remain the cornerstone of the civil service. The Centre and the States should prescribe rules and regulations for effecting transfer of officers to ensure a reasonable tenure in various posts. Reasons for any departure from this norm should be conveyed in writing to the affected officer. For heads of major public agencies

and departments, the term of service should be three to five years so that they are enabled to implement programmes and reforms necessary to ensure good performance.

5. It is necessary to encourage those who work in the government to "blow the whistle" when they come across corrupt practices. They may hesitate to report such cases to the authorities, however, for fear of retribution. This lacuna can be remedied by providing legal protection to the staff who expose corruption and wrong-doing in the government through enactment of a law on the lines of the legislation adopted by other countries to protect whistle blowers.

6. The overriding role that political executives play in personnel decisions such as the postings and transfers of even the lowest levels of officials has been a contributory factor to corruption within the government. The remedy to this would be to empower intra-service committees headed by the senior-most civil servants to deal with postings and transfers. Any departure at the ministerial level from the recommendations of such committees should be for reasons which are to be recorded in writing. They should also be open to appeal in the hands of Administrative Tribunals or specially constituted Civil Service Tribunals.

7. The cornerstone of the arrangements for tackling high-level corruption in the Centre and in the States is the creation of the Lok Pal (at the Centre) and Lok Ayukt (in the States). Both the institutions should be given constitutional status as recommended by the Administrative Reforms Commission (1966). Their jurisdiction should extend to all ministers — including the Prime Minister and Chief Minister — and the higher echelons of public servants, whether serving in governments, statutory authorities, public sector undertakings, local bodies, aided institutions (such as universities) or those belonging to any other category of public servants as defined in the Prevention of Corruption Act 1988 which may be notified for inclusion. The basic features of the legislation should be uniform for the Centre and the States, with the latter being free to introduce innovations and adaptations.

8. The Lok Pal should be appointed by the President on the recommendation of a body consisting of the Prime Minister, the Chief Justice of India, the presiding officers of both houses of Parliament and the leader of the opposition in the Lok Sabha. A similar practice should be followed for the appointment of the Lok Ayukt in the States.

It may be pointed out that the need for a non-partisan, apolitical approach to high appointments has already been recognised in the case of the National Human Rights Commission.

9. The Lok Pal/Lok Ayukt should be free to investigate any allegation relating to corruption or criminal misconduct made by a citizen or referred to it by the executive, legislative or judicial arms of the State or taken up *suo moto* by itself. They should be able to take up investigations and launch prosecutions without any prior sanction from any level in the government. They should also have the power to direct a public servant to vacate his office if considered necessary or desirable in the interests of the effective pursuit of its proceedings. The functioning of the Lok Pal/Lok Ayukt should be a model of transparency.

10. In recent months, the Supreme Court of India has taken steps to ensure that the investigations and prosecutions of the CBI are insulated from political interference and pursued in a time-bound manner without fear or favour. While judicial activism is welcome, we cannot continually depend on it in all cases. It is, therefore, necessary to institutionalise the impartiality and integrity of the CBI by providing statutory safeguards to its autonomy. This will be possible only if the CBI, and its counterpart agencies in the States, are placed under the sole administrative control of the Lok Pal/Lok Ayukt in matters falling within the jurisdiction of the latter. The governments at the Centre and in the States can have separate agencies under their administrative control to deal with other cases of corruption and with serious crimes which are now being handled by the CBI and counterpart agencies in the States. The powers of the investigating agencies at the Centre and in the States should be clearly laid down through legislation in respect of such matters as arrest, search, seizure, summoning and examining of witnesses. No restrictions should be placed on the investigating agencies initiating or pursuing investigations and prosecutions.

11. Disclosure and identification of financial and procedural irregularities in the course of audit should be followed up with investigations for possible corruption. For this purpose, a special cell should be established in each State Accountant General's office and in the Principal Central Audit offices to identify cases that need investigation. A monthly letter may be sent by the Head of the Audit Office to the concerned secretaries to the government, drawing attention to such cases. Audit offices should also keep the Vigilance

Commissioners and Lok Pal informed of these cases and act as a source of information and intelligence to them and other investigative agencies.

12. It is important to encourage close networking among the different agencies such as the Lok Pal, CBI, Income Tax Authorities, Enforcement Directorate and CAG. Appropriate and effective institutional mechanisms to facilitate the sharing of information and intelligence, and co-operation in investigations need to be put in place to improve their role in tackling corruption.

13. A procedure similar to that suggested in the case of the Lok Pal should be followed for appointments to other high level positions such as the Comptroller and Auditor General of India and the Chief Election Commissioner, which equally need to be insulated from possible political interference.

C. Empowering Citizens

Corruption can be effectively tackled only when the reform of the political process and the restructuring of government machinery are complemented by systematic efforts to inform citizens about their rights and entitlements, and to enable them to monitor and challenge abuses of the system. By reducing the opportunities for corruption, measures of deregulation and debureaucratisation will reduce the hardships that people experience, give them more competitive options, and empower them in the process. But much more should and can be done to relieve citizens of corruption. There are four important directions for empowering citizens that deserve special attention. Firstly, the culture of secrecy that pervades the functioning of the government must be broken so that citizens have access to the information that they need to understand, assess and challenge the policies, programmes and specific actions of public authorities. Withholding of information is often justified by the Official Secrets Act and other time honoured practices in government. That the right to information is fundamental to the working of a democratic society and that it can act as a deterrent to the abuse of power are still alien concepts to many of our political and bureaucratic leaders.

Secondly, in respect of most public services, opportunities for corruption arise partly because people do not know what they can expect in terms of service delivery. To alleviate this sense of helplessness and to empower people to demand public accountability, it is essential that service providers specify and announce the standards and norms they intend to meet in their areas of responsibility. They should also indicate the remedies available to the public when the assured standards of service are not met. Dissemination of this information will go a long way in increasing transparency in the working of public agencies, and to empower citizens to resist abuses and extortionary corruption by those in authority.

Finally, the inner urge and resolve of a person to combat corruption depend in no small measure on his or her basic moral values and beliefs. In the prevailing pessimistic atmosphere, it is all too easy to ignore the fact that there are public servants who resist corruption and are willing to pay the price for standing firm. Some have quit their jobs in protest rather than compromise on the principles and values they cherished. Similarly, there are many people in our society whose values militate against corrupt practices. The field studies conducted by the Public Affairs Centre in different parts of the country have shown that the vast majority of people (nearly 85 %) believed corruption to be wrong and abhorrent. Even in the world of business, which is often portrayed as a source of corruption, there are enterprises that are able to maintain their integrity and resistance to corrupt practices. An outstanding example is the Alacrity group of companies in Madras, who are known for their transparent and straightforward ways of doing business in fields such as housing and real estate.

These examples are a testimony to the power of values and beliefs in sustaining people and organisations in their resolve to resist corruption. An important lesson of this experience is that it has worked within the framework of the institutional imperfections in India. The real challenge is to see that this approach is replicated in the country on a large scale.

If, on the other hand, the guiding values of people tolerate corrupt practices and unethical behaviour, there is little hope that such individuals will revolt against corruption or help launch a collective assault on corruption in their community or society. When there is no collective urge to uproot corruption, the institutional and legal reforms proposed by our authors will not go far, and any impact they make is likely to be marginal from the larger social point of view.

Recommendations

1. By limiting the monopolistic power of public service providers, deregulation of economic activities will reduce the spread and severity of corruption that citizens face in their daily lives. However, the ability of the latter to monitor corruption and seek remedies should be increased by decentralising resource allocations and service delivery wherever possible. It is true that decentralisation by itself cannot eliminate corruption and abuses. But greater proximity to decision-making and to remedy or appeal mechanisms may empower people to monitor abuses and to seek redress more effectively. The implementation of the 73rd and 74th Amendments to the Constitution should be accelerated and made effective so as to empower people along these lines.

2. As access to information is essential to the empowerment of people, the Official Secrets Act should be suitably reformed. A Freedom of Information Act should be passed which explicitly guarantees the right of access to official documents subject to the provisions of the law. Detailed proposals have been formulated in this regard by the Consumer Education and Research Centre (CERC), Ahmedabad. Categories of documents exempt from disclosure and the limits to the right to privacy must be kept to the minimum and clearly specified. Categories of exempt information proposed in the CERC bill are advice of Cabinet to the President, information that may damage national defence and security interests, disclosure harmful to international relations and law enforcement, and information that entails the privacy of an identifiable individual. The law must also be consistent with the right to privacy that could be claimed by persons holding public office.

3. All providers of public services and regulatory agencies should be required to specify and widely disseminate information on their standards and norms of service and remedies available to the public if they are dissatisfied. Laws governing these public agencies should mandate that they fulfil this requirement. A useful approach is to enact a law that mandates public authorities to disseminate and display essential information about their services, and to give opportunities to the public to participate in the rule-making process as was envisaged in the Karnataka Administrative Procedure Bill of 1991. Public service providers should also be required to undertake periodic surveys of

their customers to identify the problems faced by them and to take steps to eliminate such problems.

4. An important cause of corruption in some public services is the failure of service providers to match services to the differing requirements of customers, and their ability and willingness to pay for well-matched services. To reduce the scope for such corruption, wherever feasible and appropriate, service providers may be encouraged to design and offer services with the required attributes such as speed and reliability and to price them accordingly. While free or subsidised services may be justified from an equity point of view, there is a strong case for a judicious blend of subsidised and cost plus recoveries. The scope for corruption and diversion of benefits is substantial when highly subsidised or entirely free services and goods are provided by the State.

5. All the major public utilities and other service providers should appoint independent ombudsmen whom citizens can approach to redress their grievances, delays, malfunctioning and inefficiency. Smaller agencies may share an ombudsman at the same location. These ombudsmen should specialise in specific sets of services. The Reserve Bank of India's ombudsman for banking services is a model to follow.

6. Empowerment of the people to resist and fight corruption will depend greatly on the values and beliefs underlying their behaviour. While behavioural changes are by no means easy to engineer, systematic efforts to inculcate values of integrity, honesty and probity in public life need to be undertaken on a large scale at all levels in the country. In the final analysis, what people see and experience are those which influence them most. Good examples from all walks of life, therefore, need to be widely disseminated and replicated. A wide range of organisations, political, religious, social and professional, can play a catalytic role in this endeavour.

D. Creating Sustained Public Pressure for Change

As noted above, legal and institutional reforms for tackling corruption need to be reinforced by pressure from citizens whose values and beliefs militate against corruption. But the power of individual concern and commitment can be multiplied and leveraged through the deliberate efforts of organised groups to encourage collective action to monitor and fight corruption. Since corruption is not a problem faced by every citizen every day, it is not easy to sustain collective interest in this issue on a continuing basis. Institutions of civil society have, therefore, to be actively involved in the mobilisation of public opinion and action in this context. The media, for example, can be a powerful source of information and education of the citizenry for this purpose. Dissemination of information of what different groups of people are doing and achieving in their fight against corruption can be both educative and inspirational to people in other parts of the country. Other civil society institutions such as voluntary agencies, religious groups and research bodies may be able to support people's movements for corruption control. Documentation of such efforts and networking among the organisations involved to leverage their impact are other important steps that deserve support.

Recommendations

1. The media is already playing a major role in exposing corruption and corrupt practices. Its influence on public opinion and values will be even greater if it can seek, emphasise and publicise the positive side of combating corruption. Dissemination of information to the public on the service standards, guidelines and norms of major service providers will be an important service to the community. Those who are doing good work by resisting corruption or taking steps to eliminate corruption need to be recognised and appreciated. It is important that the media in India devote more attention to investigative journalism so that readers can benefit from well-researched stories and their lessons. A good example is the publication of the results of the surveys of public service users with respect to the quality and reliability of services. The quality and depth of work in this area can be improved by the media linking up with specialised research institutions and related professional groups in order to draw upon their studies and insights. Media should also help disseminate information on new approaches and innovations in tackling corruption, especially experiences and lessons from other countries that are not so well known in our country.

2. Business organisations, especially associations of business and industry, can render a valuable service by making their position clear

on the subject of corruption. Business is seen as ambivalent on this issue, and on the whole reluctant to participate in any public debate on the subject. The time has come for organised business to express a collective view on the subject of controlling corruption, an issue in which it can be expected to have a vital stake. An important initial step could be for leading associations and chambers of business to recommend to the government specific measures that can be taken to minimise corruption in business-government relations. Equally important is the design of a code of conduct for governing business-government relations, on the lines that the International Chamber of Commerce and Transparency International have attempted.

3. The other institutions of the civil society such as voluntary agencies and religious groups are also critical to mobilising public opinion against corruption. They can act as support and catalytic groups to encourage individuals and communities to resist corruption and to reform the system. The Government could consult them in the process of reviewing and redesigning policies and internal systems and practices. They can also play a major role in assisting the less privileged citizens and their groups in accessing the mechanisms available to seek remedies when faced with situations involving extortion and corruption. Public interest litigation is another initiative through which voluntary groups and people's movements can challenge and expose abuse of power and corruption. Many voluntary organisations are already doing outstanding work in this area as is clear from the recent case of Jan Sunvayi in Pali District in Rajasthan which demanded access to information from the local government on public works and in the process caused a major change in the attitude of the State Government. In the last analysis, it is the awareness, resolve and demand for reform by the people that will determine the success of the many legal, institutional and policy changes proposed here for controlling corruption.

Bibliography

Adamany, David (1972) *Campaign Finance in America*, North Scituate, Massachusetts, Duxbury Press.

Alatas, S.H. (1980) *The Sociology of Corruption : The Nature, Functions, Causes, and Prevention of Corruption*, Singapore, Times Books.

— (1993) 'Corruption' in *Oxford Companion to Politics of the World*, Oxford, Oxford University Press.

Alexander, Herbert (1972) *Money in Politics*, Washington DC, Public Affairs Press.

Alexander, Herbert and Rei Shivatori (eds) (1994) *Comparative Political Finance among Democracies*, Boulder Colorado, Westview Press.

Andreski, S. (1966) *Parasitism and Subversion : The Case of Latin America*, London, Weidenfeld and Nicolson.

— (1968) *The African Predicament*, New York, Atherton Press.

Banfield, E.C. (1979) 'Corruption as a Feature of Government' in Ekpo (1979).

Baxi, Upendra (1989) *Liberty and Corruption, The Antulay Case and Beyond*, Lucknow, Eastern Book Company.

Benson, G.C.S. (1978) *Political Corruption in America*, Lexington, D.C. Heath and Co.

Bhagwati, Jagdish N. (ed) (1974) *Illegal Transactions in International Trade*, Amsterdam, North Holland-Elsevier.

Bhagwati, Jagdish N. (1982) 'Directly Unproductive, Profit-Seeking (DUP) Activities', *Journal of Political Economy*; 90.

Bhalerao, C.N. (ed) (1972) *Administration, Politics and Development in India*, Bombay, Lalvani.

Buchanan, J., Tollison, R. and Tullock, G. (eds) (1980) *Toward a Theory of the Rent-Seeking Society*, Texas, Texas A and M University Press.

Carino (ed) (1986) *Bureaucratic Corruption in Asia: Causes, Consequences and Controls*, Quezon City, JMC Press.

Chugh, R.L. and Uppal, J.S. (1986) *Black Economy in India*, New Delhi, Tata Mc Graw Hill.

Clarke, M. (ed) (1983) *Corruption: Causes, Consequences and Control*, New York, St. Martins Press.

Consumer Education and Research Centre, Ahmedabad (1995) *Judicial Pronouncements on Access to Information*, Ahmedabad.

— (1995) *Access to Information Bill (Proposed)*, Ahmedabad.

Doig, A. (1984) *Corruption and Misconduct in Contemporary British Politics*, Hammondsworth, Penguin.

Dunn, Delmer (1972) *Financing Presidential Campaigns*, Washington DC — The Brookings Institution.

Ekpo, Monday U. (1979) *Bureaucratic Corruption in Sub-Saharan Africa: Toward a Search for Causes and Consequences*, Washington DC, University Press of America.

Gardiner, J.A. and Olson, D.J. (eds) (1968) *Theft of the City: Readings on Corruption in America*, Bloomington, Indiana University Press.

Government of India, Ministry of Home Affairs, (1964) *Report of the Committee on the Prevention of Corruption (Santhanam Committee)*, New Delhi.

— Administrative Reforms Commission (1966) *Report on the Problems of Redress of Citizens' Grievances*, New Delhi.

— Ministry of Finance (1978) *Report of the Committee on Controls and Subsidies*, New Delhi.

— (1985) *Aspects of the Black Economy in India*, New Delhi.

— Ministry of Law (1988) *Prevention of Corruption Act, 1988*, New Delhi.

— Lok Sabha Secretariat (1992) *13th Report of the Estimates Committee (1991-92), Tenth Lok Sabha on Central Bureau of Investigation*, New Delhi.

— Ministry of Home Affairs (1995), *Vohra Committee Report*, New Delhi.

HMSO (1995) *Standards in Public Life, First Report of the Committee under Chairman Lord Nolan*, London.

Harriss-White, B. and Gordon White (1996) *Liberalization and Corruption*, Sussex, Institute of Development Studies Bulletin, 27:2.

Heidenheimer, A.J. (ed) (1970) *Political Corruption: Readings in Comparative Analysis*, New York, Holt, Rinehart and Wilson.

Heidenheimer, A.J., Michael Johnston and Victor T. Le Vine (eds) (1989) *Political Corruption: A Handbook*, New Brunswick, New Jersey, Transaction Publishers.

Hurstfield, Joel (1973) *Freedom, Corruption and Government in Elizabethan England*, Cambridge, Harvard University Press.

Jagannathan V. (1987) *Informal Markets in Developing Countries*, Oxford, Oxford University Press.

Kernaghan, K. and Dwivedi, O.P. (eds) (1983) *Ethics in the Public Service: Comparative Perspectives*, Brussels, International Institute of Administrative Sciences.

Klitgaard, Robert (1983) *Corruption in Mexico*, Cambridge, Harvard University Press.

— (1988) *Controlling Corruption*, Berkeley, University of California Press.

— (1990) *Tropical Gangsters*, New York, Basic Books.

Kohli, Suresh (ed) (1975) *Corruption in India*, New Delhi, Chetana Publications.

Krueger, A.O. (1974) 'The Political Economy of the Rent-seeking Society', *American Economic Review*, 64:3.

Leff, Nathaniel H. (1964) 'Economic Development through Bureaucratic Corruption', *American Behavioural Scientist*, 8.

Levi, Michael and David Nelken (eds) (1996) *The Corruption of Politics and the Politics of Corruption*, Journal of Law and Society (Special Issue) March, Oxford, Blackwell.

Le Vine, V.T. (1975) *Political Corruption: The Ghana Case*, Stanford, Hoover Institution Press.

Mac Mullen, Ramsay (1988) *Corruption and the Decline of Rome*, New Haven, Yale University Press.

Mauss, Marcel (1990) *The Form and Reason for Exchange in Archaic Societies*, London, Routledge.

Monterio, J.B. (1966) *Corruption*, Bombay, Manaktalas.

Montias, J.M. and Susan Rose-Ackerman (1981) 'Corruption in a Soviet-type Economy: Theoretical Considerations' in Steven Rosefielde (ed) *Economics Welfare and the Economic of Soviet Socialism: Essays in Honour of Abram Bergson*, Cambridge, Cambridge University Press.

Myrdal, Gunnar (1968) 'Corruption: Its Causes and Effects', *Asian Drama: An Inquiry into the Poverty of Nations*, Hammondsworth, Penguin, Vol II.

Nader, R., Petkas, P.J. and Blackwell, K. (eds) (1972) *Whistleblowing: The Report of the Conference on Professional Responsibility*, New York, Grossman Publishers.

Nehru, B.K. (1986) *Thoughts on Our Present Discontents*, New Delhi, Allied Publishers.

Noonan, J. (1984) *Bribes*, New York, Macmillan.

Noorani, A.G. (1973) *Ministers' Misdeeds*, Delhi, Vikas Publishers.

—— (1996) 'Rao & Scam', I, II and III in *Statesman, New Delhi*, March 10,11 and 12.

Nye, Joseph S. (1967) 'Corruption and Political Development: A Cost-Benefit Analysis', *American Political Science Review*, 61.

Onoge, O.F. (1982) 'Corruption in Development', Zaria, Nigeria, *Ahmada Bello University*.

Padhy, K.S. and Muni, P.K. (1987) *Corruption in Indian Politics: A Case Study of an Indian State*, Delhi, Discovery Publishing House.

Palmier, Leslie H. (1985) *The Control of Bureaucratic Corruption*, New Delhi, Allied Publishers.

Paul, Samuel (1995) *A Report Card on Public Services in Indian Cities: A View from Below*, Bangalore, Public Affairs Centre.

Rogow, Arnold and Harold D. Lasswell (1963) *Power, Corruption and Rectitude*, Englewood Cliffs, New Jersey, Prentice-Hall.

Rose-Ackerman, Susan (1978) *Corruption: A Study in Political Economy*, New York, Academic Press.

— (1987) 'Bribery' in John Eatwell, Murray Millgate and Peter Newman (eds) *The New Palgrave, The World of Economics*, London, Macmillan.

Roy, Bunker (1996) 'Right to Information: Profile of a Grass Roots Struggle', *Economic and Political Weekly*, Bombay, May 11.

Sathe, S.P. (1991) *Right to Know*, Bombay, N.M. Tripathi.

— (1991) *Administrative Law*, Bombay, N.M. Tripathi.

— (1996) *Tribunal System of India*, Bombay, N.M. Tripathi.

Scott, James C. (1972) *Comparative Political Corruption*, Englewood Cliffs, New Jersey, Prentice-Hall.

Senturia, J.J. (1931) 'Corruption, Political', *Encyclopaedia of the Social Sciences*, Vol. IV.

Singh, L.P. (1986), *Electoral Reform*, New Delhi, Uppal Publishing House.

Singh, N.K. (1996) *The Plain Truth*, Delhi, Konark Publishers.

Stacey, Frank (1971) *The British Ombudsman*, Oxford, Oxford University Press.

Tanzi, Vito (ed) (1982) *The Underground Economy in the United States and Abroad*, Lexington, D.C. Heath and Company.

— (1994) *Corruption, Governmental Activities and Markets*, Washington DC, International Monetary Fund.

Theobald, Robin (1990) *Corruption, Development and Underdevelopment*, Durham, North Carolina, Duke University Press.

Transparency International (TI) (1996) *National Integrity Systems: The TI Source Book*, TI Berlin, Germany.

Tullock, Gordon (1987) 'Rent Seeking', in John Eatwell, Murray Millgate and Peter Newman (eds) *The New Palgrave, The World of Economics*, London, Macmillan.

Wade, Robert (1982) 'The System of Administrative and Political Corruption: Canal Irrigation in South India', *The Journal of Development Studies*, 18:3.

— (1985) 'The Market for Public Office: Why the Indian State is not Better at Development', *World Development*, 13:4.

— (1989) 'Politics and Graft: Recruitment, Appointment, and Promotion to Public Office in India' in Peter M. Ward (1989).

Ward, Peter (1989) *Corruption, Development and Inequality, Soft Touch or Hard Graft?*, London, Routledge.

Williams, R. (1987) *Political Corruption in Africa*, Aldershot, Gower.

World Bank (1992) *Governance and Development*, Washington DC, World Bank.

Wraith, R. and Simkins, E. (1963) *Corruption in Developing Countries*, London, George Allen and Unwin.

Zwart, Frank de (1994) *The Bureaucratic Merry-go-round, Manipulating the Transfer of Indian Civil Servants*, Amsterdam, University Press.

About the Contributors

S. Guhan voluntarily retired from the Indian Administrative Service in which he held important positions under the Government of Tamil Nadu and the Government of India. He has been Alternate Executive Director for India in the World Bank Group and Senior Economist, Willy Brandt Commission on International Development Issues. Since 1979, he has been Professor in the Madras Institute for Development Studies. He has authored and edited books and contributed papers on a variety of topics of public interest.

K. Ganesan retired as Secretary to the Election Commission of India and was subsequently Editor, Election Law Reports. He was a consultant to the Committee on Electoral Reforms headed by the late Shri Dinesh Goswami. He has authored a number of papers and newspaper articles on electoral procedures and reforms in India.

Madhav Godbole, Ph.D., was a member of the Indian Administrative Service, and has held a number of important positions in the Government of Maharashtra and Government of India apart from working in the Asian Development Bank, Manila. He retired as Union Home Secretary in March 1993. He has authored four books and writes regularly on public issues for major newspapers.

Ramaswamy R. Iyer, formerly Secretary to the Government of India, is now a Research Professor at the Centre for Policy Research. During his civil service career, he has held several senior positions in the Indian Audit Department as well as the Government of India. He was also Senior Adviser at the International Centre for Public Enterprises, Lubljana, Slovania. He has authored three books and a number of articles and papers on a wide range of issues.

A.G. Noorani is a lawyer and author based at Bombay. He is a prolific writer on a wide range of issues and his articles appear regularly in several leading newspapers and journals in India.

Samuel Paul is Chairman, Public Affairs Centre, Bangalore. Formerly, Director of the Indian Institute of Management, Ahmedabad. He has also been an adviser to the United Nations, International Labour Organization and the World Bank.

Manubhai Shah is Founder and Managing Trustee of the Consumer Education and Research Centre, Ahmedabad. Formerly he was General Manager of The Arvind Mills Ltd. He is also a visiting Professor at the Indian Institute of Management, Ahmedabad and Administrative Staff College of India, Hyderabad.

S.P. Sathe is Honorary Director, Institute of Advanced Legal Studies, Pune. He has been Pro Vice Chancellor, University of Pune and National Fellow, University Grants Commission, New Delhi. He has authored six books and contributed numerous articles on legal issues.

C.V. Narasimhan is a member of the first batch of officers recruited to the Indian Police Service. In a career spanning well over three decades, he has held important assignments as Director General of Police in Tamil Nadu, Joint Secretary to Government in the Home Ministry and Director, Central Bureau of Investigation. He was also Member-Secretary of the National Police Commission (1977-81) set up to recommend measures to restructure the police force.

This book is an outcome of Public Affairs Centre's project on corruption. Public Affairs Centre (PAC) is a non-profit national organization dedicated to the cause of improving the quality of governance in India. Established in Bangalore in 1994, its activities include research on current issues, and advisory services to both citizen groups and government to enhance the level of public accountability and performance.

Board of Directors of Public Affairs Centre

Dr. Samuel Paul (*Chairman*)	Mr. T.R. Satish Chandran
Mrs. Anu Aga	Dr. Kamla Chowdhry
Dr. K.R.S. Murthy	Dr. G. Thimmiah
Mr. P.P. Madappa	Mr. Manubhai Shah

Index

A Crisis of Corruption, 15
Administrative Reforms Commission (ARC), 191, 214
Analysis of Official Secrets Act, 1923, 125
Anti-Defection Law, 54
Causes of Corruption, 12
Characteristics of Corruption, 10
Commissions of Inquiry, 218-250
    Suggestions, 245
Commissions of Inquiry Act, 222, 223
Consequences of Corruption, 13
Corruption, Political Interference and the Civil Service, 60-87
Corruption and Administrative Discretion, 164-188
    Administrative Instructions, 175
    Administrative Law: Types of Administrative Action, 165
    Canalisation of Discretion through Judicial Review, 167
    Corruption — Penal Remedies, 165
    Corruption: Meaning and Concept, 164
    Discretion and Rule of Law, 166
    Government Contracts, 174
    How Exercise of Discretion can be Made Accountable, 175
    Independent Administrative Agencies, 182
    Instances of Abuse of Discretion, 171
    Ombudsmanning the Administration, 185
    Peripheral Nature of Judicial Review, 169
    Principles of Natural Justice, 176
    Punishment of Corrupt Officials, 184
    Reasoned Decisions, 177
    Right to Information, 178
    The Urban Land Ceiling and Regulation Act, 1976, 173
    Town Planning: Law and Discretion, 172
    Types of Corruption, 164
Corruption in India: A Strategic Agenda for Action, 286-304
    Creating Sustained Public Pressure for Change, 302
    Empowering Citizens, 299
    Restructuring and Reorienting Government Machinery, 293
    The Political Process: Strategic Interventions for Reform, 288
Corruption in India: The Current Context, 15
Corruption in Public Service Delivery, 144-163
    Contributory Factors, 145
    Corrective Measures, 161
    Magnitude of the Problem, 149
    Preventive Measures, 154
    Remedies: Proposals for Action, 153
Corruption in the Political Process: A Case for Electoral Reform, 29-59
    Theme I: The High Cost of Elections, 29
    Theme II: Financing of Elections, 34
    Theme III: Eliminating Malpractices during Elections, 45-49
    Theme IV: Regulating the Functioning of Political Parties, 50
Definition of Corruption, 9
Dinesh Goswami Committee, 46
Election Law: Distortions and Remedies, 31
Election Manifestoes of National Parties in 1996 Elections Relating to Controlling Corruption, 25-28
Electoral Reforms relating to Probity of Legislators and Political Parties, 26
Eliminating Malpractices during Elections, 45
    Creation of a Watchdog Committee for Every Assembly Constituency to supervise the Conduct of Elections, 49
    Photo Identity Card for Each Adult Citizen, 48
    The Role of Civil Servants and Police, 45
    Use of Electronic Voting Machines, 47
Financing of Elections, 34
    Banning or Regulation of Political Donations and Contributions, 34

Income Tax Exemptions to Political Parties, 37
State Funding, 38
First Press Commission (1952), 130
Guidelines Spelt out by G. Durgabai Deshmukh, 52
Joint Committee of Parliament (JPC), 241
Lok Pal and Lok Ayukt, 189-217
Need for Public Action, 21
Official Secrets Act (1923), 80, 116, 117, 118, 122, 123, 130, 134, 135, 136, 139, 156, 194
Prevention of Corruption:Towards Effective Enforcement, 251-285
A New Lok Pal Bill, 268
Audit of the Accounts of Political Parties, 278
CBI Investigations: A Status Report, 260
Central Vigilance Commission, 264
Central Vigilance Commissioner — Terms of Appointment, 265
Classification of Anti-Corruption Measures, 251
Code of Conduct for MPs and MLAs, 277
Commissions of Inquiry Act to Continue, 271
Comprehensive Assessment of Corruption Intelligence, 275
Comprehensive Legislation for Reforms, 280
Confiscation of Property Acquired through Corrupt Means, 274
CVC's Present Role, 266
Enactment of New Law for the CVC, 267
Genesis of CBI, 254
Integration of CVC and Lok Pal, 270
Investigating Wing and Prosecuting Wing for Lok Pal, 269
Legislation for Lok Pal, 268
Lok Pals in States, 270
Monitoring of CBI Cases by CVC, 272
Monitoring of CBI Cases by the Supreme Court or High Courts, 271
MPS and MLAs to be Defined as 'Public Servant' in Law, 277
Ombudsman, 267
People's Movement for Reforms, 284
Police Reform, 279
Powers of CBI, 255
Prior Sanction for Prosecution, 273
Set-up of Vigilance Officers, 264
State Vigilance Commission, 267
Statutory Role for Civil Services, 276
Viability of Separate Staff for Lok Pal and CVC, 270
Regulating the Functioning of Political Parties, 50
Benefits, Privileges and Powers of Elected Representatives, 52
Code of Conduct for Elected Representatives, 51
Misuse of Anti-defection Law, 29, 54
Need for a Constitutional Provision, 50
Regulation of the Role of Cabinet Ministers, etc., 53
Role of Audit in Tackling Corruption, 88-113
Audit and Corruption, 92
Audit on Request, 108
Audit: An Overview, 89
Excesses Over Grants, 101
Impact of Audit Reports, 110
Need for Independent Appraisal of IAD, 103
Power of SAIS in Other Countries, 99
Pursuing Pointers to Corruption, 104
Reorientation of IAD, 96
Selection of CAG, 94
Speeding up Audit Reports, 110
Strengthening the Hands of Audit, 98
Santhanam Committee, 15, 35, 227, 252-253
Second Press Commission (1982), 81, 130, 139
Shah Commission, 114
Tarkunde Committee, 37
The High Cost of Elections, 29
The Response to Corruption, 18
The Right to Information, 114-143
Analysis of the Official Secrets Act, 1923, 125
The Background, 123
Transparency International (TI), 16
Types of Corruption, 164
Vigilance Machinery, Accountability, Transparency and Preventing Abuse of Political Power, 27

LD
77
15-12-57